Conservation on the Northern Plains

Conservation on the Northern Plains

New Perspectives

Edited by Anthony J. Amato

THE CENTER FOR WESTERN STUDIES
Augustana University

2017

Publication made possible with funding by the Anne King Publications Endowment and Ronald R. Nelson Publications Endowment in the Center for Western Studies and by the National Endowment for the Humanities. The publisher wishes to acknowledge the assistance of Hal Thompson and Ana Olivier.

ISBN: 978-0-931170-~~20-1~~ 95-9

Library of Congress Control Number: 2016941374

Number 1 in the Center for Western Studies Public Affairs Series

The Center for Western Studies (CWS) at Augustana University seeks to improve the quality of social and cultural life in the Northern Plains, achieve a better understanding of the region, its heritage, and its resources, and stimulate interest in the solution to regional problems. The Center promotes understanding of the region through its archives, library, museum and art exhibitions, publications, courses, internships, and public affairs programming. It is committed, ultimately, to defining the contribution of the Northern Plains to American civilization.

Visit the Fantle Building for The Center for Western Studies
Augustana University, 2121 S. Summit Ave., Sioux Falls
605-274-4007 • cws @augie.edu • www.augie.edu/cws • Facebook • Twitter

Cover: South Dakota Department of Tourism (front) with inset photo by Peter Carrels (back)

Printed in the United States of America

Contents

Foreword

Dennis Anderson

In 1987 I was the *St. Paul Pioneer Press* outdoors columnist, a position in which I exercised a wide range of topic choices. Perhaps this was because I was born in North Dakota, but grew up in the Upper Peninsula of Michigan—two landscapes that were, and are, different in almost every way. Add to this my college years spent in west-central Minnesota, in Morris, with its prairie heritage, and it's fair to say my interests, and writings, bore a sort of bi-polar focus, fascinated equally and often simultaneously with grasslands and forests, and the flora and fauna that flourished in each. So it was in my travels and writings that I regularly immersed myself in southern Minnesota marshes, as well as the prairie pothole region of the Dakotas and also the watery canoe country that divides Minnesota and Ontario. Each to me was comforting and an inspiration.

But even more fascinating were the people who lived in and among these terrains. To what degree, I often asked myself, had they been shaped by the land and water that surrounded them? And how had they, in turn, shaped these same resources, either by exploiting them, conserving them, or both? Intriguing as well was the variation in conservation interests I found among these inhabitants. Some were deeply engrossed in ensuring, or attempting to ensure, that clean waters and healthy lands were passed down to future generations, while others were altogether apathetic about these responsibilities.

Why this divergence of concerns existed—and still exists—among otherwise similar people is, I believe, a conundrum that goes to the heart of the human condition. Are such contradictory attitudes, for example, born of nature, nurture, or both? And, depending on the answer, if there is one answer, can people's attitudes be positively modified so that optimum conservation practices can more generally be agreed upon, and deployed? Addressing this puzzle will become more important, and time sensitive, as the Earth's human population grows and expands, while the natural resources upon which evermore people depend remain finite.

My first exposure to the notion of conservation occurred on frigid autumn mornings while duck hunting with my Dad near our home in Rugby, N.D. This was in the late 1950s and early 1960s, when I was too young to carry a gun but not too young to tag along with Dad, my brother and our Labrador retriever, and lie with them amid homemade decoys in cut cornfields.

Dad planned all year for the waterfowl season, and spent many long evenings in our basement cutting plywood profiles of ducks and geese on his jigsaw. Once shaped, these decoys needed painting, and during this process, in discussions with Dad, I learned about the size differences of waterfowl, their various featherings and also when in October and November they were most likely to arrive in fields we hunted.

When the duck season opened, everything came together. By scouting, Dad knew where the ducks were most likely to feed in the morning, and roost at night. Also, our dog had been trained to retrieve on command, limiting lost birds, and any ducks that fell to Dad's gun would be within the limits not only of the law, but—sometimes more strictly still—according to his own personal sense of right and wrong. All of this unfolded from father to son more as tradition than directive, and at day's end, to complete the cycle, we'd pluck our ducks, dip them in melted wax to remove pin feathers, and finish their skins to a butcher's standard.

These experiences, and my reactions to them, were, I liked to think at the time, unique. But in reality, I was far from the first to be smitten by the sights and sounds of the natural world, or by the rituals that preceded and followed autumn forays afield. Even the commercial punt gunners of the mid-1800s on Chesapeake Bay and, on the opposite coast, in San Francisco Bay, soulless though their missions might have been, must have been stirred by the sight of so many mallards, canvasbacks, eiders and brant landing to rest and feed en route to their final destinations.

Such scenes have been commemorated in art throughout time. Native Americans left countless petroglyphs and pictographs of birds and animals, and, in the 1800s, John James Audubon, in many ways America's first "wildlife artist," painted canvasbacks, wood ducks, pintails and other species for inclusion in his iconic book, *Birds of America*. Yet no less a figure than Aldo Leopold, widely considered to be the father of modern conservation, acknowledged in *A Sand County Almanac and Essays from Round River* that—beautiful and wondrous though the natural world is—some people are indifferent to it. "A man may not care for golf and still be human," Leopold said, "but the man who does not like to see, hunt, photograph, or otherwise outwit birds or animals is hardly normal. He is supercivilized, and I for one do not know how to deal with him."

As I aged, my love affair with wildlife and the wild places that supported them grew and expanded. But I retained, always, a particular soft spot for ducks, waiting for them in spring to return north fully plumed, and anticipating also their arrival in fall, when I would go afield with my decoys and dog to renew what was by then a lifelong tradition. The difference was that, in these more contemporary times, I was accompanied by my two sons.

Yet in 1987, seven years into my tenure at the *Pioneer Press*, the same North American ducks that had captivated so many people for so long were in tough shape, having declined by some sixty percent since the 1940s. Reasons for the drop-off were many, habitat loss being foremost. But there had also been allegations spanning many years of over-gunning, legal and illegal, along Louisiana's Gulf Coast. If true, the effects of such crimes accrued not only to waterfowl, but to Minnesotans and others in the North who, since the Dust Bowl days of the 1930s, had contributed tens of millions of dollars to restore and enhance waterfowl breeding habitats, with the goal of cultivating ever-higher mallard, teal, gadwall, and other duck populations—the assumption being that, come fall, from the beginnings of their migrations to the ends, these birds would be hunted legally and according to principles of fair chase.

In 1988, with the blessing of my editors, I undertook a year-long investigation into reasons why ducks had declined so markedly, traveling during the course of that year from Canada to Mexico to talk to hunters, waterfowl managers and policy makers. My first stop was in Louisiana. I had not hunted there, but had read a considerable amount about the state, and was aware that its vast coastal marshes, stretching up to fifty miles wide and some 250 miles long, from Texas to Mississippi, traditionally wintered about a quarter of North American ducks. I also had been advised by Minnesota waterfowl managers that I was naïve to expect that Louisiana hunters viewed ducks the same way northern hunters did. Roger Holmes, who was then the wildlife chief of the Minnesota Department of Natural Resources, said, "We raise ducks, and so we look at them differently than people do who see them only during the hunting season."

Those differences, Holmes said, also manifested themselves in ways the two states administered ducks, noting that Mississippi Flyway managers had divided themselves into northern and south-

educate that person about reasons why they should hunt legally, and show the birds respect, and they'll do it."

In his introduction to the important collection of essays that follows, Anthony Amato writes, "Conservation has retained use and holds out great promise." Now, thirty-six years after I first wrote a column for the St. Paul newspaper, and nineteen years after transitioning to a similar position at the *Minneapolis Star Tribune*, I agree wholeheartedly.

A catch phrase in contemporary conservation and natural resource management is "human dimensions." The term is necessarily broad, arguably too much so, and pertains to everything from hunters' expectations being met (or not) to the possibility of disease spreading from, say, wildlife to domesticated animals. One definition suggests that people affected by, experiencing problems with, or deriving benefits from wildlife management decisions represent the human dimensions of those decisions.

I would propose more practically that the human dimension upon which the conservation of natural resources depends going forward is kids' experiential exposure to nature beginning before they are five years old. Such introductions needn't occur in North Dakota cornfields, as they did with me. In fact the world is fast becoming urbanized, and future generations are less likely to interact with nature as hunters, anglers and gatherers, and are more likely, to the degree they get outdoors at all, to hike, bike, paddle, or bird watch. So be it. However entry to, and appreciation of, the natural world is achieved is good enough, so long as it is achieved.

I asked at the outset whether indifference to wild places and wild creatures is born of nature, nurture, or both. And whether such attitudes can be positively modified so that optimum conservation practices can more generally be agreed upon, and deployed. Whatever the answer to the first question, the answer to the second and more important question is, I believe, yes. The only issue is how quickly these changes in attitudes can occur.

Preface

Anthony J. Amato

The expressions of gratitude in this work are words of thanks first to Dr. Harry Thompson and the Center for Western Studies at Augustana University. Dr. Thompson had the vision to step off of the press's traditional path and give a book on conservation a try. He, along with board members of the Center for Western Studies, were bold enough to offer suggestions that not only improved but shaped this book from its inception. Through its previous books, conferences, and programming, the Center has a proven record of success in bringing the experiences and possibilities of the Northern Plains and the larger West to the world at large. The editor hopes that this collection of essays can reopen the Plains.

Thanks go out to all of the contributors and their informants, interviewees, guides, and assistants. Few are willing to spend the time and effort to address conservation by spending words and time on an idea. Joseph Amato (the editor's father) deserves special thanks for the original interest in this book. A winter conservation summit prompted him to wonder whether conservation was worth a book. Subsequent discussions were convincing enough for many to put effort in words into the project. Ms. Dawn Bahn, the secretary of the Southwest Minnesota State University's Department of Social Sciences, stepped up and provided technical assistance for the manuscript. Ms. Felixa Amato provided technical assistance for the manuscript at crucial junctures. Two university presses deserve gratitude. The University of Missouri Press published Lisa Ossian's *Depression Dilemmas of Iowa* and allowed a revised version of her epilogue to appear in this book. Similar thanks go to University of Nevada Press, which allowed Linda Hasselstrom to offer a revision of an essay published earlier.

This volume does not pretend to be a comprehensive study of conservation or the environment of the Northern Plains. It does not aim to capture all of the studies, moments, and efforts that have come under the heading of conservation. While each of them has made great contributions to the understanding and the shaping of places and processes, the type and scope of efforts, people, and thoughts on the Plains alone are too vast to count, let alone explain, especially over the last five decades. The extent of Franklin Delano

Roosevelt's program in the thirties, Theodore Roosevelt's conference and his childhood in the North Dakota badlands, for example, are topics for a whole volume. Rather than aim for the complete, the essays in this collection address areas, processes, and stories that define the limits of and expand the possibilities of conservation on the Northern Plains. Each essay offers insight and is a call to revisit conservation. Conservation, which is mild and moderate to many readers, is far from anodyne as a topic. Although it registers as old-fashioned with yet other readers, it is as much in the present and future as in the past.

In pursuing the extent of conservation's reach, the chapters in this book reflect the ordinary, the extraordinary, and the space in between. Veteran outdoors columnist, lifelong sportsman, and Pheasants Forever founder, Dennis Anderson opens the book by posing and answering two questions in his foreword. His answers affirm the currency and value of each of the chapters in the book. In "The Tallgrass Prairie: Raymond Lindeman, a Minnesota Bog Lake, and the Birth of Ecosystems Ecology," William Hoffman reopens the life and work of Lindeman, situating the scientist's short life of work in the thought of his day. At a time when energy systems within organisms were beginning to be understood, Lindeman created scientific ecosystems for the emerging science of ecology by introducing the concept of energy, which had been theretofore the undeveloped, unapplied, and aloof concept of the conservation of energy. In "Reflections on Conservation in the Northern Plains: From Farm Field to Biosphere," Joseph A. Amato locates conservation in times and places of conflicting sentiments and visions. Much as Keith Thomas in his *Man and the Natural World: A History of Modern Sensibility* traced the antecedents of today's attitudes toward nature, "Reflections on Conservation from the Northern Plains" follows in the tracks of conservation to points of divergence in technology, material life, and sentiment.

These points of divergence include parks. In "A Tale of Two Plains: Natural Heritage Conservation in the United States and Canada," Barry L. Stiefel revisits parks—or the absence of them—on the Plains. The creation of parks in North America could have followed many different paths. For varied reasons, national park creation missed the middle of the Great Plains, but a twenty-first-century conservation movement of park creation in the Northern Plains promises to bring together peoples, ecosystems, and countries as nowhere else.

Conservation's story on the Plains is about a larger West, its species and places. In the "Wild Horses: Conserving a National Symbol," Andrea Glessner investigates the mustang as both an icon and an interloper in the far reaches of the grassland and adjoining regions. Changing perceptions, charged symbols, and a dynamic nature have confounded the management and conservation of the herds that roam the open range. In "The War on Wheat," Miles D. Lewis surveys the land from the pinnacle of Prairie conservation (i.e., the New Deal agricultural programs). In his exploration of two counties in Montana, he demonstrates how the programs were sometimes more personal and political than ideological, and how they always carried ecological consequences. In "Elk Killers, Liberal Politics, and Tourist Magnets: Outfitter Perceptions of Wolves in Montana," sociologist Stephen L. Eliason explores the species and a livelihood, revealing the controversial nature of conservation, professions, and politics on the edge of the Plains. The underlying issues and conflicts, he suggests, stretch across the country.

In "Cattle Ranching in South Dakota: Three Variations on a Theme," Linda M. Hasselstrom presents the Northern Plains as a cattle-ranching conservationist sees them. A writer and rancher, Hasselstrom exposes the false oppositions and mistakes of people and nature in portraits of the region. She enables readers to see true life and true lives, calling for a rancher-environmentalist summit on the Plains. In "'Too much' and 'too little': Land, Food, and Farms in Rural Iowa after 1933," Lisa Payne Ossian assesses the impact of contemporary agriculture on Iowa, the Northern Plains' southeastern corner. She concludes that in Iowa, the perpetuation of lifeways and environmental elements have been traded for ever-greater efficiency in an ever-greater emptiness. In "A Grassroots Movement for Grass and Roots," Peter Carrels discovers a new group of farmer-conservationists in another stretch of the Plains. While many are heeding the present call to get bigger and use the latest products, this group has returned to ways of the past and jumped into ways of the future, making "organic" and "perennial" bywords to a new conservation.

The same post-modern life that has seen the decline of professions and the exodus from agriculture has witnessed the rise of pastimes, and the Plains is no exception in this regard. In "Why Would Hunters Quit? An Examination of Potential Hunting Desertion in Big Sky Country," Stephen Eliason documents the current departure of people from hunting. The reasons for this trend vary, but perhaps most important is that hunters have been behind many conservation movements for decades. Like other movements, it has depended on its members for its definitions. In "Saving Up on the Prairie," the editor finds that conservation is more than a hold-over from an earlier time. It has the power to encourage, guide, or even deflate efforts. Strengthened with the latest social and natural sciences, a yield and efficiency approach to people's use of the Plains can guide projects of natural restoration and human welfare.

Most of the contributors to this book are historians by training. In part, this is due to the roundup, but it is also due to the subject. Conservation, after all, is partial to the past and sees the present and future through past use. The Plains are no exception in this regard. Whether addressing the past, present, or future, each of the ten authors challenges the imagination.

The conservation presented in this volume is neither a mild nor middle-of-the-road map to compromise. The authors spare few and little. Linda Hasselstrom refers to ecological terrorism and addresses critics of meat. Lisa Ossian pronounces Iowa's landscape uninspired. Andrea Glessner points to the gaps in the rhetoric of both wild-horse rescuers and that of their critics. Stephen Eliason includes the words of many who want wolves exterminated. More significant even than these moments is the controversial nature of conservation itself. It is because of the *nature* of the topic that each of the eleven chapters provokes discussion in addition to evoking a theme or experience.

Anthony J. Amato
Marshall, Minnesota
November 2016

Introduction

Anthony J. Amato

Somewhere west of the Mississippi River, the woods and rolling hills give way to the aridity and ever-expanding horizons of the Northern Plains of the American West. The trees thin out, wither, and then vanish. The meadows become prairies, and then just prairie. The words gulch, draw, and butte take the places of the words glen, hollow, and knoll. The terrain seems to empty itself out, first losing meaning and then losing substance. Given sufficient time, the country shows its full desert side by deserting those who venture into it.[1] The Plains, alien and severe to some, are of another nature, too. The Plains invite and offer. Even while cast as stark, empty, and harsh, they have been generous, abundant, and tolerant.

The Plains are at once vast and scarce. For some, the open space has suggested that there is an open emptiness or an empty openness. It is the emptiness that might have led generations to invest mind, heart, and money in the improvement of the Plains. Seeing nothing to conserve or preserve in the open space, some thought that places needed to be created or improved, and generations of efforts to make something of the Plains created "the pragmatic of meliorism of the frontier" that Wallace Stegner mentioned.[2] The relative emptiness has also meant that all things encountered are worthy of consideration for preservation because they are rare and come few and far between. Those who have taken this view have counseled caution, restraint, and even non-activity because of scarcity. A third view has taken the Plains as a never-ending land that never runs out of resources. Down through the generations, some on the Plains have ignored all precautions about scarcity and sustainability. They have used, never suspecting that use-ups will come. Within each of these three distinct approaches there is variation as to the degree to which people see themselves at the mercy of nature. From Walter Prescott Webb to Richard Manning, beholders of the grassland have waivered like grass in the wind.

As natural as conservation might seem on the Plains, the word and the concepts that accompany it have struggled to persist in the arena of ideas. Dismissed as elitist, dated, or tendentious, conservation has slipped to the margins of rural areas and environmental movements. Where once the term abounded, concepts such as sustainability and best management practices have taken its place in the mind and on the land. For some, conservation has become "environmentalism light," and for others it has even become a rhetorical rallying point against environmentalism. Even when deployed by those with shared environmental sentiments, the word is forced to compete with newer terms such as "re-wilding" and "bioregionalism."[3] Nearly two decades into the twenty-first century, this bland and innocuous term is facing a slow phase-out. It thrives in few places in time and space outside the Sixties and the Serengeti.

Conservation is a matter of words, and the first challenges to it have been lexical. Since the late 1990s, "sustainability" has been supplanting conservation in science and public discussion. Sustainability, however, is not a synonym, and the two terms, common in environmental language, diverge. At its simplest, sustainability highlights the type of use, and conservation at its most basic refers to the items being used. Because of this, sustainability is the better term for addressing systems and processes. It is also broader in that it includes side effects (e.g., pollution) and context (e.g., economy) as conservation does not. It promises to pull people out of conservation conundrums of global sustainability that fragment and delocate the environment and its people.[4] It has even crept into historic and art preservation.[5] The vaunted s-word, however, has begun to give way to "resilience," indicating that its days are numbered and that it is far from perfect, all-encompassing, and universal.[6] All of this suggests that the movement away from the older word and concept might have been premature.

In fact, conservation has retained use and holds out great promise. It is actually the better term for addressing the materials, features, activities, and elements found in the environment. Unlike sustainability with its grand glosses, conservation efforts at times have been about specific species and places. The list of people tied to the protection of species and places includes Sigurd F. Olson and the Boundary Waters, and the Izaak Walton League and the Upper Mississippi. Above all, aside from its material focus and immediate appeal, conservation carries with it a humility and an acknowledgement of imperfection that sustainability does not.[7]

Conservation derives some of its power because of matters of words. Since World War II, cries of "Save the . . . " have enjoined millions to action, and some of these movements have drawn power from people's identity-conferring activities, such as birding. The word has had political dimensions in the vocabulary of recent U.S. politics. Those in the Wise Use movement and its successors have claimed the title of conservationists in order to oppose environmentalists, whom they have deemed radical. The term is a short hop away from "conservative," which describes the politics of many Wise-Use advocates.[8] In other parts of the world, property rights advocates have argued for "sustainability" and cast "conservation" as extreme and confiscatory.[9] The divergent rhetoric and the contests over words indicate how conservation has translated into power in policy, seen in actual applications and actions.

Conservation is partial to the past, and this past-focused bias actually enhances conservation's utility.[10] Conservation is an exercise in history, and its practice has depended on the investigation and assessment of the past. Drawing on the capacity of history to inform and guide all inquiries into the possibilities of present and future action, the past always weighs on conservation and can take precedence over the present. In fact, some efforts at conservation have even ventured so far as to entail recovering and maintaining states which were present in past nature. It is through conservation that natural history has informed and directed present policy.

The notion that conservation always has one foot in history is not just by choice. Present policies and use exists within the boundaries of legacies and depend on past use and users. As the pioneering historian of Minnesota conservation noted, "Thus, fur trader, market hunter, Indian, conservationist, sportsman, and naturalist were all vitally concerned with the wildlife of the state, and the role of each group is an important part in the story of the use and conservation of Minnesota."[11] Legislation, agencies, and orders, which are still in force, enact the mindsets and policy of the past. For example, each action and function of the Soil and Water Conservation Districts monitor and regulate the Plains, and farmers have invested authentic feelings in these districts as is seen in one farmer's description of his time on a district board as "rewarding."[12] Civic organizations have also made ideas real. The Nature Conservancy's successes unfold as a series of places in one map of the Plains. Across the United States, numerous other examples testify to the legacy of the idea.

Despite its shortcomings for a land so vast, conservation merits a reintroduction into analyses and discussions of humans and envi-

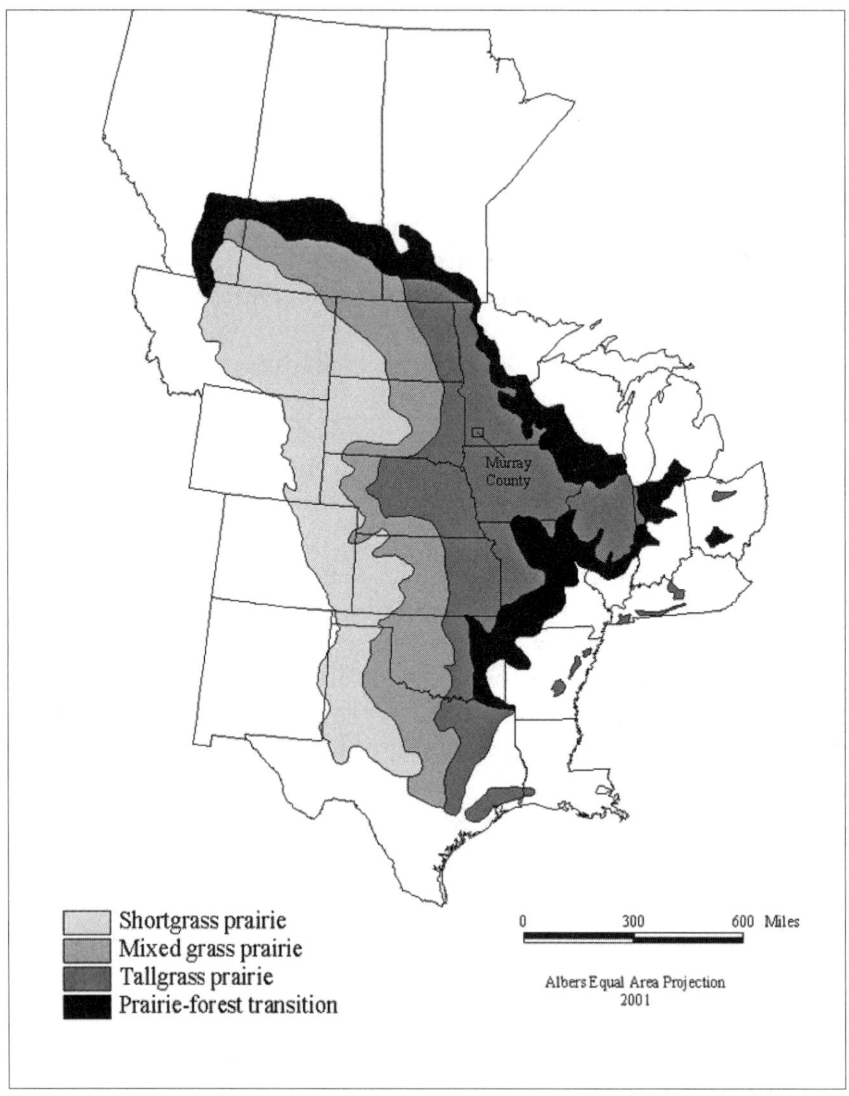

The map shows the boundaries of grassland vegetation types in the middle of North America. The county highlighted is the site of episodes discussed in "Saving Up on the Prairie," an essay later in this volume. The map is reprinted from Anthony J. Amato et al., eds., *Draining the Great Oasis: An Environmental History of Murray County, Minnesota* (Marshall, Minnesota: Crossings Press, 2001). The map was created by Charles Kost, who consulted the prairie map in David F. Costello, *The Prairie World* (Minneapolis: University of Minnesota Press, 1969).

ronment. It has great untapped potential for understanding people and nature in the Northern Plains and elsewhere.[13] Not only do efforts across this open land still come under the heading of conservation, but the concepts present in its approaches best capture the opposing realities and views of nature and people in the Plains. All endeavors in this expanse face a dynamic nature and abiding pasts of storage, accumulation, and use, and all efforts have confronted diverse places, which have been lumped together to form a specific region, but defy easy definitions for policy.

Those who seek to practice conservation in the vast middle of the United States confront uneven territory and shifting terrain. The Northern Plains deceive their beholders. Presented as monotonous, uniform expanses, the land between the Mississippi and Rockies varies on local and regional scales. The Plains, with the notable exception of the Black Hills, have had no mountain-building in recent geologic time, and they range from flat to undulating. Their most prominent features date to the Wisconsin Glaciation or earlier Pleistocene glaciations, but they also include badlands and sandhills. Embellishing the region's middle is the Prairie Pothole Region, where wetlands and shallow lakes break up the landscape. Across the vastness, soils have accumulated and disappeared according to local conditions, depositions, events, and action.

The Plains house several biomes and numerous ecosystems within each biome. The "prairie" is actually three different biomes of vegetation: the tallgrass, mixed grass, and shortgrass prairies, which stand from east to west respectively. In the tallgrass prairie, sun and wind exposure have made the southwestern hillsides' vegetation distinct, and over time these areas' susceptibility to fire have magnified the distinctions. Rivers have created ravines, floodplains, and woods sheltered from wind, sun, and fire. Even in the region's endless seas of grass, bison wallows and covered wagons' wheel tracks in swales have sustained thin bands of plants. The visitor in this vast land experiences both big botany and rare flora.

The Northern Plains assume the form of a drainage basin, which includes the Missouri River Basin and the western Upper Mississippi River Basin. The water highways and the small watercourses have formed systems through which materials, energy, and forms of life move. They have also created corridors for the movement of species, migrating and expanding. The water systems of the region have made a myriad of distinctions on the prairie.

The culture reflects nature's variety. The ninety-eighth or one-hundredth meridian has formed a line of demarcation that separates the land with sufficient precipitation for wheat from land with insufficient precipitation for wheat. This line has meant the world for residents for the past 150 years. Beyond this grand-scale division, sub-regional peculiarities have created their own distinctions. Places across the Plains have followed diverging trajectories of use. Some are steady, some are seeing booms, others stand abandoned, and yet others have been reclaimed. For instance, the lands above the Ogallala Aquifer and more recently those above the Bakken Shale have departed from their neighbors as the underworlds have supported uses above. The diverging paths of use have created different spaces for conservation. In some directions, the mirage of nature stretches out unbroken. In other places the mirror of nature is shattered by access and inroads, and yet in others it is confined to the fine cracks between construction and cultivation.

Notes

[1] These words mimic those of Walter Prescott Webb—"a semi-desert with a desert heart." For purposes of this collection, "plains" and "prairie" have two definitions each: a vegetation definition and a regional definition. Prairie is grassland of one of three types: tallgrass, mixed-grass, and shortgrass. All three types consists of perennial grasses, forbs, and legumes. Prairie is also the large areas of American land used for agriculture now, but once in prairie vegetation. In the U.S., Prairie tends to be more, but not exclusively, oriented to the areas that were tallgrass at the time of European encounter. Plains is the flat land in the middle of North America. This vast area stretches from the Mississippi to the Rockies. Additionally, Plains can be narrower and mean the shortgrass and mixed-grass prairie areas and also land used for agriculture now, but once in short- and mixed-grass prairie vegetation. In the middle of North America, the Plains also include the western tallgrass prairie. Canadians refer to all of their Plains areas as Prairie and avoid the word Plains. To the extent possible over eleven essays by ten authors, capitalization of these two words has been regularized to instances referring to specific geographic areas, such as the Northern Plains, the Plains, and the Prairie.

[2] Wallace Stegner, *Wolf Willow: A History, a Story, and a Memory of the Last Plains Frontier* (New York: Penguin Books, 1992), 306.

[3] For a description of re-wilding, see Della Hooke, "Re-wilding the landscape: Some observations on landscape" in *Trees, Forested Landscapes, and Grazing Animals: A European Perspective on Woodlands and Grazed Treescapes,* edited by Ian D. Rotherham (London: Routledge, 2013), 35-38. For a

description of bioregionalism, see Robert L. Thayer Jr., *LifePlace: Bioregional Thought and Practice* (Berkeley: University of California Press, 2003), 3-5.

[4] Thomas T. Ankersen, "Addressing the Conservation Conundrum in Meso-America" in *Bioregionalism,* edited by Michael Vincent McGinnis (London: Routledge, 1998), 171-73.

[5] See http://www.conservation-us.org/publications-resources/sustainability#.VTLWFZNKXfc accessed 18 April 2015.

[6] http://conservationmagazine.org/2013/03/good-bye-sustainability-hello-resilience/ accessed 18 April 2015.

[7] http://conservationmagazine.org/2013/03/good-bye-sustainability-hello-resilience/ accessed 18 April 2015.

[8] Hal K. Rothman, *The Greening of a Nation? Environmentalism in the United States since 1945* (New York: Harcourt Brace, 1998), 174-78.

[9] See the comments posted at http://landholders.tripod.com/id104.htm accessed 18 April 2015.

[10] See Hooke, 35, 38.

[11] Evadene Burris Swanson, *The Use and Conservation of Minnesota Wildlife, 1850-1900,* Foreword by Aldo Leopold (St. Paul: Department of Natural Resources, 2007), 143.

[12] "A Lifetime on the Farm," *Shopper's Review* of the *Marshall Independent* (Marshall, Minnesota) 8 September 2015, 1.

[13] For an overview of what to conserve in the Central North American Grassland, see Fred B. Samson and Fritz L. Knopf, eds., *Prairie Conservation: Preserving North America's Most Endangered Ecosystem* (Washington, DC: Island Press, 1996).

Chapter 1

The Tallgrass Prairie:
Raymond Lindeman, a Minnesota Bog Lake, and the Birth of Ecosystems Ecology

William Hoffman

. . . he was a field ecologist at heart, a limnologist from the prairie.

Under the summer sun of the late 1930s, as the world emerged from economic depression and reeled toward war, a graduate student would inflate his "pneumatic boat" and set out on a small lake in east central Minnesota to gather samples for his ecological studies.* One of his academic advisers at the University of Minnesota had spotted the lake during a reconnaissance flight years earlier and regarded it as a good subject for research. The student, Ray Lindeman, went about his sample collecting beneath the source of the energy that animated the ecological system of the bog-like lake he sought to understand in bold and original detail. About the same time, a Cornell University nuclear physicist, a Jewish émigré from Nazi Germany, was trying to solve the mystery of that very energy source, the sun. And solve it he did, publishing the "Energy Production in Stars" in the months before the sun set on Europe with the outbreak of war. Both the graduate student and the physicist were theoretical systems thinkers by nature. Both used thermodynamic calculations. Both were interested in energy flow, one through ecosystems and the other through stars. They had something else in common: the graduate student, naturally enough, got his hands and feet dirty doing his work; students of physicist Hans Bethe couldn't help but notice his muddy shoes when he came to class.[1]

Unlike Bethe, who was productive almost until the end of his ninety-eight years, the pioneering ecosystems ecologist Raymond Lindeman exercised his nascent yet powerful scientific imagination over the course of just a few years. He had no choice. As he collected his samples, recorded his data, wrote his dissertation, and drafted and re-drafted "The Trophic-Dynamic Aspect of Ecology,"[2] the manuscript whose publication would make him famous, he was dying. As death approached he appeared to treat the prospect as a distraction to his research and moving his ideas through scientific peer review into print, which was proving to be difficult.

Lindeman had a passion for discovering how the natural world works as a complex dynamic system. He possessed a mind well equipped to find out and work habits that enabled him to deliver the goods. The ideas about ecological energetics, food webs, and ecological succession encompassed in his paper fueled research for two generations of ecologists. The British ecologist and botanist Arthur Tansley had introduced the term "ecosystem" just as Lindeman launched his boat on Cedar Bog Lake, located north of Minneapolis, but it was Lindeman himself who gave birth to ecosystems ecology. Eugene Odum's classic textbook *Fundamentals of Ecology* (1953)[3] helped to make Lindeman's model of energy flow the key approach for studying diverse biological processes and comparing diverse ecosystems. More than seven decades after its publication, Lindeman's paper continues to be listed among essential readings in natural resource and species management and in ecosystem conservation.[4]

If the average human life expectancy worldwide is seventy-one years, in human terms the sun is about thirty-five years old. It will keep Earth habitable for life as we know it a couple more billion years by energizing Earth's ecosystems. As Hans Bethe observed in his Nobel lecture, stars have a life cycle much like animals: "They get born, they grow, they go through a definite internal development, and finally they die, to give back the material of which they are made so that new stars may live."[5] So it is with the ecosystems that sustain life on planet Earth, based on the natural metabolic processes Lindeman articulated in an aquatic system. Organisms die and decompose into simpler inorganic molecules in what he inventively termed "ooze." Subsequently these inorganic molecules in ooze are incorporated into living plants through photosynthesis and transferred through aquatic food webs, just as the sun incorporated heavy elements from earlier stars that died and became supernovas.

In ecosystems, these molecules cycle through Earth's biotic and abiotic worlds. "The *ecosystem* may be formally defined as the system composed of physical-chemical-biological processes active within a space-time unit of any magnitude, i.e., the biotic community *plus* its abiotic environment," Lindeman wrote, citing Tansley and his breakthrough idea. "The concept of the ecosystem is believed by the writer to be of fundamental importance in interpreting the data of dynamic ecology."[6] In short, the ecosystem is the key ecological unit in the natural world and an accessible avenue for the quantitative analysis of productivity and energy in ecological space.

Ecosystems are often described as self-organizing, self-regulating, and homeostatic. They are resilient to temporary changes in conditions, tending to keep them more or less in equilibrium. But what happens when people disrupt ecosystems? As Lindeman was struggling to get his transformational ideas published in the journal *Ecology*, ideas he would not live to see in print, few people aside from conservationists were concerned about environmental damage from human activity. Few talked about biodiversity loss. No one talked about human-caused climate disruption. And the debut of the term "the Anthropocene," the human age, was six decades away.

Up from the Farm

Lindeman's brief journey through life commenced on a farm set amid the gently undulating glacial-drift plain of southwestern Minnesota that the Des Moines lobe of the Wisconsin glaciation forged at the end of the last ice age. The glacial drift consists mainly of till overlaying a foundation of Precambrian bedrock. The Minnesota River, a descendant of the glacial River Warren, forms most of the northern border of Redwood County, which was home to the Lindeman farm.[7] This world, the land beneath Lindeman's feet, fired his imagination. Years later, as a graduate student, he would describe the geology and paleoecology of the Anoka Sand Plain north of Minneapolis in his article "The Developmental History of Cedar Creek Bog, Minnesota" published in the *American Midland Naturalist* in 1941, a year before his death. The Anoka Sand Plain was something of an aberration, a deflection of the Des Moines lobe as the lobe extended southward like a pseudopod creating the soil conditions on the Lindeman farm. The bog upon which Lindeman expended his graduate-student energy, as he himself described it, "was formed as an ice-block lake in a pitted sand-outwash topography."[8]

The soil upon which the farms of Redwood County rested was well suited for raising wheat, corn, oats, barley, potatoes, and prairie hay, the preferred crops of the German and Norwegian settlers there. The Lindeman 320-acre farm was next door to one of many farms in the area owned by Richard W. Sears, the founder of Sears,

Roebuck & Co. who started as a railroad station agent in Redwood Falls in the early 1880s. Both Lindeman's parents, Otto and Julia (Ash), were 1910 graduates of the University of Minnesota's Agriculture School, where they met.[9] An entry in their senior yearbook's "Class Alphabet" reads (with its misspelling of Lindeman):

L is for LINDERMAN,
The chemist so rash,
Who is always well versed
On the essentials of ASH.

Otto and Julia were married in 1913. Raymond was born in 1915. He never took to agriculture despite his parents' college degrees in the field and his father's advanced practices. A family farmhand recounted that he never saw Raymond on a tractor. According to Robert W. Sterner, who interviewed people who knew him, Raymond expended his abundant boyhood energy on nature, not agriculture. "A common and recurring theme among those who recalled Raymond was his intense and not easily satisfied curiosity about the natural world," Sterner wrote in an article published in the *Limnology and Oceanography Bulletin*.[10] Lindeman spent a lot of time outdoors observing the flora and fauna hosted by the tallgrass prairie, the area wetlands and woodlands, and the ravines and bedrock outcroppings characteristic of Redwood County. During his excursions he would capture butterflies and kept a collection of them in his bedroom. His visual acuity of the natural world suffered a setback when he accidentally damaged the cornea of

Pioneering ecosystems ecologist Raymond Laurel Lindeman (1915-1942). *Courtesy University of Minnesota.*

his right eye with iodine, leaving the eye able to distinguish only light from dark.

After attending a one-room schoolhouse and then graduating from Redwood Falls High School in 1932, Lindeman enrolled in Park College, a small liberal arts school in Missouri, graduating second in his class in 1936. In his college application he wrote that he wanted to become an experimental biologist. Lindeman was something of an idealist, and science was his first love. Science allowed one to "see and try to understand the majestic symmetry of the universe" while serving humanity.[11] Two events had a profound influence on Lindeman while he was a college student. He met his future wife, Eleanor Hall, the daughter of a professor at Albion College in Michigan. She was an indispensable partner for his scientific interests and became an algal specialist in her own right. Then in the summer of 1935 Lindeman pursued undergraduate studies at the University of Minnesota's Lake Itasca field station, where he met his future doctoral adviser Samuel Eddy, a professor of zoology and curator of fishes at the Bell Museum of Natural History. But Eddy's influence on Lindeman after he enrolled in the doctoral program the next year may have been less than that of William S. Cooper, head of the botany department, whose research centered on the postglacial history of the Anoka Sand Plain. It was Cooper who had spotted Cedar Bog Lake during a reconnaissance flight in 1930.[12]

On a December day in 1936 Lindeman traveled the thirty-five miles from campus to what was soon to be named the Cedar Creek Natural History Area and began five intensive years of collecting samples including benthos, the aquatic organisms on the lake floor. After they were married in 1938, the collecting was invariably a joint venture of Raymond and Eleanor, who were sometimes accompanied by colleagues and friends. Friends did the driving because the Lindemans didn't own a car. Sometimes their friends would loan them a car. Raymond's persistence and single-mindedness when it came to his research sometimes led him to skip his classes, which during the course of his graduate school years included protozoology, animal physiology and behavior, terrestrial animal ecology, plant ecology, aquatic ecology, entomology, parasitology, histology, ichthyology, rotifer research, aquatic biology research, and, critically, biostatistics.[13] His $600 annual stipend as a teaching assistant meant that he and Eleanor could just get by. They lived in a trailer a few minutes' walk from a basement room in the zoology building where they did their research using the analytical instruments available. Large tubs accommodated aquatic organisms and biomaterials from the lake bottom. Sieves were employed to sort the contents into two-quart canning jars for subsequent spectroscopic analysis and data collection.

View of Cedar Bog Lake with experimental plots in the rear. Cedar Creek Ecosystem Science Reserve, East Bethel, Minnesota. *Courtesy University of Minnesota College of Biological Sciences.*

A Theory Takes Flight

Ecology as an academic discipline was a half-century old when Lindeman commenced his revolutionary study of "the physical-chemical-biological processes active within a space-time unit," an effort focused on a bog lake, which according to ecological succession theory was destined to become woodland. The German biologist Ernst Haeckel coined the word "ecology" ("Ökologie") in 1866. He conceived of ecology as an anti-mechanistic, holistic approach to biology, a web that linked organisms with their surrounding environment. Haeckel's holistic view played a key role in the early intellectual development of ecology, infusing Nature with vitalism, the virtuous properties of "Mother Earth," and giving biology the upper hand over physical processes.[14] Frederic Clements, an influential Carnegie Institution plant ecologist, kept the focus on biology, the description and distribution of species, and ecological communities as communities of organisms until Arthur Tansley came along.

The botanist Tansley, a champion of landscape conservation, insisted that ecological studies needed to take into account "the whole *system* (in the sense of physics), including not only the organism-complex, but also the whole complex of physical factors forming what we call the environment of the biome—the habitat factors in the widest sense," he explained. "Though the organisms may claim our primary interest, when we are trying to think fundamentally we cannot separate them from their special environment, with which they form one physical system."[15]

After Tansley, Lindeman was the key figure in reorienting ecology from its traditional biological emphasis, writing that "the discrimination between living organisms as parts of the 'biotic community' and dead organisms and inorganic nutritives as part of the 'environment' seems arbitrary and unnatural." The organic-inorganic cycling of nutritives "is so completely integrated that to consider such a unit as a lake primarily as a biotic community appears to force a 'biological' emphasis upon a more basic functional organization."[16] Unlike Tansley, Lindeman supported his theoretical leap with copious, well-organized data systematically derived from one specific, relatively well-delineated aquatic body over five years. At the time the field of ecology was dominated by empirical science and fieldwork. Theory was fine for astrophysicists calculating how stars like the sun produce the energy that sustains biological communities, but it was regarded by traditional ecologists as questionable, if not illegitimate, as a framework with explanatory and potentially predictive power for how these communities change over hundreds or thousands of years.

Harvard University ecologist Robert Cook elucidated Lindeman's theoretical and research originality in his essay "Raymond Lindeman and the Trophic-Dynamic Concept in Ecology," published in *Science* in 1977.[17] A hydrosere is an ecological succession that occurs in an aquatic habitat. Over a period of hundreds or thousands of years, temperate zone deep lakes progress from low nutrient levels at the outset (oligotrophy) to healthy levels of nutrients (eutrophy) to deterioration and decline (senescence) to hosting mats of floating vegetation (mat stage) to bog forests and eventually to stable biological communities (climax). In Lindeman's view, to understand a hydrosere it is essential to understand both the nutritional relations of life in successive trophic (nutritional) levels of the food cycle in the aquatic environment *and* how energy dissipates through these trophic levels. Cedar Bog Lake was then as it is today a weedy, littoral body of water lying in the transition between late lake succession and early terrestrial succession. In Cook's account, Ray and Eleanor meticulously sampled the population of "aquatic plants and phytoplankton, the grazing and predatory zooplankton, the benthic fauna of worms and insect larvae, the crustaceans, and the fish." The association of an organism with a given trophic level was governed by what the organism eats and what eats it. The exercise gave Lindeman an intimate understanding of the movement of nutrients from one trophic level to another.

To integrate their data of food-cycle dynamics with current principles of community succession, Lindeman created the trophic-dynamic viewpoint, a unifying principle for understanding ecological succession. Lindeman wrote in the last chapter of his doctoral thesis: "The trophic-dynamic viewpoint, to be elaborated in this paper, emphasizes the relationship of energy-availing (food cycle) relationships within the community to the process of succession." Lindeman believed that short-term trophic functioning had implications for long-term dynamic functioning of the lake and ultimately lake succession, the hydrosere. The only way he could prove it was through rigorous quantitative assessment of the biological productivity at successive trophic levels and then integrating that information with estimates of energy expenditures at successive trophic levels. In the end what was important was not the relation of members of the same species with one another or of communities of species in a given trophic level, but the overall biomass productivity and energy use in a given trophic level and how the productivity and energy use values compared with those of the adjacent trophic levels in the food pyramid.

Pyramids and Webs

Lindeman entitled a subsection of his paper "The Eltonian Pyramid" referring to the "pyramid of numbers" conceived by the English animal ecologist Charles Elton in 1927.[18] In Elton's pyramid, simple organisms at the base of the food cycle (e.g. invertebrates) are relatively abundant. Moving toward the top of the pyramid organisms become progressively larger in size and fewer in number (e.g. mammals). Lindeman noted that the Eltonian Pyramid "may also be expressed in terms of biomass. The weight of all predators must always be much lower than that of all food animals, and the

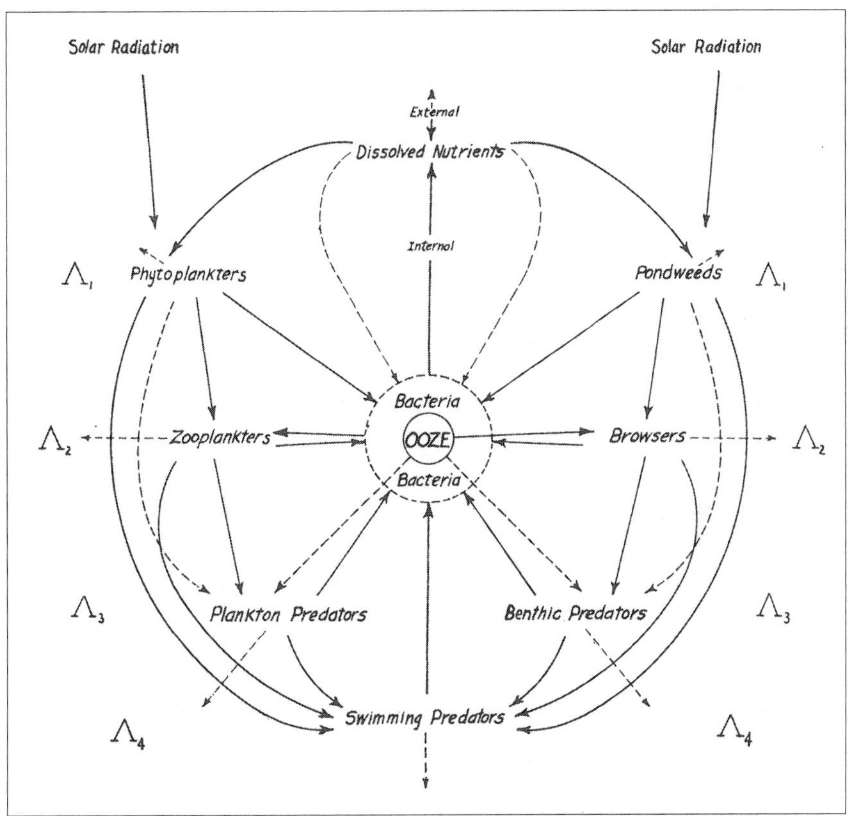

The food-cycle relationships diagram Lindeman drew for his landmark paper "The Trophic-Dynamic Aspect of Ecology." Lindeman modified the diagram he drew for his doctoral thesis, adding solar radiation input and Greek letters denoting energy and trophic levels. *Courtesy "Ecology," Ecological Society of America.*

total weight of the latter much lower than the plant production."[19] Conversely, the biomass weight of primary producers (plankton, plants) is greater than that of primary consumers (zooplankton, terrestrial herbivores) which in turn is greater than that of secondary consumers (small predators) which is greater than tertiary consumers (larger predators) and so on. Then Lindeman added: "To the human ecologist, it is noteworthy that the population density of the essentially vegetarian Chinese, for example, is much greater than that of the more carnivorous English."[20]

In today's environmentally stressed world of seven billion people, this "noteworthy" example stands out. Using Lindeman's "ten percent law" for the transfer efficiency of energy between one trophic level and the next–that is, only about ten percent of the energy is fixed in flesh and available for creatures in the next trophic level of the food web—French scientists calculated the global median human trophic level for the first time in 2013.[21] The trophic level for omnivorous humans is 2.21 on a scale in which plants and phytoplankton represent trophic level 1 and carnivorous predators like polar bears and killer whales represent 5.5, the highest trophic level in what Elton called the food cycle and what ecologists today call the food web. From 1961 to 2009 humans moved up three percent trophically from 2.15 to 2.21 "due mainly to the increased consumption of fat and meat." Populous developing countries are moving up the food web to a higher trophic level, with profound consequences for human and planetary health. No wonder, then, that the French scientists titled their study "Eating up the world's food web and the human trophic level."

Renowned ecologist David Tilman and his graduate student Michael Clark showed that demand for meat protein by Lindeman's "essentially vegetarian Chinese" surged beginning in the second half of the twentieth century.[22] Current dietary trajectories in China, India, and ninety-eight additional developing and developed countries "are greatly increasing global incidences of type II diabetes, cancer and coronary heart disease" and "are causing globally significant increases in GHG [greenhouse gas] emissions and contributing to land clearing." Tilman, who is a professor at the University of Minnesota and at UC Santa Barbara, directs the Cedar Creek Ecosystem Science Reserve, home to the Raymond Lindeman Research and Discovery Center, East Bethel, Minnesota, on the northern edge of metropolitan Minneapolis-St. Paul.

Lindeman's theoretical foundation for explaining how energy and materials move through food web trophic levels also brings together ecosystem function with biomass distribution and biodiversity. Today his descendants in ecological theory construction are developing food web models of trophic interactions between species and energy flows among species in an effort to bring together biodiversity and ecosystem function in a single conceptual framework. Quantitative analysis and modeling of food webs are already proving to be useful for managing marine and aquatic ecosystems. In its 2012 meta-review "Biodiversity loss and its impact on humanity,"[23] an international team of ecologists, including Tilman, observed that models and statistical tools can help ecologists move from experiments that detail local processes to "landscape-scale patterns where management and policy take place." One of the greatest challenges, they concluded, is to use what has already been learned to develop predictive models based on empirically quantified ecological mechanisms, models that can forecast changes in ecosystems at scales that are "policy-relevant" and that link to social, economic, and political systems. If the modeling ethos that Lindeman introduced into his field leads to reliable forecasting at such scales with such links, "we may yet bring the modern era of biodiversity loss to a safe end for humanity." The existence of a growing fraction of the approximately "9 million types of plants, animals, protists and fungi that inhabit the Earth" is at stake. What their loss means to the future well-being of the biosphere and its seven billion human inhabitants cannot be computed.

What biodiversity loss means for the productivity of the native Midwestern grasslands is something Tilman and his colleagues have analyzed and calculated following long-term field experiments performed at Cedar Creek.[24] They found that decreases in grassland plant diversity affect productivity at least as much as changes in nitrogen, carbon dioxide, herbivores, water, drought, or fire. In their natural state, the "lakes of grass," as the Lakota described the Prairie to the French explorer Joseph Nicollet, thrive as communities of grass plant relatives.

Biogeochemical Cycles and the Biosphere

Early in his paper, Lindeman acknowledges that the trophic-dynamic viewpoint he was about to describe "is closely allied to Vernadsky's 'biogeochemical' approach."[25] The Russian biologist, geochemist, mineralogist, and natural philosopher Vladimir I. Vernadsky was a remarkable figure in twentieth-century science. Vernadsky revived the term "biosphere" and secured its association with his name with the publication of *The Biosphere* in Russian in 1926. *The Biosphere* was published in French in 1929, in German in 1930, and in English not until 1998.[26] (The Austrian geologist Eduard Suess had coined the term "biosphere" in the nineteenth century. Suess defined biosphere as "the place on earth's surface where life dwells.")

In *The Biosphere* Vernadsky conceived and formulated Earth's physics as a living whole. He is regarded by many as the founder of biogeochemistry, the scientific discipline that involves the integrated study of the chemical, physical, geological, and biological processes and reactions that govern the composition of the natural environment. His was an expansive understanding of living space that involves all space that is affected by life—from Earth's atmosphere to its deep-sea vents and deepest subterranean life-supporting strata. Vernadsky imagined Earth as a structure of great concentric regions subdivided by envelopes or "geospheres." The biosphere forms the upper geosphere of one of these concentric regions—the Earth's outer shell of rock called the crust. He asserted that "a considerable amount of matter in the biosphere has been accumulated and united by the energy of the sun" and that "solar energy is transferred to the depths of the crust."[27] As Hans Bethe was calculating the energy production of stars and Lindeman was conceiving the trophic-dynamic view of ecology, Vernadsky was expanding his idea of geospheric envelopes and their biological, physical, and chemical cycles in his writings.

Lindeman may have found his way to citing Vernadsky independently, but the influence of his Yale University mentor in elevating Vernadsky in his estimation may well have been a factor because G. Evelyn Hutchinson was an early and enthusiastic supporter of Vernadsky's ideas.[28] The story of how Hutchinson used his persuasive powers as the country's most distinguished academic ecologist to midwife Lindeman's manuscript into print is well known and well told by Robert Cook in his *Science* article. Having been awarded a Sterling Fellowship to do postdoctoral research at Yale, Lindeman joined Hutchinson's laboratory in late summer 1941. With Hutchinson's guidance and his wife Evelyn's encouragement, he began to reshape the last chapter of his dissertation into a journal article for submission to *Ecology*.

Hutchinson was raised in Cambridge, England, where his father was a professor of mineralogy at Cambridge University, which he attended. While a young zoology instructor in South Africa, Hutchinson was inspired by Charles Elton's book *Animal Ecology* and his food cycle pyramid.[29] Unlike many of his colleagues, Elton among them, he embraced quantitative science, math, and model building, which he readily joined with his empirical research, setting the stage for ecosystems ecology and Lindeman's trophic-dynamic concept. Hutchinson had broad interests including chemistry, geology, and energy in addition to biology and limnology, the study of inland lakes. His studies of Linsley Pond in Connecticut helped establish his credentials as a limnologist without peer and persuaded him, as biologist and author Joel Hagen wrote, that the self-regulatory mechanisms governing the biogeochemical processes of Linsley Pond "were comparable to those operating in the biosphere as a whole."[30] Nancy Slack concludes her book *G. Evelyn Hutchinson and the Invention of Modern Ecology* writing that Hutchinson was "one of the twentieth century's most notable scientific polymaths" and "a polymath within his chosen field of ecology as well." By the mid-1930s, she notes, Hutchinson was requiring his graduate students to read Vernadsky's *Biosphere* (in French).[31]

After joining the Yale faculty in 1928, Hutchinson became acquainted with George Vernadsky, a Yale historian who introduced him to his father's writings. Later, George Vernadsky and Hutchinson collaborated to bring Vladimir Vernadsky's writings to English readers. Vernadsky died in early 1945 just before two of his translated articles, including "The Biosphere and the Noösphere," were published in *American Scientist*, of which Hutchinson was then editor.[32] Hutchinson wrote in the foreword: "The two articles together present the general intellectual outlook of one of the most remarkable scientific leaders of the present century." Three years later, in "On Living in the Biosphere," published in *The Scientific Monthly*, based on a paper he presented at an American Association for the Advancement of Science (AAAS) symposium "The World's Natural Resources," Hutchinson addressed the carbon cycle. "In the cycle of carbon we have a remarkable, possibly a unique, case in which man, the miner, increases the cyclicity of the geochemical process." The combustion of coal and oil "actually returns carbon to the atmosphere as CO_2 at a rate at least a hundred times greater than the rate of loss of all forms of carbon, oxidized and reduced, to the sediments." Here Hutchinson cited Victor Goldschmidt, a Norwegian geochemist considered along with Vernadsky to be a founder of the field. Then Hutchinson stated tellingly, "This particular process obviously cannot go on indefinitely."[33]

Leopold, Lindeman, and the Land

Had he been alive, Aldo Leopold undoubtedly would have been invited to address the AAAS natural resources symposium where Hutchinson read his paper "On Living in the Biosphere." But Leopold, a University of Wisconsin-Madison professor of game management, died tragically earlier in the year from a heart attack after trying to help a neighbor put out a brush fire that was heading toward a pine stand. It happened near his "shack," a converted chicken coop outside of Baraboo, Wisconsin, where he was awaiting publication of *A Sand County Almanac: And Sketches Here and There*. It was a book of his reflections about the natural world surrounding the shack, a book infused with the wonder of his youth as he wandered freely in the woods, prairies, and along the Mississippi River bluffs in Burlington, Iowa, at the turn of the twentieth century, a book destined to secure his place in the pantheon of the American conservation movement.

Hutchinson and Leopold had recently been among the ecologists who formed the Ecologists Union, the future Nature Conservancy. The union was "devoted to the preservation of natural biotic communities for scientific use." Protecting the wetlands of "primeval America" as "living museums" constituted Hutchinson's main interest; Leopold's main concern, as he expressed to the Union's chairman, was "the apparent raid on Western public lands" and the river damming by Army engineers "without due consideration of ecological penalties."[34]

A well-known scientist, ecologist, forester, environmentalist, and author, Leopold began writing *A Sand County Almanac* in 1942, the same year Lindeman's landmark article was published in *Ecology*. "In this influential article," wrote Leopold's biographers Richard Knight and Susanne Riedel, "Lindeman added an important element missing in Tansley's original characterization of ecosystems: energy."[35] Lindeman's trophic-dynamic viewpoint was "state of the art" when Leopold wrote "The Land Ethic," the concluding essay in *A Sand County Almanac*. Leopold laid out his environmental philosophy in the essay. A land ethic changes the role of *Homo sapiens* "from conqueror of the land-community to plain member and citizen of it." The first principle of an ethic for the land was straightforward: "A thing is right when it tends to preserve the integrity, stability, and beauty of the biotic community. It is wrong when it tends otherwise." Leopold saw the extension of ethics beyond human environments to the natural world as "an evolutionary possibility and an ecological necessity."[36]

The philosophical roots of "The Land Ethic" can be found in the speech Leopold delivered to a joint meeting of the Society of American Foresters and the Ecological Society of America in Milwaukee in 1939. In it he called ecology "a new fusion point for all the natural sciences" and one that challenged the "balance of nature" approach to discovering where utility ends and conservation begins.

"If we must use a mental image for land instead of thinking about it directly, why not employ the image commonly used in ecology, namely the biotic pyramid?" he asked.[37] Leopold revealed a modified version of Charles Elton's food cycle pyramid to represent a soil-biota energy circuit. In the scheme energy flows up the food cycle from soil through plants, plant-eating insects, insect-eating birds and rodents, herbivorous mammals, bird- and rodent-eating mammals, to carnivores, with each group returning energy to the soil. "Land, then, is not merely soil; it is a fountain of energy flowing through a circuit of soils, plants, and animals."

But *energy* does not cycle. It arrives via the sun, flows, and dissipates into nature's entropic sinks. In his book *Thinking Like a Planet: The Land Ethic and the Earth Ethic,* environmental philosopher J. Baird Callicott wrote that if Lindeman was not in Leopold's audience when he read his plenary address, "G. E. Hutchinson would have been."[38] Callicott poses the question of whether Leopold's address directly influenced Lindeman or indirectly influenced him through Hutchinson. Leopold never adopted Lindeman's "field-defining" trophic-dynamic viewpoint of energy flow. Writing "The Land Ethic" as Lindeman's unifying concept was inspiring some key ecologists, Leopold repeated his "fountain of energy" error. He merely renamed his biotic pyramid the "land pyramid." It was a curious scientific blunder in an otherwise powerful environmental vision, a vision that lives on in natural resource conservation and ecosystems management.

Ecosystems, Earth's "critical zones," and the Anthropocene

From its earliest days knowledge integration was key in the intellectual development of ecology, serving a deep-seated desire to see "ultimate order, balance, equilibrium, and a rational and logical system of relations," in the words of ecologist Frank Golley. The rise of ecosystems ecology with Lindeman's unifying principle of energy flowing through a complex that inextricably entwined the living and nonliving fed the prevailing ethos even though it was, in a sense, as Golley described it, "machine theory applied to nature."[39]

Unlike the early affiliation of conservation with academic departments of applied economics in schools of agriculture, ecology grew up in departments of biology "fractured into botany, zoology, and other taxonomic or functional 'ologies,'" as Golley put it.

Naturally the "biotic" dimension of the biotic-abiotic complex that Lindeman described was emphasized. Moreover, aquatic systems were preferred over terrestrial systems for study. Ponds, streams, lakes, and rivers have characteristics that lend themselves to metabolic study. The water column is relatively easy to sample, aquatic organisms can be retrieved more readily than terrestrial and soil-based organisms, and the instruments needed to analyze photosynthesis and respiration in aquatic systems were available in the 1930s.

Lindeman made numerous comparisons of aquatic systems to terrestrial systems in formulating his trophic-dynamic viewpoint. But in the end he built his theory from the study of an aquatic system, comparing his data mainly with that of Chancey Juday's study of Lake Mendota in Wisconsin.[40] Not until the 1960s was ecology able to produce reliable metabolic data sufficient to show how energy flows through trophic levels in marine and terrestrial ecosystems. A review of its application to food webs in marine ecosystems seventy years after Lindeman concluded that "trophodynamics as an organizing theme is robust and valuable for marine ecological research."[41] Terrestrial trophodynamic research also was on the move. By the 1970s ecologists were able to show that terrestrial ecosystems, including soil, were responsible for a large fraction of carbon dioxide in the atmosphere. Two decades later, with rising atmospheric CO_2 levels becoming a growing concern, the role of Earth's surface materials and their alteration from human activity came into sharper focus, culminating in the formulation of Earth's "critical zones" concept by geophysicist Thomas Jordan and sedimentologist Gail Ashley.[42]

A critical zone is defined by the National Science Foundation's Critical Zone Observatory program as "a living, breathing, constantly evolving boundary layer where rock, soil, water, air, and living organisms interact."[43] The term "critical" was used to highlight the human factor in the profound alterations occurring in structure and function of the Earth's outer skin. Critical zone observatories around the world coordinate observation, experimentation, and modeling of the dynamic processes that drive the atmosphere and tree canopy layers, the soil, and subsoil regions down to the deepest aquifers and regions of biogeochemical reactions in what Vernadsky termed the Earth's "crust." The communications system is a sort of Earth sciences "Internet of things," the interconnection of computing devices and sensors embedded on the Earth's surface and beneath its surface. The wireless system monitors the availability of life-sustaining resources, including food and water, and the interactions that regulate natural habitats.

One critical zone observatory, based at the University of Illinois, focuses on intensively managed landscapes in Illinois, Iowa, and Minnesota. The core site for Minnesota is the Minnesota River basin where Lindeman grew up. Land use in the basin has undergone profound changes since the beginning of European settlement in the 1830s. Settlers drained wetlands, cut down the hardwood forests, and converted the tallgrass prairie to row crop agriculture, which now covers more than three-fourths of the basin. Faculty and students from the Department of Soil, Water, and Climate at the University of Minnesota, Lindeman's alma mater, are studying how natural and human-induced landscape change can influence the movement of sediment and the water quantity and quality into the Minnesota River.[44]

Lindeman's trophic-dynamic approach to ecology is poised to help make comprehensible how critical zones and terrestrial ecosystems function, in the view of ecologists Daniel Richter of Duke University and Sharon Billings of the University of Kansas. They see metabolism and energy flow as fundamental to both terrestrial ecosystems and critical zones. Richter and Billings propose that deeper sub-surface regions be examined "to connect the biogeochemistry and hydrology of the above-ground ecosystem and its soils with groundwater, streams, lakes, and rivers."[45] They stress the words of Tansley and the spirit of Lindeman, Hutchinson, and Odum that an ecosystem is "one physical system." Lindeman could easily have substituted terrestrial systems into his text about lakes, which Richter and Billings imagine might read, "to consider such a unit as a forest, a grassland, or a wetland primarily as a biotic community appears to force a 'biological' emphasis upon a more basic functional organization."

Richter and Billings say terrestrial ecosystem metabolism can only be resolved by quantifying the full effects of respiratory carbon dioxide released by organisms at their deepest level. Measurements should proceed from soil to weathering geologic substrata—the layer where rocks are broken down into small grains and soil—to the base of the critical zone. That requires bringing the Earth sciences of hydrology, geology, geomorphology, geophysics, ecology, pedology, geochemistry, and biogeochemistry fully into terrestrial ecosystem science. "At a time when Working Group of the International Commission on Stratigraphy is evaluating 'the Anthropocene' as a new, contemporary unit of geological time," they write, how better to promote understanding of the human forcings of the planet than by accelerating interdisciplinarity across all the Earth sciences? Critical zone science "may become the science of the Anthropocene."[46]

Ecosystems, Life Code, and Conservation

In his account as Lindeman's classmate, lab partner and friend at the University of Minnesota, Charles Reif told the story of how Lindeman had built "a set of detachable rods and a piston-type coring device with which he sampled the subsurface layers of the bog."[47] He used the device to gather materials from the lake's benthic layer at specific sites across the length of the lake. Benthos is home to aquatic organisms that live on, in, or near the bottom, from algae, aquatic plants, zooplankton, and protozoa to microflora like bacteria and fungi to macroinvertebrates like clams, snails, worms, and crayfish. It represents both producing and consuming trophic levels in the food web.

When Lindeman was writing his doctoral dissertation based on his intensive study of Cedar Bog Lake, most scientists believed protein was the carrier of genetic information. Not until 1944, two years after his death and publication of his landmark paper, was deoxyribonucleic acid, DNA, found to be the molecule responsible for transmitting heritability.[48] In the decades that followed the code of life was deciphered, the chemistry of life was explained, and the transfer of genetic material from one organism to another gave birth to a new industry, biotechnology, now four decades old.[49]

The development and deployment of powerful new tools based on advances in physics, chemistry, and computer science beginning in the 1980s are transforming the study of the "biotic" component of Lindeman's biotic-abiotic complex. Ecosystem genomics is to the biosciences what the critical zone is to the Earth sciences. Both constitute rapidly emerging fields of inquiry enabled by new tools and by reframed visions about how to explore and conserve the natural world, including the substantial ecological services natural and modified ecosystems provide to human beings.[50] Both are enhanced by the information revolution and Moore's Law, the axiom that computing power per cost input doubles every two years. Whether it be the rising tide of "omics"–genomics, proteomics, transcriptomics, metabolomics, and microbiomics–or the ubiquitous wireless sensors, communications and imaging devices, and earth-bound and satellite networks, technological innovation is opening a big window on the biosphere.

The genome is an organism's complete DNA sequence including all of its genes. Genome sizes vary widely, for example, from a couple hundred thousand DNA base pairs in the smallpox virus to 3.2 billion base pairs in the human genome to 22 billion base pairs in the loblolly pine genome. Ecosystem and conservation genomics use new genomic techniques to solve problems in environmental science and conservation biology. Because genetic fitness is key to healthy populations, genomic approaches are currently being employed to study animals as diverse as wolves, bison, and bighorn sheep to inform care and breeding practices in captive or managed populations and monitor trends in wild populations.[51] In the unseen world, metagenomics is revolutionizing microbiology and related fields. Today Lindeman would be able to draw a sample from the benthic layer of Cedar Bog Lake, sequence the genomes of all species in the sample as a single community, and gauge the entire community's productivity and energy transfer potential.

The application of genomics to ecosystems "is an especially important advance as this field has not previously incorporated genetics into studies of fundamental processes such as energy flow or nutrient cycling," wrote an international team of scientists in "A Framework for Community and Ecosystem Genetics: From Genes to Ecosystems" published in *Nature*.[52] In a study providing a genetic basis for trophic-level interactions, researchers showed that small genetic changes in cottonwood trees along Utah's Weber River increased the density of aphid galls on the host trees, which in turn spurred birds preying on the aphids.[53] Does genetic variation influence the way energy flows among organisms in an ecosystem?

Knowledge of microbial genes and the organisms in which they are expressed can be used to develop screening instruments to assess how these genes and organisms fix carbon dioxide (photosynthetic micro-organisms), break down organic matter, reduce metals, remediate hydrocarbons, transfer energy, and otherwise influence biogeochemical cycles. Metagenomic studies in the Gulf of Mexico following the Deepwater Horizon oil spill, for example, showed that indigenous sediment microbes perform a valuable ecosystem service by degrading spilled oil through hydrocarbon-reducing genetic pathways.[54] Other microbial genetic pathways helped to make oil from decomposed food-web plant and animal matter over hundreds of millions of years. Microbes are versatile. They perform on the global stage and have a long run.

The genetic revolution has much to offer natural resource, energy and ecosystems conservation, remediation of environmental damage, sustainable photosynthetic harvests, and adaptation to climate change. The new genomic editing technologies can be used to create "gene drives," genetic systems that greatly enhance the odds that a specific trait will be passed on to offspring in sexually reproducing wild populations.[55] Gene drives have the potential to help protect endangered species and suppress or eradicate invasive species and disease-bearing insects. They and other genetic technologies are poised to become useful tools for twenty-first century ecosystems management and conservation practice, though their adoption by practitioners in the field will not occur unless their safety and value can be persuasively demonstrated.[56]

A Tribute and a Legacy

Lindeman died in June 1942 at age twenty-seven, two weeks after surgery to treat a rare form of hepatitis. He had written to Charles Reif in May that "there is a better than even chance I won't survive the summer."[57] If there was a consolation to his rapidly failing health it was the letter from *Ecology* editor Thomas Park he received in March. "I have carefully considered your revised manuscript and am herewith accepting it for *Ecology*," Park wrote. "I rather imagine that the original referees will still object to certain of its basic premises but I think it best to publish your paper regardless. Time is a great sifter in these matters and it alone will judge the question."[58]

As he would with the passing of Vladimir Vernadsky three years later, Lindeman's Yale mentor G. Evelyn Hutchinson wrote a tribute to him in an addendum to the trophic-dynamic paper, which was published in the October issue of *Ecology*:

> Knowing that one man's life at best is too short for intensive studies of more than a few localities, and before the manuscript was completed, that he might never return again

> to the field, he wanted others to think in the same terms as he had found so stimulating, and for them to collect material that would confirm, extend, or correct his theoretical conclusions. The present contribution does far more than this.

The "father of modern ecology" ended his tribute by calling his late postdoc "one of the most creative and generous minds yet to devote itself to ecological science."[59] That mind, born of the tallgrass prairie, could grasp and integrate questions about the length of food chains; the efficiency of trophic transfers; the rates of primary productivity; energy value adjustments for losses due to respiration, predation, and decomposition; and the role of bacteria and microorganisms in cycling dead organic matter.[60] Despite criticism of Lindeman's trophic level concept,[61] it has endured. "Lindeman was able to see beyond the immediate form of ecosystem relationships to perceive the underlying thermodynamic generator for much of organized behavior," wrote theoretical ecologist Robert E. Ulanowicz.[62]

The laws of thermodynamics operated exactly the same when fossil fuels were being formed from dead organic matter eons ago as when Hans Bethe discerned how the sun produces the energy that radiates to Earth and Lindeman proffered a unifying theory for energy flow in ecosystem food webs. The energy demand for life itself, for metabolism, respiration and reproduction, has not changed. The energy demand for human life, as humans prefer to live it, has changed enormously, running up against constraints posed by ecology and thermodynamics.[63]

In *On the Origin of Species*, a book in which the word "energy" does not appear, Darwin wrote that "plants and animals, most remote in the scale of nature, are bound together by a web of complex relations." Lindeman figured out how energy flows through Darwin's web in a few short years, mostly when he was a graduate student and briefly as a postdoctoral fellow. He was a mere decade removed from life on a prairie farm, from his letter to Park College in which he expressed his interest in science because it allowed one to "see and try to understand the majestic symmetry of the universe." It was this orderly balance that Darwin understood, invoking Newton at the end of his book with the observation that endless forms have been and are being evolved while "this planet has gone cycling on according to the fixed law of gravity."

Yet Darwin's theory of evolution by natural selection lacks the symmetrical structure of Newtonian physical laws. Its apparent randomness and contingency were out of sync with science's prevailing "balance of nature" paradigm, the concept that an implicit order underlies the natural world and is just waiting to be discovered.[64] In ecology the balance of nature implies that ecosystems are normally in a stable equilibrium. Here Lindeman hedged, qualifying the natural symmetry he had hoped to confirm. "Natural ecosystems may tend to approach a state of trophic equilibrium under certain conditions, but it is doubtful if any are sufficiently autochthonous [indigenous] to attain, or maintain, true trophic equilibrium for any length of time," he wrote in his paper. The less-than-stable equilibrium was principally a function of local conditions, however, conditions that in his mind could be overcome when framed in a larger context, say as a single global biogeochemical mechanism. Under Hutchinson's influence, Lindeman reached again for the "majestic symmetry of the universe" that he had envisioned when he was a high school senior in Redwood Falls, Minnesota, writing, "The biosphere as a whole, however, as Vernadsky so vigorously asserts, may exhibit a high degree of true trophic equilibrium."[65] To view the biosphere as asymmetrical, intangible, contingent, and stochastic was to rob it of its harmony and beauty. That may have been the case as much for a pioneering ecosystems ecologist as it would surely be for a twenty-first-century environmental activist.

The biosphere and its ecosystems are not zones of harmonious order, and neither is their energy source. As Lindeman collected his samples on Cedar Bog Lake beneath the summer sun and calculated energy flow through trophic levels of ecosystem food webs, Hans Bethe was calculating the energy production in stars using quantum mechanics, the very embodiment of scientific uncertainty in the invisible world of energy flow. Indeed, quantum effects are found in photosynthesis itself.[66] Yet ecologists are uncomfortable with indeterminacy, so the search goes on for a plausible explanation of ecological dynamics. More than a century after it first appeared on the scene, Robert Ulanowicz wrote in 2003, "ecology today still appears to many to be too diverse and conflicted to be able to coalesce around any one coherent theory."[67] What is needed, in his view and that of others, is a more encompassing metaphysics, one that can accommodate metaphor and bridge the divide between ecological science and environmental ethics.[68]

Lindeman likely would have agreed. Bethe did not see his thermodynamic calculations of nature's energy source as inconsistent with his being an outspoken critic of the world's prevailing post-World War II environmental threat, the buildup of thermonuclear weapons. Besides, although Lindeman is remembered chiefly for a breakthrough theoretical concept of energy flow in ecosystems, he was a field ecologist at heart, a limnologist from the Prairie. His description of the natural history of Cedar Bog Lake echoes his limnological forebears, with origins in Stephen Forbes's classic description of "The Lake as a Microcosm" (1887) and Henry David Thoreau's account of Walden Pond (1854). Indeed, the transcendentalist Thoreau, regarded by some as America's first limnologist, spent a day at the Indian agency in Redwood Falls while touring Minnesota in 1861, botanizing along the way.[69]

In his journal Thoreau described *Decodon verticillatus*, swamp loosestrife. "What stout, woody, perennial rootstocks!" he exclaimed.[70] Lindeman observed in his *American Midland Naturalist* article that most of Cedar Bog Lake "is bordered by an invading front" of *Decodon*, "a plant rare in Minnesota but very abundant in the Cedar Bog." *Decodon* is better adapted than *Typha latifolia* (cattail), its rival in the battle for invasion supremacy from the shoreline, particularly with high water, he wrote. Both *Decodon* and *Typha* are key contributors to the vegetative mat that, based on the ecological principles of lake succession, will be transformed into peat-like soil that can support the growth of trees including *Thuja occidentalis*, the white cedar after which Cedar Creek with its bog lake was named.

The ecological principles of lake succession are no longer the exclusive province of the natural world. Seen from the sky on a clear summer day, Cedar Bog Lake is like an oval mirror framed in green felt. We can imagine that the mirror reflects not just a summer sky beneath which a graduate student once collected samples but an atmosphere dramatically altered by human agency in ways we struggle to comprehend because we cannot see it. The sunlight that animated ecosystems eons ago, now effectively packed in organic materials from *Decodon* and *Typha* and other plants and animals, is being massively resurrected from Earth's subterranean vaults. These materials are burned at eight times the rate they were when Lindeman extended his sampling rod into Cedar Bog Lake.[71] Their combustion produces tens of billions of tons of waste compounds each year that cannot readily be gathered and stored or shipped. For now, living things and their ecosystems have little choice but to adapt to having these waste compounds in their midst.

In time, the relentless biotic encirclement and encroachment of the lake Lindeman came to know so intimately will transform it, as he envisioned the natural course of lake succession. The oval mirror will go dark, covered over by sedge mat succeeded by bog forest. Meanwhile, an unnatural ecological transformation flowing from laws governing energy and heat, breathtaking in scope, is well underway.

Modern ecology constitutes the interplay of science and conservation, an interplay reflected in the research of young investigators who receive the Raymond L. Lindeman Award for aquatic science.[72] Lindeman undertook his ecological and developmental studies of Cedar Bog Lake just as public attitudes towards prairie wetlands were shifting. In his book about the wetlands of the American Midwest, geographer Hugh Prince describes how growing interest in wildlife conservation, elevated by Aldo Leopold, dramatically slowed the massive draining of prairie wetlands for agriculture that came with Euro-American settlement.[73] Wetland ecosystems, he concluded, are culturally constructed representations of deep history.

The Cedar Creek upland forest-wetland mosaic that Lindeman came to know stretches across the heart of the Anoka Sand Plain. The ecological succession of the bog lake he explored proceeds largely as nature would have it proceed. In contrast, the prairie-wetland mosaic of Redwood County at the time of Thoreau's visit has been transformed into a food production grid. Like much of Earth, southwestern Minnesota no longer possesses a natural history unaltered by human design. But it produced Lindeman just as the wetlands preservation movement was beginning to flower on the Prairie. It gave the world a keen intelligence for imagining and describing the life-energy dynamic of an aquatic system, an ecosystems dynamic animated by energy from the sun.

Notes

*Acknowledgments: The author is indebted to Joseph A. Amato for his helpful comments and guidance in the development of this chapter. Duke University soil systems ecologist Daniel deB. Richter also provided valuable suggestions concerning Raymond Lindeman, Arthur Tansley, Vladimir Vernadsky, and the chapter subsection "Ecosystems, Earth's 'critical zones,' and the Anthropocene." University of St. Thomas thermal engineer John Abraham kindly read the manuscript. The University of Minnesota Archives provided valuable assistance in locating the portrait used in this article and granting permission for its use as well as locating information about School of Agriculture graduates Otto Lindeman and Julia (Ash) Lindeman, Raymond Lindeman's parents.

[1] Bethe's classic paper is H. A. Bethe, "Energy Production in Stars," *Physical Review* 53 (1939): 434-56. The reference to Lindeman's dirty hands and feet can be found in Robert W. Sterner, "Raymond Laurel Lindeman and the Trophic Dynamic Viewpoint," *Limnology and Oceanography Bulletin* 21 (May 2012): 47. The reference to Bethe's muddy shoes is from the account of his student and future famous physicist in his own right Freeman Dyson in his memoir *Disturbing the Universe* (New York: Basic Books, 1979): 47.

[2] Raymond L. Lindeman, "The Trophic-Dynamic Aspect of Ecology," *Ecology* 23 (1942): 399-417. Lindeman's paper was drawn from the final chapter of his doctoral thesis "Ecological Dynamics in a Senescent Lake" (1941). Gary W. Barrett and Karen E. Mabry in "Twentieth-Century Classic Books and Benchmark Publications in Biology," *BioScience* 52 (2002): 282-285, rank Lindeman's paper third among journal articles that biologists considered to have had "the greatest impact with respect to their career training" based on a survey of American Institute of Biological Sciences (AIBS) members. They wrote: "Lindeman's 1942 paper . . . not only set the stage for both Odum's classic text [see next note] but also provided a functional (energetic) basis for this emerging science."

[3] Eugene P. Odum, *Fundamentals of Ecology* (Philadelphia: W. B. Saunders Company, 1953). In his book *A History of the Ecosystem Concept in Ecology* (New Haven, CT: Yale University Press, 1993), ecologist and environmental historian Frank B. Golley wrote that "Eugene P. Odum's use of the ecosystem concept as an organizing concept . . . in his popular, widely used textbook, *Fundamentals of Ecology*, transformed a specialized technical idea into a concept with vast theoretical and applied significance."

[4] Paul R. Krausman and Bruce D. Leopold, *Essential Readings in Wildlife Management and Conservation* (Baltimore: Johns Hopkins University Press, 2013): 213-33.

[5] H. A. Bethe, "Energy Production in Stars" Nobel Lecture, December 11, 1967, 233, accessed January 17, 2015, http://www.nobelprize.org/nobel_prizes/physics/laureates/1967/bethe-lecture.html. In his Nobel lecture, Bethe observed that in a supernova explosion much of the material of the star, probably containing heavy elements, is ejected into interstellar space and can then be collected again by newly forming stars. "This means that most of the stars we see, including our sun, are at least second generation stars, which have collected the debris of earlier stars which have suffered a supernova explosion."

[6] Lindeman (1942), 400.

[7] George R. Shiner and Robert Schneider, "Geology and Ground-Water Conditions of the Redwood Falls Area, Redwood County, Minnesota," U.S. Geological Survey Water-Supply Paper 1669R (Washington, DC: United States Government Printing Office, 1964), R1-R2. See also the contributions of Thomas Dilley on geology and Neal S. Eash on soils in Murray County adjacent to Redwood County in *Draining the Great Oasis: An Environmental History of Murray County, Minnesota,* Anthony J. Amato, Janet Timmerman, and Joseph A. Amato, eds. (Marshall, MN: Crossings Press, 2001). Contributors to Joseph Amato and David Pichaske, eds., *Southwest Minnesota: A Place of Many Places* (Marshall, MN: Crossings Press, 2000) explore the history, land, culture, and character of the Redwood Falls region.

[8] Raymond L. Lindeman, "The Developmental History of Cedar Creek Bog, Minnesota," *American Midland Naturalist* 25 (1941): 101-12.

[9] Franklyn Curtiss-Wedge, "The History of Redwood County, Minnesota," Volumes I and II (Chicago: H. C. Cooper, Jr. & Co., 1916). The verse citing Otto Lindeman and suggesting his future wife Julia Ash is from "The Senior," the 1910 senior yearbook of the University of Minnesota (University of Minnesota Archives).

[10] Robert W. Sterner, "Raymond Laurel Lindeman and the Trophic Dynamic Viewpoint," *Limnology and Oceanography Bulletin* 21 (May 2012): 38-51. Sterner's is the best account of what is known about Lindeman concerning his upbringing on the farm (40-41), his collegiate, graduate school and postgraduate experiences (41-44), and those who influenced him (44-46). Sterner also explains the conceptual background for Lindeman's trophic dynamic viewpoint and its development while Lindeman was a Yale University postdoctoral fellow working under G. Evelyn Hutchinson (46-49).

[11] Joel B. Hagen, *An Entangled Bank: The Origins of Ecosystem Ecology* (New Brunswick, NJ: Rutgers University Press, 1992): 87-88.

[12] Sterner, 45.

[13] Ibid., 44.

[14] Anna Bramwell, *Ecology in the 20th Century: A History* (New Haven, CT: Yale University Press, 1989): 41-42. Golley, n. 3 above, 2-3.

[15] A. G. Tansley, "The Use and Abuse of Vegetational Concepts and Terms," *Ecology* 16 (1935): 284-307.

[16] Lindeman (1942): 400.

[17] Robert E. Cook, "Raymond Lindeman and the Trophic-Dynamic Concept in Ecology," *Science* 198, 22-26. Lindeman's doctoral thesis, quoted on page 8, is R. L. Lindeman, "Ecological Dynamics in a Senescent Lake," University of Minnesota (1941).

[18] Charles Elton, *Animal Ecology* (New York: Macmillan Co., 1927).

[19] Lindeman (1942): 408.

[20] Ibid.

[21] Lindeman proposed that about ten percent of energy is stored in organisms populating each ascending trophic layer of the food pyramid. Thus about ten percent of the net productivity of primary producers is incorporated by herbivores, about ten percent of the net productivity

of herbivores is incorporated by first-level carnivores, and so on. J. L. Chapman and M. J. Reiss, *Ecology: Principles and Applications* (Cambridge, UK: Cambridge University Press, 1999), 142. For an estimation of the median human trophic level in the food pyramid or food web, see Sylvain Bonhommeau, et al., "Eating Up the World's Food Web and the Human Trophic Level," *Proceedings of the National Academy of Sciences U.S.A.* 110 (2013): 20617-20620.

[22] David Tilman and Michael Clark, "Global Diets Link Environmental Sustainability and Human Health," *Nature* 515 (2014): 518-22.

[23] Bradley J. Cardinale, et al., "Biodiversity Loss and Its Impact on Humanity, *Nature* 489 (2012): 59, 65.

[24] David Tilman, Peter B. Reich and Forrest Isbell, "Biodiversity Impacts Ecosystem Productivity as Much as Resources, Disturbance, or Herbivory," *Proceedings of the National Academy of Sciences U.S.A.* 109 (26) (2012): 10394.

[25] Lindeman (1942): 399.

[26] Vladimir I. Vernadsky, *The Biosphere* (New York: Springer Science & Business Media, 1998). For accounts of Eduard Suess coining the term "the biosphere" and the publication of Vernadsky's *The Biosphere* in different languages, see Nicholas Polunin and Jacques Grinevald, "Vernadsky and Biospheral Ecology," *Environmental Conservation* 15 (1988): 118.

[27] Ibid., 91.

[28] Nancy G. Slack, G. *Evelyn Hutchinson and the Invention of Modern Ecology* (New Haven, CT: Yale University Press, 2011). For Hutchinson's upbringing in Cambridge, see Chapter 2, 15-41. For Elton's influence, 144-45. For Vernadsky's influence, 171-73. In the foreword, Harvard biologist and author E. O. Wilson called Hutchinson "the last great Victorian naturalist, a pioneer of modern ecology and justifiably called its founder, the one who brought the discipline into the Modern Synthesis of evolutionary theory." Eville Gorham in "Biogeochemistry: Its Origins and Development," *Biogeochemistry* 13 (1991): 199-239, acknowledges "the inspiration of G. E. Hutchinson and his academic descendants" in his valuable overview of the biogeochemical concept with origins that preceded Vernadsky. Gorham conducted pioneering studies of the effects of acidic precipitation and carbon cycle perturbations on lakes, bogs, and peatlands as a University of Minnesota ecologist.

[29] Slack, 134-35.

[30] Hagen, 65.

[31] For Slack's concluding remarks about Hutchinson being a polymath, 371. For her reference to Hutchinson requiring his graduate students to read Vernadsky's *Biosphere*, 173.

[32] V. I. Vernadsky, "The Biosphere and the Noosphere," *American Scientist* 33 (1945): 1-12. The word "noosphere," the "sphere of the mind or intellect," was coined in Paris in the 1920s by the French scientist and Jesuit priest Pierre Teilhard de Chardin, the French philosopher Edouard Le Roy, and Vernadsky. See Paul R. Samson and David Pitt (eds.), *The Biosphere and Noosphere Reader* (London: Routledge, 1999), 4.

[33] G. E. Hutchinson, "On Living in the Biosphere," *The Scientific Monthly* 67 (1948): 393-97. For Hutchinson's acquaintance and collaboration with George Vernadsky, see Nicholas Polunin and Jacques Grinevald, 119, n. 26 above.

[34] Permanent Constitution: Ecologist's Union, adopted December 31, 1947. The Aldo Leopold Archives, accessed January 17, 2015, http://uwdc.library.wisc.edu/collections/AldoLeopold. For Leopold's interest in protecting Western public lands, see his letter to Ecologist's Union chairman Curtis L. Newcombe, December 17, 1947. For Hutchinson's interest in protecting the wetlands of "primeval America" as "living museums," see Slack, 308-10, note 28 above.

[35] Richard Knight and Susanne Riedel, *Aldo Leopold and the Ecological Conscience* (New York: Oxford University Press, 2002), 93.

[36] Aldo Leopold, *A Sand County Almanac, and Sketches Here and There* (New York: Oxford University Press, 1949), 203-04, 224-25.

[37] Aldo Leopold, "A Biotic View of the Land," *Journal of Forestry* 37 (1939): 727-30.

[38] J. Baird Callicott, *Thinking Like a Planet: The Land Ethic and the Earth Ethic* (New York: Oxford University Press, 2014), 84-86. Callicott argues that Leopold had anticipated both energy transfers and materials cycling before Lindeman integrated them in his paper. Leopold failed to understand that energy flows rather than cycles, "but he did understand that energy is more fundamental than food—that energy, not food is the burning question in the biotic community."

[39] Golley, 2-3.

[40] Lindeman (1942): 409.

[41] Simone Libralato, et al., "Trophodynamics in Marine Ecology: 70 Years After Lindeman," *Marine Ecological Progress Series* 512 (2014): 6.

[42] Jordan T, et al., *Basic Research Opportunities in Earth Science* (Washington DC: National Academy Press, 2001).

[43] National Science Foundation's Critical Zone Observatory program, accessed January 17, 2015, http://criticalzone.org/national/.

[44] Minnesota River Basin, Intensively Managed Landscapes, National Science Foundation's Critical Zone Observatory program, accessed January 17, 2015, http://criticalzone.org/iml/infrastructure/field-area/minnesota-river-basin/.

[45] Daniel deB. Richter and Sharon A. Billings, "'One Physical System': Tansley's Ecosystem as Earth's Critical Zone," *New Phytologist* (2015): 1-13, doi: 10.1111/nph.13338.

[46] Ibid., 3.

[47] Charles B. Reif, "Memories of Raymond Laurel Lindeman," *Bulletin of the Ecological Society of America* 67 (1986): 20-25.

[48] Oswald T. Avery, Colin M. MacLeod, and Maclyn McCarty, "Studies on the Chemical Nature of the Substance Inducing Transformation of Pneumococcal Types: Induction of Transformation by a Deoxyribonucleic Acid Fraction Isolated from Pneumococcus Type III, *Journal of Experimental Medicine* 79 (1944): 137-58.

[49] William Hoffman and Leo Furcht, *The Biologist's Imagination: Innovation in the Biosciences* (New York, Oxford University Press, 2014).

[50] Cardinale et al., 60 (see n. 23 above). Ecosystem services include provisioning services such as the production of renewable resources (e.g. food, wood, fresh water) and regulating services such as those that lessen environmental change (e.g. climate regulation, pest/disease control). Concerning the latter, an international scientific team reported in 2015 that the carbon sink services provided by the Amazon rainforests have been in decline since the 1990s, suggesting these rainforests are becoming saturated just as their environmental services are needed most to modulate global climate change. R. J. W. Brienen et al., "Long-term Decline of the Amazon Carbon Sink," *Nature* 519 (2015): 344-48. Tropical rainforests account for roughly half of all the carbon scrubbed from the atmosphere by the land biosphere. Lars O. Hedin, "Signs of Saturation in the Tropical Carbon Sink," *Nature* 519 (2015): 295.

[51] Fred W. Allendorf, Paul A. Hohenlohe and Gordon Luikart, "Genomics and the Future of Conservation Genetics," *Nature Reviews Genetics* 11 (2010): 697-709.

[52] Thomas G. Whitham, et al., "A Framework for Community and Ecosystem Genetics: From Genes to Ecosystems," *Nature Reviews Genetics* 7 (2006): 510-23.

[53] Joseph K. Bailey, et al., "Importance of Species Interactions to Community Heritability: A Genetic Basis to Trophic-level Interactions," *Ecology Letters* 9 (2006): 78-85.

[54] Olivia U. Mason, et al., "Metagenomics Reveals Sediment Microbial Community Response to Deepwater Horizon Oil Spill," *ISME Journal* 8 (2014): 1464-75.

[55] Kevin M. Esvelt, Andrea L. Smidler, Flaminia Catteruccia, and George M. Church, "Concerning RNA-guided Gene Drives for the Alteration of Wild Populations," eLife (2014), 10.7554/eLife.03401.

[56] Aaron B.A. Shafer, et al., "Genomics and the Challenging Translation into Conservation Practice," *Trends in Ecology & Evolution* 30 (2015): 78-87.

[57] Letter from Raymond Lindeman to Charles Reif, May 16, 1942, Lindeman papers, Yale Archives. Reported in Robert W. Sterner, 43, n. 10 above.

[58] Cook, 24.

[59] Ibid., 25.

[60] Golley, 59-60.

[61] Steve Cousins, "The Decline of the Trophic Level Concept," *Trends in Ecology & Evolution* 2 (1987): 312-16.

[62] Robert E. Ulanowicz, "Ecosystem Trophic Foundations: Lindeman Exonerata" in *Complex Ecology: The Part-Whole Relation in Ecosystems*, Bernard C. Patten and Sven E. Jorgensen, eds. (New York: Prentice Hall, 1994), 559.

[63] James H. Brown, et al., "Energetic Limits to Economic Growth," *BioScience* 61 (2011): 19-26. Herman E. Daly, *Ecological Economics and Sustainable Development* (Edward Elgar Pub, 2008), 143-45. Adam Frank, "Is

a Climate Disaster Inevitable?" *The New York Times*, January 15, 2015. An astrophysicist at the University of Rochester, Frank notes that no matter on what planet they live "any species climbing up the technological ladder by harvesting energy through combustion must alter the chemical makeup of its atmosphere to some degree" because chemical byproducts from combustion "can't just disappear."

[64] Jason Simus, "Metaphors and Metaphysics in Ecology," *Worldviews* 15 (2011): 185-202.

[65] Lindeman (1942): 411. John Kricher discusses Lindeman and his revolutionary paper in the context of the "balance of nature" paradigm in his book *The Balance of Nature: Ecology's Enduring Myth* (Princeton, NJ: Princeton University Press, 2009): 75-77. According to Golley, 59, n. 3 above, one of the organizing principles of Hutchinson's theoretical work was "the familiar concept of system equilibrium or balance. He thought that systems evidenced processes of self-regulation that produced and maintained equilibrium conditions."

[66] Jessica M. Anna, Gregory D. Scholes and Rienk van Grondelle, "A Little Coherence in Photosynthetic Light Harvesting," *BioScience* 64 (2014): 14-25. The authors write that because biological systems are so complex, statistical approaches are employed to determine averages in cellular processes such as respiration and enzymatic activity. As a result, quantum mechanical (or *coherent*) phenomena are hidden. A new technology called two-dimensional electronic spectroscopy is being used to identify coherent [quantum] contributions to energy transfer dynamics in photosynthetic complexes.

[67] Robert E. Ulanowicz, "Some Steps Toward a Central Theory of Ecosystem Dynamics," *Computation Biology and Chemistry* 207 (2003): 523.

[68] Robert E. Ulanowicz, "Limits on Ecosystem Trophic Complexity: Insights from Ecological Network Analysis," *Ecology Letters* 17 (2014). See also Jason Simus, "Metaphors and Metaphysics," no. 59 above.

[69] For Thoreau's account of his visit to Redwood Falls, see Letter to F. B. Sanborn (at Concord) from Henry David Thoreau, Redwing, Minnesota, June 26, 1861 in Franklin B. Sanborn, *The Familiar Letters of Henry David Thoreau* (Boston: Houghton Mifflin 1894), 445-53. For Thoreau's visit to Minnesota in 1861 including his journey to Redwood Falls via the Minnesota River, see John T. Flanagan, "Thoreau in Minnesota," in *Minnesota* History, 16 (1935), 35-46, and Harriet M. Sweetland, "The Significance of Thoreau's Trip to the Upper Mississippi in 1861," *Transactions of the Wisconsin Academy of Sciences, Arts and Letters* LI (1962): 267-86. For a short description of Thoreau's walking, botanizing, and description of American landscapes, see Joseph A. Amato, *On Foot: A History of Walking* (New York: New York University Press, 2006), 141-47.

[70] Henry David Thoreau, *The Writings of Henry David Thoreau: Journal*, edited by Bradford Torrey and Franklin Benjamin Sanborn (Boston: Houghton Mifflin, 1906), 308.

[71] Angus Maddison, *Contours of the World Economy 1-2030 AD: Essays in Macroeconomic History* (New York: Oxford University Press, 2007). See

Chapter 7, Table 7.11, World Consumption of Primary Energy, 1820-2030 (metric tons of oil equivalent), fossil fuels (million tons).

[72] Information about the annual Raymond L. Lindeman Award can be found at http://www.aslo.org/information/awards.html. The award recognizes an outstanding paper written by an author who is no older than 35 years and published in a peer-reviewed journal in the aquatic sciences.

[73] Hugh Prince, *Wetlands of the American Midwest: A Historical Geography of Changing Attitudes* (Chicago: University of Chicago Press, 2008), 1, 347.

Chapter 2

A Grassroots Movement for Grass and Roots

Peter Carrels

"We viewed our farm as land to be used, and we were following the quickest route to making money without thinking about the environment. There are still too many farmers who do that."
—Rick Smith, farmer-rancher, Hamlin County, South Dakota

There's a certain inevitability about the emerging collective of farmers and farmer-ranchers in South Dakota who are distancing themselves from a status-quo agricultural paradigm that encourages devoting one's land to planting, protecting, and harvesting annual grains, particularly corn. Those in this collective say the weaning process was bound to happen because the warning signs are mounting.

Which demographics in the agricultural community have heeded these warning signs and are separating themselves from conventionality? We know that those in the organic farming and gardening movement have for many years demonstrated alternative approaches to industrial agriculture. So have many who are engaged in hobby-farm enterprises. But a somewhat surprising eco-progressive element in the ag sector just beginning to bloom is found among so-called regular, full-time farmers and farmer-ranchers. These can be second-or third-or fourth-generation producers, and they're often big operators, many with a land base of three, four, five thousand acres or more. Another surprising aspect of this authentic and important conservation movement is the direction from which it is flowing.

It's not fair to say that an eco-progressive approach to large-tract land management is new to the ranching community. There have been for decades many outstanding stewards among ranchers. Relying on grasslands, and with greater worries about drought, keeps them close to the natural rhythm of the land. Closer, most certainly, than conventional grain farmers. It's welcome news that this movement—let's call it ecological agriculture—exists at all. What's more

High corn prices stimulated record corn planting and yields in South Dakota. In 1995 South Dakota farmers harvested fewer than 200 million bushels of corn. In 2013 they harvested 813 million bushels. Pictured is a corn storage and train-loading facility operated by South Dakota Wheat Growers, a large farm cooperative that now has far less to do with wheat than corn. *Photo by author.*

interesting is that it has spread from west to east, from conscientious ranchers to established farmer-ranchers and farmers who have begun to naturalize their strategies and tactics when using the earth.

I've discovered that these men and women, these newly minted practitioners of ecological agriculture, are the ones who have their hands in the dirt. They're looking for earthworms and microbes to gauge the health of the soil. These are the farmers who watch for bobolinks and butterflies to assess the health of their land, and they have redefined for their own satisfaction the meaning and pursuit of land management. This shift came when each detected deteriorating soil biology and shrinking biodiversity because their fields had been subjected year after year to a grain-crop treadmill reliant on inorganic agri-chemicals.

The idea of regularly dousing their land with synthetic fertilizers and biocides became increasingly uncomfortable for these farmers. Not only were soils compromised, so was water. They knew aquifers were being unsustainably depleted and degraded by intensive farming. They knew ponds and lakes suffered from pollution as a consequence of chemicals creeping off or seeping through treated farm land. They read about hypoxia in the Gulf of Mexico and worrisome nitrate levels harming rivers and streams. They watched their neighbors install tile drainage systems that disrupted natural flow patterns and served as conduits further concentrating pollutants in water.

In the first fifteen years of the twenty-first century, rising corn prices encouraged many South Dakota farmer-ranchers to destroy native prairie in order to plant more corn. Cattle numbers dropped as grazing pastures were converted to grain-growing land. Here is newly plowed prairie, left, and surviving native prairie, right, in northern Brown County, South Dakota. *Photo taken by author, fall 2012.*

But what most bothered many of these conservation-minded farmers and ranchers was the widespread conversion of native prairie and pasture to grain fields. That tendency–plowing and destroying prairie–swept the western-most reaches of the tallgrass prairie region and the eastern portions of the mixed-grass prairie with the arrival of the new millennium, and it continued for at least the next fifteen years. In just one short burst of time, from 2006 to 2011, more than one million acres, much of it native tallgrass and mixed-grass prairie that had never been plowed, was transformed from perennial grasslands to annually-planted, grain-growing tracts. Scientists proclaimed that tallgrass prairie was the most endangered ecosystem in North America. Indeed, since European settlement, some ninety-nine percent (more than 150 million acres) of the continent's tallgrass prairie landscape has been destroyed.

Some time ago I started interviewing members of the South Dakota Grassland Coalition and writing about their eco-friendly agricultural operations. Each person I interviewed had converted from conventional farming. And from most of them there echoed surprisingly similar explanations for that conversion. It might sound overly dramatic but really it's not. Nearly all of the people I interviewed experienced an epiphany of sorts.

The Grassland Coalition has existed only since 1998. With help from a federal agency known simply as the Natural Resources Conservation Service (NRCS), a couple of dozen rancher-farmers formed the coalition, nurtured it, and shaped it to be most useful as an organization providing education about native prairie and pasture. Membership trickled upward as word spread about the pragmatic knowledge being sought and shared, and by 2015 membership approached 500. The organization now sponsors regular workshops and forums, convenes each year for an annual meeting, and presents awards for grasslands stewards who practice exemplary land and soil management.

To describe conservation-based land-use strategies, profiles of three individuals involved with the South Dakota Grassland Coalition—Gabe Brown, Jim Faulstich, and Rick Smith—follow. Choosing only three subjects was challenging, but each of the three represent values and ideas consistent with others in the organization.

Gabe Brown is the only North Dakotan among those I've interviewed. He's also the so-called "guru" of the Northern Plains agrarian conservation movement and is revered by his fellow stewards as a leader, innovator, and visible representative and spokesperson of their movement. Brown is in great demand across the nation as a speaker, and he travels as frequently as his farm obligations allow.

He'll admit that his ecological land management practices were earned through hardship and necessity, and he describes four straight years of economic turmoil (1995-1998) when hail or drought wiped out crops on his substantial farm and ranch in Burleigh County, near Bismarck. Nearly broke and lacking access to credit and capital, Brown desperately needed to figure out how to grow something to generate income without resorting to expensive seeds, synthetic fertilizers, and farm chemicals. "That series of four years was hell to go through," remembers Brown, "but it was the best thing that could have happened to me. It changed the way I farm, and it changed the way I look at agriculture and soils." Brown had already abandoned soil tillage in 1993, so he was inclined to seek out improved land management practices. By the late nineties, faced with losing his operation, he was ready to make another big move.

The next step, he determined, was to gain a more intimate understanding about the soils on his property. Precipitation in his area is low—about fifteen inches per year—and he understood the importance of keeping precious moisture in his land. Testing revealed that the infiltration rate was only about half-an-inch per hour, a sub-standard amount. "The aggregate stability of the soil," Brown explains, "had been destroyed by tillage." Although he'd stopped this practice years earlier, the damage persisted.

Brown also determined the organic levels of his croplands, and he discovered rates ranging from 1.7 to 1.9 percent. This, he dejectedly understood, was dismally low and unacceptable. Brown began reading about and studying sustainable farming practices, including the writing of Thomas Jefferson. "I learned that long before industrial farming came to dominate agriculture, farmers operated differently, and that they had been successful. I wanted to know how they'd done that."

Cover crops became a focus of his investigations and planting strategies, and it was soon apparent that his land dramatically benefitted by their use. Brown began growing a great variety of cover crops during all seasons on his land. "We now grow cover crops on all our crop land every year," he says. "This might be before a cash crop, as a companion crop or mixed in with a cash crop, or after a cash crop has been harvested." "The objective," he explains, "is to protect the soil and maintain living roots in the soil at all times." He emphasized that "It's the presence of living roots that feeds soil biology and starts nutrient cycling."

Today, after some fifteen years of perfecting his cover crop and other land management strategies, Brown has tripled the organic levels of his soils and increased moisture infiltration rates by 1600 percent. His ecological approach also builds new topsoil.

Brown abandoned synthetic nitrogen fertilizers when cutting costs, and he eventually learned he did not need or want them, even when he could afford them. "The irony and reality of synthetic fertilizers," he declares, "is that they destroy soil health." Despite his aversion to chemical fertilizers, Brown's corn fields out-yield the county average by twenty percent. He also learned to live without certain biocides. "We sparingly use herbicides," Brown notes, "but we completely avoid pesticides and fungicides. When you apply something to kill a pest, you also kill beneficial species. I want living things in my soils. I treat my farm and ranch like an ecosystem."

Diversity is the over-arching theme of Brown's operation. He runs 350 cow-calf pairs and up to 800 yearlings on 100 carefully tended pastures. There is no confinement feeding. He also has a flock of sheep, pastured hogs, and 600 free-range laying hens. His crops are grown mostly from organic seed, and he's raising corn, oats, barley, sunflowers, spring and winter wheat, alfalfa, and other crops. Of his 5,000 acres, 2,000 are in native prairie, 2,000 are cropped, and 1,000 exist as what he calls "tame prairie" or pasture. "We're trending toward more grasslands," he explains. "We're continually seeding cropland back to perennial pasture."

Brown refers to his operation as a re-generative agricultural business relying on "stacked enterprises" creating multiple income streams. Much of what he sells, including his line of grass-fed beef, is directly marketed to consumers. He did not and does not participate in the farm program and complains that the farm program has restricted progressive agricultural practices. His message to other farmers carries extra weight because it is accompanied by a candid confession. "It's not easy to admit that I farmed the wrong way for many years," he said. "I'm now trying to prove that there's another way, a better way, to farm." Fair and comprehensive assessment reveals the proving part is done.

One of Gabe Brown's disciples in South Dakota is a Hyde County farmer-rancher named Jim Faulstich. The Corn Belt has shifted westward, into areas that were not so long ago dominated by native prairie and grazing cattle. Faulstich's sprawling 8,000-acre operation, lying between the ninety-ninth and hundredth meridian near latitude 44.6 degrees north, is surrounded by plowed fields planted into grain. On the edges of those fields, near fence lines, are mounds of fieldstone excavated by landowners during the process of making their lands annually plantable.

Jim Faulstich has spent the last ten years doing the exact opposite of what his neighbors are doing. Instead of converting prairie to grain, he's expanding his acres into grass by restoring prairie. He's now up to 5,000 acres of grasslands, and he says that number will continue to increase. "We watch for birds to monitor how we're doing with the land," he says, as his truck slowly moves from his yard onto vast, grassy fields. Then he rattles off a list of what he's looking for: grasshopper sparrows, sharp-tail grouse, greater prairie chicken, and ring-neck pheasant. "If the birds aren't doing well, we're not doing something right," he declares. "When you run your operation in tune with nature, wildlife prospers and the land prospers, too. That's what I call managing for the big picture. Some use the word 'sustainable.'"

He is a learned, studious man who also has his hands in the dirt. He describes how his land was recovered from rough shape to fertile and fit earth. He talks about insects, worms, and micro-organisms thriving in a vibrant soil world. Cover crops are planted in all grain fields. Grazing practices for some 500 head of Red Angus cattle are dictated by ecological influences. Diversity in his plant regime, grasslands, and even in his marketing plan is critical. "We're not as diverse as we'd like to be," says Faulstich. "But we're getting better. We believe that diversity is a huge factor in protecting the land. We practice diversity not only within our crop mix, because managed diversity is better for soil and natural resources, but also because it's a safer approach for our operation's economics."

Rick Smith is another soil guy, another farmer-rancher deep inside the movement to protect resources and earn a living based on the natural carrying capacity of the earth. Smith runs a tidy, tightly-run spread in Hamlin County, 140 miles east of Jim Faulstich's Daybreak Ranch. Though driving from one to the other requires fewer than three hours, the biological and ecological differences are remarkably significant.

Plowing prairie with a tandem disc. More than one million acres of grasslands in the western reaches of the corn belt, including eastern South Dakota, were plowed under between 2006 and 2011 in order to grow more corn. Half the corn was used for ethanol. Not since the 1930s had so much prairie been so quickly destroyed. *Photo taken by author in Brown County, SD, fall 2012.*

Daybreak Ranch is in mixed-grass prairie country, while Smith's place occupies the western edge of the tallgrass prairie region. Faulstich's land is open to the horizon with a very modest roll. A casual observer would call it the Plains. Rick Smith tends a landscape geomorphologists describe as prairie coteau. This is a highlands region, with the James River and Minnesota River lowlands on either side. Although some glacial ice sheets overrode this coteau country, its stature was sufficiently elevated and influential to deflect the main masses of ice, creating calmer, shaved-down landscapes flanking the coteau. Up on top of the coteau the land undulates, with gullies, ravines, and some fertile, flatter stretches, too. The Smith farm includes decently farmable land, a sizeable length of lakeshore, and some highly erodible, steep-sloped topography. Most would call it a fine, pretty place.

Smith was in college when his dad died, and suddenly his life changed. It became his responsibility to run the family farm. "When I started farming in the early seventies," Smith recalls, "I did things like they'd always been done on our place and on most other farms." His dad had planted seventy-five percent of their operation to corn and small grains, and he'd also run a few cattle on some hay and grazing ground, with some hogs and sheep too.

Smith followed that grain-oriented cycle for many years, and when prices for corn dramatically rose he destroyed some of the grassland his dad had restored. "I'm not proud of it," he admits, "but I actually did plow under grasses established by my dad so I could grow more corn." "Back then," Smith laments, "when I pursued practices like plowing under grasses established by my dad, I didn't think about things like soil biology, moisture retention, water quality, and bio-diversity like I do now. And just about everybody thought that as long as you had some type of cash-crop growing on the land it was okay. We viewed our farm as land to be used, and we were following the quickest route to making money without thinking about the environment. There are still too many farmers who do that."

Smith's epiphany was slow, cultivated as he struggled through steep business challenges in the eighties. Low crop prices and rising expenses for chemicals and fuel forced frugality and a re-thinking of his farm practices. He watched bankruptcies claim plenty of places that had been profitably run for years. He needed to reduce input costs, and that meant changing the way he farmed.

The transition from annual grains to perennial grass may have been prompted by his desire to avoid high input expenses, but he noticed that his soils were improving as native species like big bluestem and others replaced corn and soybeans. And the market for prairie seeds took off as CRP sign-ups escalated. He started adding more cattle to graze his new grasslands. He started learning about pasture management, including rotational grazing, and he began reading books by land-use pioneers Allan Savory and Stan Parsons.

As the new century began, Smith was re-orienting his relationship to his land. "I came to understand," he reveals, "that I'd been farming for a quarter century, and I had never before paid sufficiently close attention to the ground, to the soils." His steady, careful transition to running a farm dominated by grass continued, even when corn prices jumped and conventional, corporate agriculture advised planting more corn. Recalling how he resisted the temptation, Smith observes that "Corporate agriculture has its own set of goals. Unfortunately, those goals don't always match what the earth can endure."

As he began the most difficult field transitions–converting his oldest grain-growing land to grass–he discovered the rate of soil recovery wasn't as complete or as satisfactory as he wanted. Then he started studying the work of Ray Archuleta, a respected agronomist who champions healthy soils and ecological agriculture. "In 2012 the light bulb really went on for me," says Smith. "That's when the concepts of protecting and restoring soils while earning an income from the land really clicked."

Exposed to sky for the first time. Freshly plowed virgin prairie, Brown County, South Dakota, fall 2012. Rich prairie sod, hundreds of years in the making, can be quickly transformed into corn growing ground. A tandem disc will cross-disc the broken prairie a second time, further pulverizing dirt and vegetation. Corn was planted here the following spring. *Photo by author.*

Rick Smith's farm now functions in a completely different mode than the enterprise he took over as young man. Soil health is the undisputed centerpiece of land management decision-making. Smith no longer rents any land, and of the 600 acres he owns 500 grow perennial grass, and only 40 are planted to corn. The commercial component of his operation revolves around feeding and selling livestock. Smith runs about 100 cattle, 150 ewe sheep, and up to a couple hundred lambs each year. "All our farm income comes from animals," he explains. "Everything I grow on the farm is used to feed our animals. A businessman might describe Smith's enterprise as being more vertically integrated than it had been. Smith says his new approach requires more thought and more labor, and it delivers more satisfaction.

It's 2015, and Jim Faulstich is serving as Chair of the South Dakota Grassland Coalition's Board of Directors. He reminds me that his comments about agriculture do not necessarily reflect the viewpoints of the organization. A reserved and modest man, Faulstich is not prone to hyperbole or self-serving clichés. As we sit in his well-used truck, surrounded by dense, healthy prairie, I ask about contemporary agriculture and how the movement he helps lead can change the future of land use. "Sustainability is a buzz word now," he says. "But are we sincere about what it means? What are we really doing to the land and other resources? We have already lost lots of diversity and lots of grassland. Are we caretaking our land or are we mining the soil? We need to embrace sustainability and diversity, and we need to earn profits and compete in a world market without government subsidies while protecting the environment. That's what we're doing here, on this place."

Chapter 3

Cattle Ranching in South Dakota: *Three Variations on a Theme**

Linda M. Hasselstrom

Environmentalists and the public need to give ranchers an opportunity to prove cattle raising can be not only sustainable but beneficial to the land and all its inhabitants; they'll be surprised at the ecological health of a well-managed ranch.

I own a South Dakota ranch that has been in our family since my grandfather, a Swedish cobbler, homesteaded here in 1899. As a rancher, I take care of the land in order to benefit my cattle and my livelihood, but like many ranchers I understand that taking care of the land means I am sustaining the health of my community and nation as well as myself.

Besides being a rancher determined to improve the local habitat, I am a writer, exploring topics centered on sustainable ranching; that is, on how my ranch raises cattle in a way that enhances the land and community. Each of the three connected essays that follow were written at different times. I have extensively revised each to be sure that the viewpoint presented still represents my thinking and current ranching practices, but the basis of each is a reflection on the philosophy of conservation as practiced by single-family ranches. My family and I have maintained this small ranch in western South Dakota for more than a century, supporting ourselves while improving the habitat for wildlife as well as cattle. My intent is to explain how a family ranch operates, and to show the sense of responsibility embodied in this work. I use statistics sparingly because I've learned from hundreds of talks and workshops that statistics are outdated within minutes of compilation, and readers avoid them the way a smart horse avoids a rattlesnake.

Since 1980 I've also worked actively in various plans to improve the environment, including statewide efforts to limit or halt uranium mining in fragile ecosystems and to prevent the establishment of a nuclear waste facility and radioactive waste dump. After my father's death, I moved to Wyoming for sixteen years, leasing my land to a neighbor who grazes his cattle under conditions calculated to enhance the land's condition. Our lease limits the number of cows he can run and includes provisions requiring him to maintain improvements that benefit wildlife as well as cattle, such as windbreak trees that shelter deer and grouse in winter. In 2008 I moved back to the ranch and now supervise the work done here.

Because of my activities, I've been disturbed by leaders who assert that the interests of ranchers and environmentalists must differ. In fact, numerous recent studies show ranching may be the best choice the West has to protect its wildlife, air, water, and other natural resources, as well as surrounding communities with open space filled with scenery for subdivision residents to enjoy. Each of these essays expands upon that belief.

Who Cares for the Land?

In 1985 David Foreman, a founder of Earth First!, published a technical manual to "monkey-wrenching," a guide to environment sabotage. Reprinted several times, the book devotes fourteen pages to instructions for vandalizing ranches, from stealing salt blocks, plugging water pipes, smashing water tanks, and disabling windmills to cutting fences. Publications available on the Earth First! website include several free and downloadable "direct action manuals," with chapter headings such as "Police Intimidation and Torture Tactics," "Chains and Cables," "Backwoods Actions," "Making Life Hell," and "Misc Deviltry."

"Some experts estimate that 100 people cutting fences on a regular basis around the West could put the public-land ranchers out of business," wrote Foreman encouragingly. The April 1998 issue of *Earth First! Journal* noted "rampant fence cutting" in Wyoming and advised, "Dust off those wire cutters, folks!"

This respected environmental leader encouraged ecological terrorism, suggesting environmentalists destroy public and private property! And Earth First! is following devotedly in his footsteps.

"We believe in using all of the tools in the toolbox, from grassroots and legal organizing to civil disobedience and monkey-wrenching," says the Earth First! website. "When the law won't fix the problem, we put our bodies on the line to stop the destruction."

If this man was leading a monkey-wrenching crowd in a city, he'd probably be jailed immediately for terroristic threats but his words, and those published on the Earth First! website against ranchers, apparently are not taken seriously by law enforcement officials.

Even if his method of removing cattle from *public* lands was legitimate, his advice makes no distinction between ranching using public or private land except in the throwaway phrase "public-lands ranchers." Many ranchers do not use a single acre of public land—but most grazing land isn't labeled with signs on the fences.

"Earth First! does not accept a human-centered worldview of 'nature for people's sake,'" says the website. "We believe that life exists for its own sake." Yet wildlife may depend on ranchers' water tanks, hay, and salt licks for their survival. The folks who destroy ranch property may put their "bodies on the line," but they aren't the ones dying of thirst. "Earth First!'s direct-action approach . . . saves lives," says the website, but cattle, deer, antelope, or elk may be killed by the destruction.

In June of 1998, during the Wyoming Stock Growers Association annual meeting in Casper, someone who was never identified drove a hundred miles on dirt roads in the rough Gas Hills uranium mining area of the Rattlesnake Range, cutting barbed wire fence in hundreds of places.

"Just in time for the welfare cowboys' convention," read signs nailed to fence posts. No group admitted the action; no arrests were made.

In fact, members of the WSGA own more than 120 million acres of land outright. Because they also manage grazing on additional public lands, they are subject to public scrutiny. A separate group within WSGA, the Public Lands Council, deals with Bureau of Land Management and Forest Service regulations and related issues affecting the ranchers who do use public land.

Following the fence-cutting, Wyoming agricultural groups acknowledged that fence-cutting had increased; the incidents weren't publicized because members hoped to keep the conflict quiet. One Wyoming rancher whose fence was cut in sixty places said, "For their own safety, they better lay off. If the right group finds them, they might get shot." Another notes, "Any number of my neighbors are now carrying rifles."

So besides causing thousands of dollars' worth of damage to ranching businesses that may have been entirely on private land, the fence-cutters also created a hostile atmosphere. There's no indication they attempted to use legal means to reform public land use, or to talk to the ranchers before they began their day of destruction. No news organization reported whether *any* of the land affected by the fence-cutting was public; every fence might have been on private land. Ranchers who experienced or heard about this incident may now be less likely to talk to a stranger about any topic at all.

Oddly, in our statistical age, it's difficult to collect reliable information about how much of the nation's ranch land is privately owned, because the U.S. Department of Agriculture does not differentiate between farm and ranch land. All rural operations are called "farms." But farming involves plowing soil. Farmers plant single crops and therefore contribute to loss of species diversity, employing chemicals to protect fragile non-native plants that have been introduced into the ecosystem. Historically, ranching has not relied on farming methods, though, sadly, some ranchers have been persuaded by so-called agricultural experts to use growth hormones and to spray poisons to control weeds and insects that feed on domestic animals. The trend, however, is toward sustainable ranching practices which utilize native grass without the aids of products sold by the agricultural industries, whether the grazing takes place on public or privately-owned grassland.

Studies also indicate that private lands are critical to preserving wildlife habitat in the Great Plains, because they provide buffers around federal public lands where citizens enjoying their rights to use public lands often abuse them. Several surveys have indicated that the best habitat for ninety-five percent of all federally threatened and endangered flora and fauna was on private land. Considering 262 threatened and endangered flora and fauna, researchers found that nineteen percent survived *only* on private land.

Here's just one example of ranch stewardship. In 2014 the family-owned Ladder Ranch on the Wyoming-Colorado border won one of the most prestigious awards in private lands conservation, the Leopold Conservation Award, proclaimed by the state's governor on Wyoming Environmental Stewardship Day. The Wyoming Stock Growers Association led a tour of the ranch to highlight efforts of the Salisbury/O'Toole family in conservation. Owner Patrick O'Toole says, "There is no inherent contradiction between production and conservation." Proof is visible on land leased from the Bureau of Land Management for lambing grounds, where the O'Tooles work with the U.S. Fish and Wildlife Service and other partners to conserve habitat for the greater sage-grouse. Also on or near the ranch are thriving populations of elk, deer, and antelope, as well as more than 250 species of birds.

A variety of organizations work with ranchers, rangeland managers, environmentalists, and universities in diverse coalitions to improve and protect western working landscapes. Among them are the National Grazing Land Initiative, Partners for Conservation, Society for Rangeland Management, the Noble Foundation, Quivira Coalition, and, in-state, the South Dakota Grassland Coalition and the Dakota Amphibian and Reptile Network. Scientific and practical studies conducted by various interest groups have determined ranching may be one of the best ways to protect the wildlife, pure air, water, and natural resources of Western land. Ranches also provide open-space protection at no cost to the communities they benefit. Privately-owned ranches often buffer public lands from development and high intensity land uses that might conflict with the attractions of wildlife, scenery, and recreation, and with management practices such as controlled burning.

Unfortunately, this makes ranches next to public land particularly attractive to developers. As many as forty-five percent of U.S. ranches are being sold each decade, and ranchers are often an aging population, "land rich and cash poor."

While ranchers use millions of acres of public land in some states, that is not the case in my home state of South Dakota. Still, in this state where nearly everyone knows everyone else or their cousin, we experience most of the misunderstandings that arise nationally between ranchers and environmentalists. For years, in my writing and in talks before varied groups, I've urged ranchers and environmentalists to get acquainted, to listen to each other's positions.

When folks interested in protecting the environment drive with me through our pastures, they can't see the difference between the land we lease from the government and the land we own. My father treated both kinds of pasture the same: with care. (I later gave up our lease so no one could scream the often-used slur that I am a "public lands rancher.")

My father lived on the ranch almost all of his life, and knew to the cow how many head of livestock a particular pasture would comfortably support in any weather. In a dry year, he began selling cows in early summer to avoid overgrazing, because grass damaged in summer will not recover enough by the next spring to support grazing. He habitually under-grazed, keeping grass in reserve in case a prairie fire or a hard winter reduced the amount of pasture we had available. Most of our neighbors do the same, as does the man who now leases my land. The ranchers we know might not call themselves conservationists, and certainly would not call themselves environmentalists, but they know taking care of their land is good business. And most, like us, are equally respectful of the other life forms that share this land with us. Several neighbors have told me of seeing unusual wildlife–a pair of wolves, a mountain lion–and cautioned, "Don't tell anybody! Somebody'd come in and shoot it," implying the killer would be an outsider, not a fellow rancher.

The day I wrote the first draft of this essay, in the 1980s, my husband and I had been trucking cattle to our summer pasture, a ten-mile trip across land owned by a couple of neighbors. As usual, we saw many native animals living natural lives in the midst of our cattle operation, just as we intended: several herds of deer and antelope, and a half-dozen coyotes. We always talked about bringing a rifle to fire out the windows, to teach the animals that they should fear vehicles, but we always forgot.

In another pasture, burrowing owls ruffled their feathers and crouched in old prairie dog holes as we passed. Later in the spring, owlets would gather at the burrow entrance, climbing on each other's shoulders to see out.

We had let the prairie dogs live their lives naturally, too, until they destroyed most of a hay field in an area where we often sorted cattle before taking them to the home corrals. Sorting, we often had to do tricky high-speed turns on horseback. Several times my horse stepped in a prairie dog hole and fell with me, wrenching my shoulder, tearing ligaments in my leg, and hurting me badly enough so it was difficult to ride a horse, or do the other work that constitutes my living.

Because of those injuries, and the severe damage to the hay ground, we decided to try to reduce the number of prairie dogs. We studied the various methods recommended by authorities like the county extension service and finally determined that "bombing" the rodents was the most humane: asphyxiating them in their burrows. We chose not to use poison, because it might kill the surrounding population of coyotes, owls, and other predators. We never bombed a hole with owl scat outside it, but no doubt we did kill other creatures, like snakes, that lived in the borrows. The bombing reduced the prairie dog numbers but did not eradicate them. Eventually, I decided suffocating the prairie dogs wasn't working and began keeping cattle out of the area to let grass grow, hoping natural predators would eat more prairie dogs. This reduced the grazing acreage available to the cattle, and required me to keep fewer cattle in that pasture, cutting my income for the year. We did see more eagles, hawks, and coyotes in the neighborhood, but the prairie dogs thrived.

Poison hadn't worked; natural predators didn't succeed. I discussed with my lessee what we should try next. We were both frustrated by our inability to strike a balance. In national and state parks near us, we could see hundreds of acres of grass turned to unproductive dust by the depredations of the prairie dogs protected by federal law there. We talked to experts. One suggested flooding the burrows. The burrows covered several acres, and were many feet deep. Our nearest water was a windmill with a limited output. We debated. Trapping prairie dogs is only successful fifty percent of the time. We laughed about a Japanese businessman who was trapping the animals and shipping them to his homeland to be adopted as pets. While we dithered the rodents multiplied.

One day my lessee used his D-9 Caterpillar to bulldoze the mounds flat, filling in the holes so grass would grow over the area. The prairie dogs have not reappeared in that pasture.

I don't condone what he did, but I understand and empathize with the frustration that drove him to it. Some prairie dogs probably dug out of the smashed holes, and some burrowing owls, snakes, and other animals sheltering in the prairie dog holes died. We'd tried to coexist with the varmints, but my lessee, an honest and hard-working rancher, feared for the welfare of his horses and kids, who had to move cattle through the hole-pocked territory. He knew the species would thrive, even if the dogs didn't remain on our land. Plenty of prairie dogs live on public land east and west of us, handy for tourists who call them "cute" but don't know they are susceptible to plague and that their burrows often harbor black widow spiders.

Usually, our treatment of the land is more benign. When driving through the pasture, we stick to the trails we've used on this land for sixty years. Even driving over grass buried under snowdrifts leaves trails of broken grass that will be visible next spring. And everywhere we can see the trails of hunters who have avoided our No

Trespassing signs and driven all over the pasture. The tracks from a single drive over the grass remain visible for several seasons.

When I drive visitors through the pasture, we stop often to collect trash while I explain that hunters and railroad repair crews often toss out soda cans, tin foil, and plastic bags. On windy days, Styrofoam cartons from fast-food sandwiches tossed from cars on the highway fifteen miles away hop across the pastures like white rabbits. This junk could be fatal to any animal that eats it, whether it's a cow, bird, or other wildlife. Passersby often use the broad entrance to our private road to empty their bladders and waste baskets. We don't mind the former, but we dream of finding an address in the piles of garbage we gather every year, so we could return the compliment. Meanwhile, we haul their garbage and our own to town and pay to dump it in the city landfill.

Our neighbors' pastures, too, are wildlife havens, as we learned whenever we rode there to collect our cattle when they trespassed. One day I counted ten deer, seven antelope, two coyotes, and dozens of smaller animals including a great horned owl. The grass was knee-high on my horse, and the bottoms of draws overflowed with water from the last snowstorm. I once saw two turtles larger than wash tubs mating (or fighting) in one of the ponds. Passing through, we always startled deer or antelope bedded in grass so deep they didn't hear us coming. Once, we saw a mountain lion. Grouse gobbled buffalo berries and wild grapes. Little streams supported an abundance of water life. The edges remained grassy because the number of cattle was never large enough to trample it down.

Counting the animals set me thinking that this and others pastures like it in this area are really "wilderness," as defined by the *American Heritage Dictionary*: "Any unsettled, uncultivated region left in its natural condition." Of course, the pastures are fenced, but so are most parks. We usually turn cattle into summer pastures in late June and move them to another pasture in October or November.

Eventually, my neighbor died, and his land was sold at auction; it remains in private hands. Posted against hunting and trespassing, the land is in better shape now than it was when its first white resident, a homesteader, gave up and left. Recently its owner saw a pair of golden eagles.

Not every rancher is so careful with his land, because not all ranchers understand that care of their land is directly related to the success of their cow business. But anyone concerned about the effects of grazing on prairie grass and wildlife should look over neighboring ranch lands before commenting, and should never accept broad generalizations about "grazing in the West" without examining local conditions. Be brave; drive in and talk to a rancher. Ask how long the family has been there. Investigate before condemning. A visitor may discover more interests in common than she can imagine.

Unfortunately, most land owned either by individual or corporate ranchers is not open to the public, because some of us have suffered damage from trespassers. If a person asks permission, she may be allowed access within limits: don't smoke, and don't drive everywhere. This won't help everyone, of course, because if we let in everyone who promises to be kind to the land, the thundering herds would trample it by their sheer numbers. If this land was a park, the two-track trail would be worn down to dust before it was replaced by a paved road at taxpayers' expense. The streams would be clogged with beer cans and toilet paper. Toilets and trash cans would stand on concrete pads beside asphalt paths leading to concrete parking lots. Stout fences would keep some folks from driving straight up ridges to prove their four-wheeler was "truck tough," ripping sod and starting erosion. The young and athletic would climb the limestone ledges and roll boulders down to hear them bounce.

Still, perhaps those who care about prairie can be content knowing that someone is watching over it, regarding themselves as only caretakers for the future. Healthy ranch land contributes to the health of the planet by harboring plants and animals important to all of us.

Why Giving Up Meat Won't Save the Planet

To be memorable, a good slogan should be short and simple. That's probably why "Save the planet! Stop eating meat!" has made it onto the bumpers of cars, even in my agricultural corner of the West. Unfortunately, a good slogan doesn't have to make sense.

I'm a rancher, so when I want meat, I pick out a likely heifer from the hillside and encourage her to stroll calmly into a small corral containing feed. While she eats in a familiar place, she's killed with one bullet in the center of her forehead and her throat is cut the instant after she drops. Chain is wrapped around her back ankles and a tractor lifts her body so we can skin and gut her. We haul her head and innards to a hillside where the coyotes will feast for several nights. I cut and wrap the meat for my own freezer and serve it to my guests as organic beef. I know—because I was present every day of that cow's life—that all she ever consumed was grass, hay raised without herbicides or chemicals, pure water, and salt. Each beef we butcher is chosen because she's not quite good enough for sale or for raising calves for our herd: she may be crippled, or she may have lost a calf the season before.

For those who do not have such a clear and active involvement in the way meat gets to their plate, here's a brief overview of the three major phases of the beef cattle industry.

First, farmers and ranchers own basic herds and produce breeding cattle, or yearlings sold as feeders. They keep the breeding cattle and sell the yearlings at a market where the price is determined by supply and demand, and by bidders.

In the second phase of the beef cattle industry, when ranchers sell their cattle, they have no opportunity to add costs of materials to the product, thus passing expenses on to the consumer as most businesses do. Ranchers take the price offered on sale day, or take the cattle home–where they will require more care at more expense.

The third phase of the industry may be confinement to feedlots: muddy, stinking enclosures for forty-five days or more while they consume huge quantities of pesticide-laced grain designed to add fat. These CAFOs or "concentrated animal feeding operations" (sometimes also referred to as "confined animal feeding operations") produce immense amounts of polluted runoff, drawing the attention of environmentalists. These facilities are generally operated by corporations that control feeding, butchering, and in some cases supermarket sales of meat, grain, and associated products; this is "industrial agriculture," or "factory farming," and accounts for much of the milk and meat, including chicken, pork, and beef, consumed by Americans. Because these feedlots buy grains grown in America, they are considered to be beneficial to Americans—surely a contradiction since such grains are fossil-fuel intensive and heavily subsidized, and thus damaging to the ecosystem.

By contrast, most domestic meat-producing animals evolved eating grass to produce healthy fat and safe meat without antibiotics. Grasslands harbor more biodiversity and sequester more carbon than cornfields or annual forage.

By 2011 about 35 million cattle were slaughtered in the U.S. annually by 60 major beef-packing operations processing around 26 billion pounds of beef. Four companies control more than eighty percent of all beef slaughtered: Tyson Foods, Cargill, JBS USA, and National Beef Packing Company. These monopolies, which also control a considerable amount of the nation's grain, flour, pork, egg, and poultry production, pass on their costs to the consumers, but the farmers and ranchers who raised the animals do not share in those profits. Enormous corporations are tough to attack and difficult to affect; it's much easier to cut fences or poke holes in water tanks in remote pastures owned by individual ranchers.

Most urban Americans buy beef wrapped in plastic from a well-lighted supermarket. City dwellers should relish that steak while they consider the life of the animal that furnished it.

The calf may have been born on a ranch like mine, where someone helped the cow if necessary. The calf grew up roaming the open prairie, watched almost daily by a rancher to be sure it was healthy. When it was six months old, we quietly herded the cows into the corral and separated them from their calves. Within an hour, we'd loaded the calves into a truck and drove it to the sale. Unloaded at the sale ring, the calf hardly had time to miss its mother before it entered the ring with fifty other calves and was sold to the highest bidder.

Then a trucker crowded as many calves as possible into his truck and sped east to a feedlot where the calf was dumped into a lot so crowded it might not have had space to lie down. Shoulder to shoulder, hundreds of calves struggled to a feed bunk to eat corn that has been produced and grown with herbicides. The biggest calves, like schoolyard bullies, ate the most. Some of the weakest were injured or died in the pen. When it wasn't eating, my calf stood knee-deep in muddy manure until it was killed for someone else's dinner.

My father used to say, "It makes me sick to think about."

Some people who advocate giving up beef to "save the earth" quote statistics showing that millions of people could eat the grain fed to cows, an extremely pathetic fallacy. First, while this statement plays on sympathies for starving people, most grain fed to cattle can't be fed to humans because our bodies can't absorb it. Second, cows don't need to eat grain to be healthy, edible, or even delicious. They developed as grass eaters so grain makes them ill.

Third, cattle graze in good health on land where crops cannot grow, so we can have both meat and grow crops; we need not choose.

When a guest's feet are under my table, the meat on the menu has been formed from grass and hay produced by old-fashioned sun and rain in our pastures. In the winter, cattle may get a supplemental ration of hay or a cake composed of grains, vitamins, minerals, and molasses. Most of the cows I've eaten lived the way cattle did for centuries before humans started interfering: largely undisturbed on prairie grass.

Once my cattle are owned by "industrial agriculture," they are no longer individuals. They are vulnerable to disease, exposed to germs carried by cattle imported from other countries. Runoff from feedlots pollutes streams and even underground water, not only with the contents of the cow manure, but with the chemicals used to grow the grains. Cattle raised on a diet of grass suffer diarrhea until their systems adjust to eating only grain while their flesh inflates with unhealthy fat.

Today much of our food production industry is dependent on monopolistic companies, not individual ranchers. Driving ranchers off public lands and out of business won't stop either the unhealthy feedlots or the pollution. Fewer than four percent of the nation's beef cattle graze on federal lands, according to the Department of Agriculture. The rest live on private ranches.

When family ranchers sell out, their holdings are often bought by corporations, giving big business tighter control over food production and thus over the price the consumer pays to eat. Land owned by such corporations is likely to be managed according to a formula devised without any particular knowledge of the landscape, and carried out by hired hands with no previous experience.

Feisty individual ranchers who object to centralized commerce may be called "un-American" or worse. But without them, dinner would be more costly and consumers would have less influence over what it contains. Major companies often ignore or subvert pollution laws, arguing that food is necessary for national security. Close alliances with government agencies may give them more control over public lands than ranchers ever had. And let's not forget the so-called ag protection laws ("ag-gag"), often reinforced by lawsuits, that prohibit anyone from filming CAFOs or writing anything bad about their products.

None of this is necessary. The whole complicated scheme is an elaborate edifice built to create profits. Range-fed beef is lean, organic, and healthy. If meat-eaters bought beef directly from a local rancher, both parties would profit and both would be helping to preserve their right to independent action. The buyer might supervise his or her future steak's daily life, monitoring the amount of fat in the eventual steaks. The buyer might choose to do the butchering, earning dinner up close and personal. If ranchers had a ready market for beef raised without chemicals, they could operate more cheaply. Both buyer and seller would be working together against monopoly and pollution, and more surplus grain would be available for hungry people in the world.

Before buying supermarket beef, research Department of Agriculture inspection regulations. Within the last few years the agency has reclassified a frightening collection of animal diseases as being "defects that rarely or never present a direct public health risk," and has allowed "unaffected carcass portions" to be passed on to consumers. In other words, meat workers are supposed to simply cut out cancer, lymphomas and tumors, sores, and intestinal worms, among other things, and send the carcass down the line to be wrapped and sold to you. Feedlots are often owned by the same companies that own factory farms where the corn is produced, the meat packing plants where animals are slaughtered, and the grocery chain stores where the price is affixed.

On my ranch, calves range over miles of pastures, free to romp, grazing on native grass. Their wastes are deposited on the ground and scattered by bugs and birds. Rains wash a little manure into stock dams, but the cattle are spread so widely over the land that their waste is probably absorbed by the earth before it reaches water used for human consumption. Feedlots, which produce too much waste for natural absorption, are regularly granted "permits to pollute" rivers and streams by county or state governments, which believe such permits will help bring jobs to impoverished rural residents. While it's illegal for CAFOs to dump waste directly into rivers, their sewage lagoons often overflow in heavy rains. They are supposed to apply the waste to land, but this method can overwhelm the land as well, and is also subject to flooding runoff.

Want to save the planet but like meat? If you live where grass grows, take a spring drive and locate cows with calves at their sides. They won't be far from the ranch house. A problem ranchers have been facing in recent years is impromptu rustling, where someone stops on the highway, slings a calf into the car's trunk and sells it at the sale ring. So don't stroll around a pasture without permission. Drive to the ranch house and introduce yourself. Explain why you want healthy meat. Most ranchers will happily explain their operation. You might be able to pick out your calf the day it's born, name it, and watch it grow.

Drive into the country regularly to visit your future dinner. Wear old clothes and waterproof boots. If ranchers believed that "time is money," most of us wouldn't be ranching. Offer to pitch hay or fix fence. Talk over local issues. In an exchange of views, both will probably learn.

A few years ago, I read a manifesto of "Green" political proposals that sounded as if it had been written by my rancher father. Yet the accompanying commentary suggested the concepts were "idealized" and "politically unrealistic."

But self-reliance, one of the core ideas of the manifesto, is our way of life. We didn't spend more than we made; we bought only the equipment we needed for our "small is beautiful" operation. We worked to match raising cattle with the harmony nature established on our ranch.

We practiced nonviolence, handling our cattle with horses and on foot much of the time, never striking any with a whip. We never shot coyotes, though we shot over their heads if they ventured into the yard where children and pets played. We never shot the deer that used our haystacks or salt licks.

I found only one Green desire we didn't already practice in its fullest sense: diversity. Most of our income was produced from one product: cattle. Still, we raised chickens for meat and eggs to use and sell, and harvested a large garden. We sometimes collected seed from a late alfalfa crop to sell if the price was high or to use in replanting exhausted fields. We bought black bulls to breed our Hereford heifers because my father noted that the first cross was always full of vigor. "Works that way in people, too," he said reflectively.

Defining the Sustainable Ranch

Every week someone somewhere mentions "creating a New Paradigm for Western Environmental Policy," probably in a meeting where experts declare the need to remove cattle from public lands. Environmental leaders hint darkly that cows exist only because "Powerful Ranching Interests Control Congress." Most of the ranchers I know take seriously their duty to vote and aren't afraid to call their state legislators. But rural populations are in decline, and ranchers don't hold enough voting power to control many legislators at any level.

People who advise rural folks on economic strategies seldom live in the West or have the foggiest notion of how and why ranchers survive here. Public figures offering counsel on the West's problems appear not to grasp the reality every ranch kid knows at ten years old: resources—especially the soil and water imperative for life—are scarce. If short-sighted people govern the West in ignorance, job-hunting ranchers in worn boots will jostle each other on every city street corner while public lands become dusty zoos full of starving elk.

Only grass keeps most of the West's thin soil from blowing east in swirling clouds to fall into the Atlantic Ocean. Evolved over millions of years, grasses utilize combinations of nutrients and water in specific ways unique to each Prairie region. Grass is the main product of Western rangelands. Disturbing the surface of the earth—plowing for crops and bulldozing for houses, highways, and parking lots—destroys grass and encourages weeds. Every farming method tried on arid prairies has been less successful than nature's. Few crops could thrive as well as grass does under these tough conditions.

Therefore, the most sensible way to sell grass—or "realize its market potential"–is inside a grazing animal. If, as Aldo Leopold commands, we make the land's needs basic to planning in the West, we must consider two resources—water and grass—first. By Leopold's gauge, sustainable ranching is the most logical and practical profession on the Plains. If a ranch has been in business for a hundred years, its owners or managers are working to maintain its water, grass, and therefore its wildlife.

Of course, my rancher father didn't say we should "sustain a naturally-functioning ecosystem." He taught me, "This land will take care of us if we take care of it." He didn't call it an ecosystem, but I learned by watching his actions that he considered antelope, deer, badgers, and coyotes important to our ranch. The antelope and deer still graze among the willows, trimming them; badgers and coyotes help keep the prairie dogs and moles from overpopulating.

Folks who live in town rarely consider predation relevant to their lifestyle unless they meet a mugger. Visiting Yellowstone Park, they expect to gawk at elk and geysers but be protected from grizzlies and forest fires. Managing the park for those isolated elements has nearly eliminated the varied animals and vegetation that create a healthy environment. As a rancher, I battle predatory blizzards, bankers, and environmentalists, but I try to remember that nature thrives on conflict. Survival requires skill and intelligence, not necessarily power.

Undoubtedly, the West was settled by a rugged tribe chasing profits in cattle and grass. Gradually, though, they deduced the reasons why too many cows or too many people destroyed their livelihood. Ranchers who came West in the 1800s knew nothing of ecosystems, but if their descendants are still here, they know that any sustainable economy proposed for western prairies must start with consideration for grass and water. How did my grandfather, trained as a cobbler, learn to sustain cattle in the shortgrass prairie? He had to learn from the land.

Environmentalists and the public need to give ranchers an opportunity to prove cattle raising can be not only sustainable but beneficial to the land and all its inhabitants; they'll be surprised at the ecological health of a well-managed ranch. Most alternatives are more destructive. Before banning cattle from public lands, we should examine the consequences.

Slouched in my saddle following cows, I've spent hours considering the possibilities of domesticating other grazing animals. The primary product of a ranch is grass; it would be harder to sell if it was packaged in a wilder critter than a cow. Recent immigrants to my neighborhood, for example, raise bison, touting their lean flesh and ability to survive Northern Plains winters without human help. Disadvantages are less obvious unless you share a fence line with the herd, as I do. Bison stay together even when grazing, while cattle spread out. Tired of their range, bison march through the tightest, tallest fences. They're quick-tempered and hard to herd; they can gut a horse with one sweep of their horns.

Deer and elk? Too fast to catch with a horse or the average pickup, they can jump most fences and are darn hard to rope. Pronghorn? It's hard to confine or harvest an animal able to run sixty miles an hour and duck under a barbed wire fence four inches high. Horses? Like bison, they gallop in groups, destroying plants, and though the meat is relished in some countries, it is unlikely to be added to the American menu because we have made cowboys, and their horses, into mythical heroes. A cow is a sensible compromise.

Cooperation between ranchers and their critics is the way to find an answer to the challenge of land use in the West. Antagonism arises because neither faction knows enough about the other's position. Ranch publications make environmental issues sound like the clamor of an invading horde, while folks in favor of preservation portray ranchers as barbarians. As an environmentalist born and raised on a ranch, I don't like to visit national parks or cities. Both resemble zoos too much for my taste, noisy, crowded, artificial environments, in strong contrast with the well-managed ecosystem where I live: a family ranch.

*One version of "Cattle Ranching in South Dakota: Three Variations on a Theme" appeared in my book *Between Grass and Sky: Where I Live and Work,* published in 2002 by the University of Nevada Press. The essay has been extensively revised and updated. As I worked toward the thinking in that piece, my essays on related topics were published in magazines like *High Country News* and *South Dakota Magazine.*

Chapter 4

"Too much" and "too little": *Land, Food, and Farms in Rural Iowa after 1933*

Lisa Payne Ossian

"Witness my home, Iowa, the most ecologically altered state in the union."
—David S. Faldet, *Oneota Flow* (2009)

"It was the 1980s farm crisis in Iowa and people were disappearing."
—John T. Price, *Man Killed by Pheasant and Other Kinships [A Memoir]* (2008)

"Dairy families lived in this neighborhood thirty years ago," explains David Faldet about the long-term consequences of New Deal government policies on Iowa's farmers, "but the pattern and use has changed. The steady money, from the markets and subsidies of the farm security agency, is no longer in small dairy operations." Explaining the irony of that government agency's title, Faldet continues, "The money has gone to row crops and the hogs that consume a steady diet of subsidized grain from infancy to slaughter." He further details the long-term consequences of such a government policy in that a contemporary farmer along the Upper Iowa River with "steeper fields shifted to corn and beans" now harvests 4.5 tons of corn per acre of tilled soil each year, but the loss of topsoil from that intense harvest can be almost ten times that amount in a single growing season. "The formula," as Faldet concludes, "does not allow for a long future of farming."[1]

Despite its acreage limitations, the New Deal's agricultural adjustment administration ultimately encouraged an industrial approach to agriculture with its emphasis on row crops and specialized livestock. To manage agricultural market prices, the federal government directed and limited to specific crop acreages and livestock production, but yields still increased because of the newly developing hybrid corn along with scientific animal husbandry. Still, market prices never rose significantly because American farms continued to overproduce, and thus the financial independence of the family farm subsequently eroded.

In September 1939, with Europe's sudden emergence into the Second World War, Iowa's farmers found themselves at the forefront of "Food for Freedom," a national campaign creating the "farm front" by encouraging all-out production with specific crop and livestock specialization along with increased mechanization. Dramatic, short-term profit resulted from the urgent, global need to feed the United States military and allies. The Second World War changed American agriculture in many dramatic and probably permanent ways.

Concepts of diversification and conservation, which had created progressive ideals such as alternative crops and contour plowing during the Depression era, would be shoved aside as almost treasonous in this escalating world war against the Axis enemies. Severe wartime shortages of farm labor pushed many family farmers out of business if they could not keep pace with the all-out production model and its corresponding requirements. Tractors had become tanks on this farm front, and even growing soybeans could now be an act of military revenge for Pearl Harbor. Corn in particular became the wartime ammunition.

The all-out production model during the Second World War and into the postwar era developed rapidly and expanded geometrically. By the 1970s, as Iowa farmer Bruce Carlson explains Iowans' new approach to the land, only a few farmers had "followed their instincts and never left crop rotations, wind breaks, and the many practices that farming fence-to-fence with lots of chemicals and big equipment seemed to make passé." Carlson also questions the turmoil of the state's later farming generations: "We speak of tolerable soil loss. Why do we farm on a limited and depletable medium and speak of its demise as tolerable?"[2]

"Traction engine" was a gas-powered tractor during the Great War. "A heavy, expensive, and not very maneuverable machine," explains Iowa historian David Faldet. "By the thirties it became useful, reliable, and affordable. By the end of the Second World War there was one tractor for approximately every two hundred acres of Iowa farmland. Tractors did not need oats or hay, never got tired, and could provide power for speeded-up machinery." Faldet concludes with a litany of rural Iowa's changes: "Horses would disappear, hired men and women became less necessary, and children were less essential as extra hands. Farm size had grown in the sell-off period of the Depression, and new cash demands for machinery and fuel pushed farmers to increase the acreage they farmed to meet their expenses."[3]

Northeastern Iowa farmer Greg Welsh makes a similar comment concerning the 1970s as he describes the extreme industrial movement encouraged by U.S. Secretary of Agriculture Earl Butz, who began what many citizens believed symbolized an earnest assault on America's land and the family farm. "Expansion, yield, fence-row to fence-row production, 'feed the world,'" as Welsh lists the rapid changes and challenges and then the almost complete demise of the family-centered farm operation. "It was a question both of 'too much' and 'too little.' Too much productivity that meant too much work, too much debt, too much anger, with too little return, too little communication, too little time for love."

Another farmer, named Richard Sandry, also expresses his frustration regarding the rapid governmental changes during the seventies as the seemingly uncontrollable storm of industrial agriculture swept over him. "How the clouds on the horizon of my sunrises sometimes later in the day," writes Sandry, "turn into the black clouds of fear, of despair, of anger, of uncertainty, and of depression."[4] Agricultural change had not only brought irreparable soil erosion but extreme emotional turmoil.

"Will you cut corn acreage?" asked *Wallaces' Farmer* at the beginning of 1950 within an editorial series titled "Fit Your Farming to the Fifties." Sixty percent of the polled Iowa farmers responded they would cut the recommended fifteen percent from their corn acreage through the 1950 government-directed program if they would otherwise be deprived of future federal corn loans. Twenty-four percent of Iowa's farmers still refused to cut corn acreage, however, preferring to take the varied risks and possible rewards accompanying all-out agricultural production.

"Many farmers claimed," commented *Wallaces' Farmer*, "they had followed good farming practice, had corn acreage down where it should be, and should not be asked to cut further. They were like this man from Kossuth County who declared, 'I don't market any corn to speak of. If they cut me too much, I won't have enough corn. I've been following good farming practice. The ones who should be cut are those who plowed up everything to raise more corn.'"

Wallaces' Farmer still encouraged Iowa's farmers to limit their corn acreage with soil-conservation goals as the main reason: "we need more acres back in grass to keep soil fertility up. Farmers have been putting too much of their land in row crops."[5] This generational move toward more and more row crops would be almost impossible to suppress, however, in the years to follow as corn presented the ideal technological response to changing postwar markets.

"Let's skip the crazy talk about 'push-button farming,'" joked *Wallaces' Farmer* that same year regarding an absolutely modern agricultural approach. "You'll probably never be farming from an easy chair." With the multiple yearly increases in available electricity, lighter farm chores would be possible, softening the daily routine and responsibility of rural life. Over 70,000 miles of rural electrification association lines had increased the number of Iowa farms with available electric service from 25,000 before the Second World War to more than 190,000 farms by 1950. Electricity would present just one of the many elements of dramatic rural change, and by the 1960s the catchphrases illuminated such agricultural changes: "power farming," "most modern operations," and "today's stepped-up farming."[6]

"Farm families for the next twenty-five years," explains agricultural historian Joseph Anderson, "continued to deal with fewer hired men, smaller family size, and a contraction in the number of farm operations." In this period from 1945 to 1972, Anderson characterizes the changes as "an agricultural revolution" in which farmers were the revolutionaries, yet vacant homes stood as stark symbols of this rapid technological and social change. "Iowa farmers were the ones who industrialized the rural landscape," states Anderson, "creating a very different landscape in Iowa but still one dedicated to agriculture. These physical manifestations of technological change were signs that Iowa, the heart of the Corn Belt, was an industrial landscape as much as it was a rural one."[7]

In an official letter written in 1973, long-standing Governor Robert D. Ray detailed Iowa's witness to these tremendous agricultural changes. "The last 50 years in agriculture—as in human existence generally—have seen the swiftest change which mankind has ever experienced," began Governor Ray. "Fifty years ago it took about 30 minutes of man-time to raise and harvest a bushel of corn; now an Iowa farmer can produce a bushel of corn with less than three minutes work."

By the early 1970s Iowa farmers profited with $4.5 billion realized gross farm income each year. "This fantastic increase is in spite of fewer farms today," explained Ray. "Within the last 10 years, the number dropped from 183,000 to 141,000 with an average size increase from 190 to 247." Fewer farms meant fewer people living on the land but with an increased agricultural production—a process perhaps only possible with an industrialized approach.

"Specialization came to the farm," proclaimed Ray regarding this new future of Iowa's farming. "With changes came a big investment in more efficient production methods, new techniques and new equipment. Of necessity, the farmer became a scientist, financier, marketing expert, and production specialist. He became skilled in management, law and politics and modern business practices." The governor and other Iowans were very proud of these agricultural shifts toward business and science rather than art and culture as Ray would conclude his report: "Due to these changes, farm productivity has risen nearly 500% since 1945. Big business farming produces more than twice as much wealth as all the gold mines in the world on 25% of the nation's grade 'a' land, producing 10% of the nation's food supply."[8]

The total number of Iowa acres in row crops (specifically corn and soy beans) increased from 11.7 million acres in 1950 to 20.2 million by 1975. "By 1980," reported Iowa's Secretary of Agriculture Robert Lounsberry in his 16th Biennial report, "we had 22 million acres in row crops. In 1982, Iowa had a total of 25.8 million acres of cropland in production." The secretary then examined the consequences of this rapid doubling of row crops from eleven to twenty-two million acres in just thirty years: "These figures indicate the pressure Iowa farmers are putting on the soil's resources. Erosion has always been a problem in the Prairie states, but it is being accelerated as more acres of row crops are planted on steeper, unprotected slopes, resulting in greater movement of both soil and water from the land."[9]

"Looking back, we see that since 1950," reflected Lounsberry, "new techniques, new equipment, and relatively high profits have brought about rapid and significant changes in farming: fewer and larger farms, fewer people living on farms, increasing costs, higher yields, and higher product prices are only a few of the changes that have been, and are currently, taking place. Major changes have occurred in the past 33 years in Iowa's crop production."[10]

"Iowa begins to look a little different," counters environmentalist Michael Pollan, "when you think of its sprawling fields as cities of corn, the land, in its own way, settled as densely as Manhattan for the very same purpose: to maximize real estate values. There may be little pavement out here, but this is no middle landscape. Though by any reasonable definition Iowa is a rural state, it is more thoroughly developed than many cities." As Pollan poignantly points out, "almost everything in this rural farm state has been remade: the only thing missing from this man-made landscape is . . . man."[11]

Pollan then depicts his overtly critical viewpoint of agricultural industrialization through the story of Iowa farmer George Naylor, who raises nothing but corn and soybeans on a fairly typical Iowa farm that feeds 129 Americans within this modern agricultural ratio. "Measured in terms of output per workers," explains Pollan, "American farmers like Naylor are the most productive humans who have ever lived. Yet George Naylor is all but going broke—and he's doing better than many of his neighbors." The Naylor farm has survived over the last several decades, not from increased corn and soybean production, but because of Peggy Naylor's paycheck from a social service career and annual subsidy payments from the federal government.[12]

Though the abundant years in Iowa lasted much longer following the Second World War, this prosperity through the 1970s would also end with a severe crash in the early 1980s, further echoing the earlier boom and bust cycles. After the 1929 national collapse, the resulting early Depression years presented many dilemmas—troubled scenarios and limited choices for Iowa's rural citizens as modernization compounded by difficult economic times presented a crisis but also an opportunity to explore creative ideas and possible solutions. Industrialization of agriculture seemed to present the answers to some farmers, although this approach required increased financing with ever more intricate systems of mortgages, loans, and government involvement, and as the decades advanced through the century, this industrialization created a complex agricultural system overly financially dependent on mechanization—tractors and combines—along with chemicals—fertilizer, herbicides, and pesticides.

The most extreme change for Iowa's farms since the early years of the Depression has certainly been this level of industrial scale and corresponding technology. "Chemical fertilizers, herbicides, and insecticides weren't available yet [in 1933]," writes Iowa farmer Bob Leppert. "About this time, hybrid corn became available and would be standing in the fall when it was time to harvest. This seemed unreal, because the open pollinated corn seemed always to be laying on the ground." Leppert then begins a proud litany of his own farm's mechanical progress: first, a rubber-tire tractor, a two-cylinder John Deere Model B in the 1930s; then in 1946 a new John Deere Model A tractor with a two-bottom plow and cultivator for $810; during the 1950s, his first diesel powered tractor. "During this time," Leppert explains, "the popular statement was, if you are having financial problems, get bigger."[13]

The move to "clean" coal and ethanol in this next century has still not solved the energy-production dilemmas of Iowa and has only brought more turmoil and tension along with a lack of complete answers. Within an interesting inversion on the old concept of burning cheap corn rather than costly coal, Iowa's industrial agricultural operations now manufacture corn ethanol as a fuel additive with potentially crucial long-term environmental consequences.

"The state of Iowa now subsidizes an ethanol industry based on surplus corn," Iowa writer David Faldet points out. "Conventional corn demands petrochemical fuel, fertilizer, and chemicals to produce. Political spin sells ethanol as a 'green fuel.' If it were produced from a perennial low-input crop like switchgrass or hemp, that would be true. But based on corn, ethanol does little to reduce the nation's dependency on petroleum and exacts a high cost from the soil and water of farm states like Iowa and Minnesota and every place downstream."[14] In an almost colonial economy, Iowa now risks its irreplaceable resources of soil and water to provide for other Americans an additive to their fossil fuel.

The industrialization of agriculture has also removed many of the labor needs for hired hands along with older brothers and sisters on the family farm who followed the lure of the increasing number of city jobs. Although mechanization brought its tensions of farm financing, tractors along with combines have eliminated some of the stresses caused by human relationships, such as unfair employment practices and uneven inheritance patterns. With a touch of hyperbole, a green John Deere tractor could never physically suffer from the green-eyed monster of jealousy like an angry hired hand or an anxious older son.

Despite the initial financial costs, mechanization did seem to provide more of a simple, safe, and straightforward answer. Though the Prairie farms of Iowa's pastoral landscape have enjoyed a romantic image and reputation for a peaceful coexistence with its residents, these homes had in reality suffered from aspects of isolation and various violent expressions of anger, jealousy, and despair among its family and labor members. The early Depression-era economic crisis only intensified the fragility of these bonds and boundaries, leading more and more to thievery, murder, and suicide.

Rural survival in the early Depression era had required increased stoicism, renewed pragmatism, occasional optimism, and sheer perseverance. And now what remains of that era's spirit? Sixty years later around the kitchen table in a northeastern Iowa farmhouse, a more reflective view of the past dilemmas concerning rural Iowa emerges: "the impact of technology on farming practices, the land, and the community." "Over food and coffee," begins editor Robert Wolf in his 1992 book *Voices from the Land*, "we would discuss the loss of community, the decline of the national economy, the problems of the family farm, and ways to counteract the dissolution we saw everywhere." Wolf compliments this rural neighborhood's informal organization and resulting "folk writing" as "a record of community that once existed here, of the growing costs and instability of farming, of the love of the land."[15]

"Farming was more than a chosen profession," comments Wolf in his second collection of Iowa farming memoirs titled *More Voices from the Land*. "Underlying the very foundations of traditional societies was the knowledge that to lead a fully human existence a person must have an art that he follows all his life." Wolf then defines the distinction between "work" and "labor" in that work is "imbued with art" and shaped by that concept—its dedication and passion—while labor simply lacks art—neither the creativity nor the energy.[16]

Farming, particularly on Iowa's rich prairie soil, was once such an art form. Another writer, Iowa farmer and poet James Hearst, recalls in a similar, poignant tone the sale of his grandfather's prized purebred cattle. The herd had remained a proud possession of the family for decades since Hearst's grandfather's presidency of the Iowa farm Bureau in the difficult years of the 1920s. "Everybody was stock market crazy and farmers were slowly sinking into a sea of debt," notes Hearst of that earlier era. When the sale closed, Hearst wonders about his grandfather who had never concerned himself with "financial reports or cash flow or bank credit." As this grandson suddenly realizes, "I sensed a change in our farming. It was a move from what sentimental editors called a 'way of life' to farming as a business." Hearst's ancestors had once produced fresh eggs, dairy products, garden vegetables, orchard fruit, and a variety of meat on their farm, while only "staples" such as coffee and sugar were purchased at the town grocery store.

"Now the farm had to pay its way," eulogizes Hearst. "Bookkeeping, accounts, income tax forms, charge accounts, and bank credit all became part of our concern. The luxury—if it could be called that—of being independent of the world outside the farm had disappeared. A different way of farming had begun." Despite Hearst's sense of realism, he does end on a rather poignant note: "I wondered which balance sheet, if one could be drawn at the end of the year, gave the most satisfaction."[17]

Ironically, the crest of the family farm had occurred in those same early years that marked the depths of the economic crisis of the Great Depression. At that time master farmers were judged on family relationships and community responsibilities as well as successful agricultural practices. Although phrases like "the romance of farming," "the rural way of life," and "the love of the land" seem rather nostalgic today in a world of capitalist-styled agriculture, those sentimental beliefs began to be subsequently countered during the midst of the Great Depression with such phrases as "the wave of the future," "the dollars and cents of farming," and "fields becoming factories."

By the immediate postwar era, five of the six master farmers of 1949 either owned larger farms from 300 to 500 acres or specialized in greater numbers of livestock such as 4,000 hogs a year. Only one of the selected master farmers owned a half-section that he had dedicated his life to creating "a fertile, productive farm from poor land." In 1960 one production motto simply explained the popularized necessity of these increasingly larger hog confinement operations: "it takes more pigs to buy a car now!"[18]

And by 1970 all five of Iowa's master farmers represented "large-scale producers who used the latest technology." As agricultural historian J. L. Anderson explains the era's shift in perspective, "this generation's legacies were larger operations, more intense livestock production, serious environmental consequences, and government regulation relating to waste management on modern farms."[19]

The industrialization of agriculture has systematically removed many rural residents from Iowa's land over the decades of the twentieth and into the twenty-first century, along with their votes and the state's political power. Iowa dropped from eleven congressional districts in 1929 to nine in 1930, losing another in 1940, yet another in both 1960 and 1970, still one more in 2000, and yet another disappearing district with the 2010 census. In short, within eighty years Iowa's political strength has plummeted from thirteen electoral votes in 1929 to only six in 2011.

"Today the small Iowa farmer knows," concludes editor Robert Wolf in an essay titled "The Jeffersonian Ideal," "that his years are numbered, and he knows that his and other Midwestern farm lands are being transferred into the hands of fewer and fewer owners." After the Second World War, when this "triumph of efficiency" became "the standard by which to judge agricultural techniques," the tremendous agricultural changes challenged both the environmental and social worlds of Iowa. "When you think about it," Wolf points out, "it seems remarkable that organic farming, which farmers had practiced for millennia worldwide, should have been wiped out in a matter of decades."[20]

"Beginning in the fifties and sixties," begins Pollan's environmental analysis, "the flood tide of cheap corn made it profitable to fatten cattle on feedlots instead of on grass, and to raise chickens in giant factories rather than in farmyards. Iowa livestock farmers couldn't compete with the factory-farmed animals their own cheap corn had helped spawn, so the chickens and cattle disappeared from the farm, and with them the pastures and hay fields and fences." This became the agricultural turning point, the plummet of the family farm. "In their place," as Pollan details, "the farmers planted more of the one crop they could grow more of than anything else: corn. And whenever the price of corn slipped they planted a little more of it, to cover expenses and stay even. By the 1980s the diversified family farm was history in Iowa, and corn was king."[21]

Dilemmas involve difficult choices, realizing Iowa's rural landscape has never evolved naturally or accidentally. As Esther Welsh emotionally recalls for many Iowa farm families, the early 1980s would be remembered as "truly hard times." "The value of our land, our equipment, and farm production slid to a devastating low," observes Welsh, "while farming input costs increased and interest rates climbed to a high of twenty-two percent. Those same capital investments that we had planned for, and that appeared sound to us only months before, had now become unmanageable debt. Financial difficulties and forced decisions are painful. Feelings of defeat, depression, and desperation cast a cover of gloom over farm families and farming communities."[22] As Iowa's secretary of agriculture during the early 1980s, Robert Lounsberry also attempted to explain this dramatic farm crisis emerging in Iowa. "Consequently, hard times on the farms during the recent U.S. recession," began Secretary Lounsberry, "has brought economic hardship to thousands both on the farm and in the city. Unfortunately, Iowa's recovery from the recession is still not complete and there has been an effort to diversify agriculture in Iowa with less dependence on corn, soybeans, and livestock which are the mainstays of Iowa agriculture."[23]

In a first-of-its-kind survey by the Iowa Department of Agriculture and the Iowa Corn and Livestock Reporting Service in March 1984, government officials reported that "10 percent, or more, of Iowa farmers will likely have exited the farm by the end of 1985." In a single year, from June of 1983 to June of 1984, an estimated two percent net loss of farmers in Iowa had already occurred. Following the policy numbers, the report turned more poignant. "What is wrong?" echoed the voices of farmers who testified at the hearings, blaming their problems on "high interest, low market prices, high cost of production, and low or non-existent profits, and a sharp drop in the export market."[24]

Still, farmers were not innocent victims or bystanders in this entire industrial process. "While advertisers, agricultural extension agents, scientists at land-grant schools, bankers, and policy makers had a voice in how farmers conducted business," prefaces agricultural historian Joseph Anderson within his detailed monograph on Iowa's industrial farming process during the postwar era, "farm families were the ones who allocated resources to invest in new technology and who lived with the anticipated and unanticipated consequences of using it."[25]

"Entwined in this problem is the family farm," elaborated Secretary Lounsberry, "a concept that is dearly embraced in the hearts of most Americans. It is difficult to define a 'family farm,' but we would like to see a continuation of the Iowa farm structure of today, where many families, individually or together, have an opportunity to farm their land. We believe this to be in the best interest of all. We need many farms in the hands of many; not a few large farms in the hands of a few."[26]

The more recent agricultural figures, however, are presenting another image further removed from the family farm. In 1980, the number of Iowa's rural residents reached 1,485,545 but by 2000 the number stood at 1,362,732 and in 2008 at 1,310,507. To translate, Iowa now has 175,038 fewer rural residents within the last twenty-eight years, while urban residents have increased from 1,428,263 to 1,563,592—gaining over 135,000. And "rural resident" does not necessarily equate with "farmer." The poverty rate in rural Iowa, however, has increased only slightly in that same time frame—from 11 percent in 1980 to 11.6 percent in 2008. Remaining consistent have been the top three commodities for the state: corn, soybeans, and hogs. Corn still reigns as Iowa's absolute king, yet the monarch has unwittingly created a kingdom containing fewer and fewer people.[27]

Iowa's rural dilemmas have certainly continued into the present century. As the former director of Iowa's Department of Natural Resources in 2001, Paul Johnson urgently wished to replace commodity subsidies with "conservation commodities." "Every farm should have subsidies for helping produce bluebirds as well as corn," Johnson emphasized. "If we don't do that, life on earth is in trouble."[28] Johnson's political tenure, however, was cut short for a variety of political and personal reasons.

Other officials' views of Iowa have remained slightly less romantic. "Iowa's and my commitment to preserving our soil and improving our water quality," stated Secretary of Agriculture Patty Judge, in 2000, "without detrimental damage to the agricultural industry, shall be forefront." Judge, too, echoed a family-farm rhetoric: "agriculture will always be of utmost importance for Iowa. The world believes that we are its breadbasket. With this daunting history—my department and I are committed to preserving Iowa's quality for the next millennium."[29]

The irony of Secretary Judge's determined words within her 2000 agricultural report of Iowa is depicted within the cover's illustration, which still proudly portrays an era almost completely vanished: a farm portrait shaped by a traditional red wooden barn and silver steel windmill as an orange sun sets in the background, a landscape of Iowa's rural life that has been systematically eliminated in the years since the early Great Depression. Iowa's rural spaces are now mostly composed of an austere array of barren images: endless rows of identical hybrid or genetically modified corn and soybean plants, plain prefabricated steel Morton buildings of bland beiges and browns, and monstrous white power turbines dominating the horizon, creating a sparse, stark sterility of an uninspired landscape and an unfertile imagination. Perhaps new rural Iowa dilemmas should resound?

The new champion of "the local food revolution" is, perhaps ironically, the U.S. Department of Agriculture's Secretary Tom Vilsack, as the USDA reports in 2009 a national increase during the last five years of 108,000 new farming operations with sales of less than $10,000. "There is a real opportunity for us," believes Secretary Vilsack, "to grow these small operations to mid-income-sized operations, and the way to do that is by creating opportunities locally for local production to be consumed locally."

Local food—"surprising words," some political and agricultural analysts contend, from a politician perceived as "too friendly with big business." "He was, after all, the governor of Iowa," states a National Public Radio commentary in 2009, "where some say support for corn subsidies is practically required to win local office. But Vilsack says the momentum behind local food is building." Perhaps an older agricultural dilemma of Iowa might finally be resolved with this increasing number of promising smaller farms and growing families prospering in a renewed rural life.[30]

Notes

[1] David S. Faldet, *Oneota Flow: The Upper Iowa & its People* (Iowa City: University of Iowa Press, 2009), 38.

[2] Robert Wolf, ed., *Voices from the Land* (Lansing, IA: Free River Press, 1992), 44, 45, and 46.

[3] Faldet, 193.

[4] Wolf, *Voices from the Land*, 55; and Robert Wolf, ed., *More Voices From the Land* (Lansing, IA: Free River Press, 1994), 3.

[5] *Wallaces' Farmer* (Des Moines, IA), January 7, 1950, 5, 9; January 21, 1950, 6, 14.

[6] *Wallaces' Farmer*, February 4, 1950, 14; March 5, 1960, 25.

[7] J. L. Anderson, *Industrializing the Corn Belt: Agriculture, Technology, and Environment, 1945-1972* (DeKalb, IL: Northern Illinois University Press, 2008), 140, 193, and 194.

[8] Iowa Department of Agriculture, *"Iowa Agri-Culture Serves the World": Biennial Report-June 1, 1971 to June 30, 1973*, opening letter.

[9] Iowa Department of Agriculture, *Iowa Book of Agriculture, Biennial Report-July 1, 1981 to June 30, 1983*, 2.

[10] Ibid., 2.

[11] Michael Pollan, *The Omnivore's Dilemma: A Natural History of Four Meals* (New York: Penguin Press, 2006), 34.

[12] Pollan, 37, 38.

[13] Wolf, *Voices from the Land*, 21, 22.

[14] Faldet, 197.

[15] Wolf, *Voices from the Land*, 1, 2.

[16] Wolf, *More Voices from the Land*, 55, 56.

[17] James Hearst, *My Shadow Below Me* (Ames, IA: Iowa State University Press, 1981), 125-27.

[18] *Wallaces' Farmer*, March 4, 1950, 8, 9; January 2, 1960, cover.

[19] Anderson, 137.

[20] Wolf, *More Voices from the Land*, 48.

[21] Pollan, 39.

[22] *Iowa Department of Agriculture, Iowa Book of Agriculture, Biennial Report-July 1, 1983 to June 30, 1985*, 28.

[23] Ibid., 2.

[24] Ibid., 3.

[25] Anderson, 5.

[26] *Iowa Department of Agriculture*, 2, 3.

[27] www.ers.usda.gov/statefacts/ia. The characteristics of Iowa's farms have changed with the average remaining somewhat steady at 331 acres in 2007 while cropland has reached 26,316,332 acres.

[28] Faldet, 197.

[29] Iowa Department of Agriculture, "Iowa Agri-Culture Serves the World": Biennial Report 2000, opening letter by Patty Judge, n.p.

[30] Guy Raz, "Farmer Markets: Fresh, Local, and Government-Approved," *All Things Considered*, www.npr.org (October 4, 2009).

Chapter 5

A Tale of Two Plains:

Natural Heritage Conservation in the United States and Canada

Barry L. Stiefel

While the emphasis of the first established national parks, Yellowstone and Banff in the United States and Canada, respectively, soon refocused on unique geological formations, majestic alpine terrain, and tourism, it was the Great Plains that continued to serve as the catalyst for environmental conservation within a "park" or "preserve" framework in both countries.

This chapter's investigation will focus on how the Great Plains (as called in the United States) and the Prairies (as called in Canada) played a pivotal role in the development of the national park model, both regionally as well as internationally. Several of the national parks within the region, on both sides of the American-Canadian border, were important to the emergence of wildlife conservation, with the species of significance being the American bison and the early success story of its salvation from extinction. Example parks include Yellowstone National Park (the first national park in the world, the eastern end falling within the great Prairies), Wood Buffalo National Park (for early bison conservation), and Waterton-Glacier International Peace Park (the first bi-national peace park in the world). All of these are listed on the UNESCO World Heritage List, testifying to their global importance.

Other park and natural areas of national, regional, and local significance will also be discussed as important case studies. Questions that will guide the investigation include: what were the causes for the establishment of these important parks in the Great Plains/Prairie region? The study will also investigate if the conservation approaches within each country have been similar or different, as well as gauge their development. For instance, has conservation policy within one country affected preservation practice in the other? If so, in what ways? Lastly, indigenous cultural heritage in relation to prairie ecosystems, as well as significant events related to transnational environmental conservation, will be explored specifically within the national park system context.

Conserving the environment of the Great Plains in the United States is a noble undertaking; however, it cannot take place unilaterally in order for it to be successful. Not only do the Great Plains span several state lines, but also the international border with Canada. Fortunately, relations between the United States and Canada are relatively positive, with the boundary spanning from Maine/New Brunswick to Washington/British Columbia, as well as Alaska/Yukon, creating the longest demilitarized border in the world. The two nations have had different yet parallel destinies in respect to the settlement of North America following the conclusion of the American Revolution in 1783, and so there is an important environmental and cultural history that must be considered here as part of planning for future conservation. Moreover, the indigenous peoples of North America have also played an important role within the region's land-use. Indeed, there is a very real triangular relationship among indigenous cultural heritage, bison conservation, and the prairie ecosystem. The aboriginal reservations and reserves within the Great Plains, sometimes with a relationship to national parks, have been leading the way for new approaches to environmental conservation in both countries within recent decades, especially in respect to restoring the natural rangeland ecosystem of the American bison. Through an inquiry into indigenous heritage, bison, parks, and prairie habitat, a more holistic understanding of conservation can be achieved, particularly as it pertains to the relationship between people and the land on the North American Great Plains.

North America's Great Plains: Cradle of National Park Conservation

George Catlin (1796-1872), an American artist renowned for his portraits of native peoples, first advocated in the 1830s that a great national park should be established for the purposes of preserving some wildlands from settlement for both "man and beasts" (*man* implying indigenous peoples), which would extend across parts of the western North American frontier, from the border with Canada in the north to Mexico in the south.[1] During the following decades, the writer and philosopher Henry David Thoreau also recognized the value of "Indian wisdom" in respect to the understanding and appreciation of ecology; however, the concept of a "national park," as we conceive it today, was never part of his proposal.[2] Decades would pass before anything materialized in respect to a national policy of land conversation.

During the second half of the nineteenth century, both the United States and Canada were looking to their respective westward frontiers as possible answers to internal problems. With the end of the American Civil War in 1865, the war-torn Union needed a project to bring Northerners and Southerners together. Additionally, following the British North America Act of 1867, the Dominion of Canada was created. The founding provinces, which had until recently been separate colonies under independent administration, also needed a common project to unite them. (Building something, such as a new nation along with a reinvented identity, can be an incredible rallying point.) In this way, new cities, communities, states, and provinces, as well as industries were created. Immigrants from the eastern seaboard, as well as Europe, settled land made vacant by the aboriginal peoples' removal policies of each country. It was from this *zeitgeist,* with much of the world having been colonized or explored by Europeans and their North American counterparts, that the protection of natural scientific curiosities and parts of surviving wilderness, where still intact, became socially important so that future generations could also experience them. However, this first step towards environmental conservation was primarily due to a nineteenth century romantic nostalgia for the past, not of ecological concern, which came about during the twentieth century.

In 1872–the same year as Catlin's death–the United States government created the world's first contemporary national park at the headwaters of the Yellowstone River, an area where the ecological biomes of the Rocky Mountains and Great Plains converged. While the vegetation of Yellowstone National Park is comprised of eighty percent forests, it was Catlin's interest in the Great Plains (both through writings and art work) that began his dreamy idea of a national park on the American western frontier. At this point, public park development in and of itself was still a nascent phenomenon within the United States. New York City's Central Park, co-designed by Frederick Law Olmsted and Calvert Vaux, was first opened in 1857 but not completed until 1873. Prior to the mid-nineteenth century, parks, both urban and rural, were primarily the exclusive retreat for the privileged. Central Park was specifically created for purposes of public recreation and leisure so that New Yorkers could quickly escape the squalor of urban life, even if only for a moment or two. Yosemite Valley was set aside as a park for purposes of protecting the scenic valley and groves of giant sequoia trees and tourism in 1864. The federal government granted the land to the State of California for management purposes, and so, while an important precedent for conservation purposes, Yosemite became a state-level undertaking, and not a federal one. Eventually, this land grant was transferred back in 1906 and joined with other federal lands to make a larger national park.

Conservation, as socially understood during the late nineteenth century, was not how we conceptualize it today. There was an implicit emphasis for proactive human use of the park, which did not consider ecology. The media of the period expresses this mindset best in the *New York Herald* from February 1, 1872, which was also reprinted in Toronto's the *Globe*:

> The Yellowstone National Park. – The bill has passed the Senate setting apart, as a national park, that wonderful district, some forty miles by fifty, on the head waters of the Yellowstone River, among the Rocky Mountains, in the Territory of Montana, embracing those strange mountain peaks, cliffs, castles and canyons, and those numerous wonderful warm springs, hot springs, boiling springs, geysers, &c., of which, the other day, we gave a general description for the information of our readers. Now let the friends of the bill in Congress push it through the House, and then, by simply marking the boundaries, we shall have the grandest and most wonderful national park, and, in a year or two, the most popular resort of summer travelers in the world.[3]

This recreational purpose for the park was also delineated in the Yellowstone Act, ratified on March 1, 1871, declaring, "Yellowstone . . . is hereby reserved and withdrawn from settlement, occupancy, or sale under the laws of the United States, and dedicated and set apart as a public park or pleasuring-ground for the benefit and enjoyment of the people."[4] Environmental conservation, from an ecological perspective, was not a priority at this point. Additionally, the vision of what a national park should be had shifted considerably from Catlin's initial proposal in the 1830s to the actual creation of Yellowstone National Park in 1872. First was the redirected interest from the expansive North American Great Plains to site-specific geological curiosities and scenic views; though the park boundaries do include some prairie grasslands where the Plains give way to the Rocky Mountains. Second, the indigenous peoples of Yellowstone were not allowed to reside within the landscape, and were purposely removed. This began a precedent-setting policy of removing native peoples from national parks the world-over for nearly a century.[5] Only tourists and park rangers were permitted within national parks.

The redirected interest in Yellowstone as a national park for the purpose of protecting some wilderness for both "man and beasts" was not unique to the national park movement. It was a reflection of political and economic priorities during the period. For instance, the American Antiquities Act of 1906, which came about as a response to defend historic and prehistoric ruins or "any object of antiquity"–specifically to save the Pueblo ruins on federal lands in the Southwest from pot hunter pillaging–also include a clause for "objects . . . of scientific interest."[6] This is how Devils Tower, a volcanic laccolith also in Wyoming, was established as the first American national monument. Its importance had nothing to do with it being a sacred mountain for the Arapaho, Crow, Cheyenne, Kiowa, Lakota, and Shoshone peoples.[7] The laccolith had peaked the interest of the American public as a scientific wonder, as had Yellowstone's geysers and hot springs.

When Yellowstone National Park was established in 1872, the Tukarika Shoshone, Bannock, Crow, and Blackfoot peoples were known to have lived there, along with other tribes, for many generations. By the 1880s the local tribes were confined to reservations, preventing access to their traditional hunting grounds in the Yellowstone area. This policy became full-bodied in Yellowstone when violent members of the Nez Perce tribe killed and abducted several tourists from a park hotel in 1877. The removal of indigenous people, as well as others (such as Euro-American inhabitants of the Smokey Mountains during the 1920s and 1930s, who had also lived on the land for multiple generations) spread as new parks were established across the United States.[8]

Native peoples of the Yellowstone area, either Shoshoni or Arapaho, shortly after their removal. In a manner of speaking, these people look out of place, confined to a sedentary life on a reservation. From *Journey through the Yellowstone National Park and Northwestern Wyoming, 1883*. Photograph by Frank Jay Haynes. *Courtesy Library of Congress Prints and Photographs Division.*

The tourist aspect of national parks quickly became a success, as predicted in the *New York Herald* article from 1872. Besides entrepreneurs in the Yellowstone area, railroads also profited in the transport of people from East Coast and Midwestern cities to the American West. This is why the Canadian Pacific Railway pushed for the establishment of Banff National Park in 1885 in Alberta. Indeed, in Canadian newspapers we find that the U.S.-based Northern Pacific Railway advertised in French, "La seule voie ferrée se rendant au Parc National de Yellowstone"[9] [that they were "the only railway traveling to Yellowstone National Park"]. The French Canadian advertisement by an American company is also revealing of how broad of an audience the Yellowstone National Park model appealed to. Not only as a matter of national pride, but also as an economic engine, Canada needed its own national park too.

Banff National Park began as Banff Hot Springs Reserve, at what is now Cave and Basin National Historic Site, a thermal mineral hot springs where a small resort was soon established for tourists. Though it lacked geysers, it is no coincidence that the first park was established at a site that contained natural hot springs, one of the main attractions at Yellowstone. Beginning in 1887 with the Rocky Mountains Park Act, Banff was subsequently expanded over the years to include scenic vistas and other outdoor opportunities. Establishments like Chateau Lake Louise and Banff Springs Hotel were built by the Canadian Pacific Railway to cater to Eastern Canadian, American, and European tourists. For example, in 1902 Canada's Parliament expanded Banff National Park by twenty times its original size so that it would "be larger than Yellowstone Park," as well as "be stocked with all native Canadian animals." Additionally, while the Northern Pacific Railway had advertised to Canadians to visit Yellowstone, in 1901 "over 9,000 tourists," largely Americans, visited it [Banff]," spending "in the park over $1,000,0000."[10] Similar to Yellowstone, between 1890 and 1920 the Assiniboine people were also incrementally removed from Banff as the park grew.

Recreational activities at national parks in both countries included some game hunting, which was permitted on a limited basis in Yellowstone National Park until 1894 and in many Canadian national parks until the 1900s.[11] However, as the late nineteenth century turned into the early twentieth, passengers on west-bound railcars witnessed a landscape that fell short of their expectations, especially in terms of the lack of American bison that had been known to cover the landscape in massive herds. Newspaper readers in eastern cities would learn the following:

> Excepting a few scattered bands of antelope on the plains north of the Missouri river and the small number of black and whitetail deer in the timber along the river bottoms, what little is the large game we have left in the northwest is congregated in the Yellowstone National park. Of course there are more or less elk, mountain sheep, and deer in the

mountains (Big Horn and Rocky ranges), but they are a mere handful to what the county could boast of ten years ago. The laws of the National park forbid the hunting of game within its confines, and it does indeed appear as if our big game were cognizant of the fact, for nearly all the remaining species seem to have sought refuge there.[12]

RULES AND REGULATIONS 939

OF THE

Yellowstone National Park.

DEPARTMENT OF THE INTERIOR,

WASHINGTON, D. C., May 4, 1881

1. The cutting or spoliation of timber within the Park is strictly forbidden by law. Also the removing of mineral deposits, natural curiosities or wonders, or the displacement of the same from their natural condition.

2. Permission to use the necessary timber for purposes of fuel and such temporary buildings as may be required for shelter and like uses, and for the collection of such specimens of natural curiosities as can be removed without injury to the natural features or beauty of the grounds, must be obtained from the Superintendent; and must be subject at all times to his supervision and control.

3. Fires shall only be kindled when actually necessary, and shall be immediately extinguished when no longer required. Under no circumstances must they be left burning when the place where they have been kindled shall be vacated by the party requiring their use.

4. Hunting, trapping and fishing, except for purposes of procuring food for visitors or actual residents, are prohibited by law; and no sales of game or fish taken inside the Park shall be made for purposes of profit within its boundaries or elsewhere.

5. No person will be permitted to reside permanently within the Park without permission from the Department of the Interior: and any person residing therein, except under lease, as provided in Section 2475 of the Revised Statutes, shall vacate the premises within thirty days after being notified in writing so to do by the person in charge; notice to be served upon him in person or left at his place of residence.

6. *THE SALE OF INTOXICATING LIQUORS IS STRICTLY PROHIBITED.*

7. All persons trespassing within the domain of said Park, or violating any of the foregoing rules, will be summarily removed therefrom by the Superintendent and his authorized employes, who are, by direction of the Secretary of the Interior, specially designated to carry into effect all necessary regulations for the protection and preservation of the Park, as required by the statute; which expressly provides that the same "shall be under the exclusive control of the Secretary of the Interior, whose duty it shall be to make and publish such rules and regulations as he shall deem necessary or proper;" and who, "generally, shall be authorized to take all such measures as shall be necessary or proper to fully carry out the object and purposes of this act."

Resistance to the authority of the Superintendent, or repetition of any offense against the foregoing regulations, shall subject the outfits of such offenders and all prohibited articles to seizure, at the discretion of the Superintendent or his assistant in charge.

APPROVED:

S. J. KIRKWOOD,
SECRETARY.

P. W. NORRIS,
SUPERINTENDENT.

Rules and regulations of Yellowstone National Park. Note item number 4, regarding hunting within the park. Department of the Interior, Washington, D.C., 4 May 1881. *Courtesy Library of Congress Prints and Photographs Division, Washington, DC.*

"The far west – shooting buffalo on the line of the Kansas-Pacific Railroad," *Frank Leslie's Illustrated Newspaper*, 32: 818, (3 June 1871), 193. *Courtesy Library of Congress Prints and Photographs Division, Washington, DC.*

During the first decade of the twentieth century, both American and Canadian citizens and governments responded to the dwindling herds of mega fauna. In 1905, the American Bison Society was established at the Bronx Zoo in New York where several lived in urban captivity. Founding members of the American Bison Society included William T. Hornaday and President Theodore Roosevelt. Congress was subsequently lobbied, along with fundraising for purposes of protecting bison, which resulted in the establishment of the National Bison Range in Montana in 1908–the first wildlife refuge to be created in the United States by Congress.

At the same time, Canada's Parliament established Buffalo National Park in Alberta (1909), a national park with a specific purpose as a wildlife refuge, instead of tourism or geologic curiosity protection. Many of the bison for Buffalo National Park came from American rancher Michel Pablo, who was of Mexican and indigenous ancestry.[13] In the following years, additional parks with the priority of wildlife conservation (especially bison) were also established, including Nemiskam, Wawaskesy, and Wood Buffalo national parks in Alberta, and Menissawok National Park in Saskatchewan.

Oddly, after completing their intended purpose of reinvigorating American bison populations, Buffalo, Nemiskam, Wawaskesy, and Menissawok national parks were subsequently closed during the 1930s and 1940s. In the United States, the American Bison Society also closed in 1935 due to the belief that their mission had been accomplished since bison were no longer on the brink of extinction. In 2005 the Wildlife Conservation Society restarted the American Bison Society, though many bison survived in domesticated captivity.[14] Only Wood Buffalo National Park persists, which is presently a UNESCO World Heritage Site as well as the second largest national park in the world. According to its statement of significance, Wood Buffalo National Park is recognized today as the "most ecologically complete and largest example of the entire Great Plains-Boreal grassland ecosystem of North America, the only place where the predator-prey relationship between wolves and wood bison has continued, unbroken, over time."[15]

Thus, we can see the development of national parks, in tandem with each other in the United States and Canada, as places that began ideologically (through the art and writings of Catlin) as a concept for enabling a bygone past to continue into an institution with a purpose of protecting exceptional scientific and geological formations for western tourist development (the Yellowstone and Banff models), only to reinvent itself again for the purpose of conserving endangered wildlife and its necessary habitat on an ecosystem scale. It was also respectively, in 1911 and 1916, that Parks Canada (first called the Dominion Parks Branch) and the National Park Service were created as distinct government agencies to manage the growing number of national parks in each country.

Ecology in Parks Beyond Borders

While primarily within Alberta, Wood Buffalo National Park also spans the province's northern boundary into Canada's Northwest Territories, comprising an ecosystem where grasslands meet frozen tundra. However, Wood Buffalo National Park was not the first to transverse a boundary considering that parts of Yellowstone National Park are within Montana and Idaho, besides Wyoming. Therefore, national parks have a long history of overlapping jurisdictional borders, and it is also in North America where they would first engage each other internationally.

In 1895 Canada established Waterton Lakes National Park in Alberta, and in 1910 the United States created Glacier National Park in Montana; both were established as destination parks and developed in a similar manner to Yellowstone and Banff in respect to accommodations for tourists. Indeed, Glacier National Park was specifically established "as a national park and playground."[16] Coincidentally, both were located at the edge of each country, along the international border between Canada and the United States. While both parks are noted for their mountain vistas and alpine terrain, what should not be forgotten, like Yellowstone, is that the Great Plains and species common to the Prairies are important parts of these parks along their eastern edge.

At a 1931 Rotary Club meeting in Waterton, Alberta, where the chapters of Alberta and Montana were in attendance, the members initiated the idea that the two parks should be joined as a symbol of friendship and peace between their countries. Both chapters soon lobbied their respective members of Parliament and Congress to pass legislation formulating the first international peace park, which came about in 1932. Besides goodwill, park management and conservation would be coordinated and conducted together across Waterton Lakes and Glacier national parks. The idea of an international peace park, like Waterton-Glacier International Peace Park, did not come out of a vacuum. Another citizens group, comprised of both Americans and Canadians, had formed in 1929 to create the International Peace Garden, a 3.65 square mile (5.87 square kilometer) park on the international border separating Manitoba and North Dakota.[17] This park was created by the donation of prairie lands by the respective provincial and state governments, not the federal governments, thus making it significantly smaller in size and scope.[18] The International Peace Garden has also been the focus of horticultural partnerships, instead of tourism or wildlife conservation, but nonetheless, it was an important precedent that was established on the Great Plains. In the late 1970s, the partnering national parks of Waterton and Glacier were designated as Biosphere reserves by UNESCO, and in 1995 a joint natural World Heritage Site. Waterton-Glacier International Peace Park, and by extension the International Peace Garden, has been the inspirational model for multinational peace parks and conservation initiatives elsewhere.

Perhaps the most significant multinational park partnership in respect to the conservation themes of the Great Plains and the bison are the Białowieża and Belovezhskaya Pushcha national parks, between Poland and Belarus. These parks have been instrumental in saving the European bison (*Bison bonasus*), an endangered/vulnerable species and cousin to the American bison (*Bison bison*).[19] Other notable international peace park partnerships include Kluane/Wrangell-St. Elias/Glacier Bay/Tatshenshini-Alsek (Canada and the United States), Talamanca Range-La Amistad Reserves/La Amistad national parks (Panama and Costa Rica), and Sangha tri-national park (Cameroon, Central African Republic, and Congo).

Despite the early role the Great Plains played in the idea of a multinational park between internationally recognized foreign governments, this was not the case per se for the federal governments of Canada and the United States with their respective indigenous peoples. Not until the 1960s, almost a century after the establishment of Yellowstone National Park, did a change in national park development policy occur in respect to its relationship with indigenous peoples. The change began first in 1961 at Xingu National Park in Brazil, where the Xingu, Xavante, and other peoples were permitted to remain (instead of being removed), though the government still maintained its supremacy in management decisions for the park.[20] The practice of allowing people to remain as part of the environment in national parks soon spread, including Botswana (Central Kalahari Game Reserve, early 1960s), Venezuela (Canaima National Park, 1962), Sweden (Padjelanta National Park, 1963), and Columbia (Sierra Nevada de Santa Marta National Park, 1964). Similarly, the United States began to entertain the idea of Native American peoples in national parks in 1975, when the National Park Service signed an agreement to allow the Havasupai tribe to use parts of Grand Canyon National Park for traditional purposes, including grazing. Canada began considering First Nations rights in 1972 within certain northern national parks, with greater guarantees beginning in 1979, as well.[21] The evolving attitude that indigenous peoples should have greater rights to their ancestral lands and traditional practices came about as a worldwide phenomenon during the 1950s, 1960s, and 1970s with the decolonization of Africa, Asia, and Oceania and expanded acceptance of human rights as a whole.[22] Within North America, examples include the passing of the American Indian Religious Freedom Act of 1978 in the United

States and the Canadian Charter of Rights and Freedoms, which both provided for greater aboriginal rights.

Within the heart of the North American Rocky Mountains are the Confederated Salish and Kootenai Tribes of Mission Mountain, Montana, where they had made a significant attempt of their own volition to create an indigenous owned and managed "national park" for the purpose of environmental conservation on tribal lands with the United States government, beginning in 1936. The effort was unable to materialize due to political disagreements between the two that concerned management rights in respect to wilderness conservation. The issues of contention for the proposed park revolved around who would have ultimate authority and decision-making power over management and land-use. Later, during the 1970s, the Confederated Salish and Kootenai Tribes unilaterally created their own Mission Mountain Tribal Wilderness area as well as the Tribal Wildland Recreation Department.[23] However, it must be understood that what was achieved was completely within the jurisdiction of the Salish and Kootenai peoples' reservation–it did not transcend a border. In contrast, a similar joint agreement was successfully accomplished at Canyon de Chelly National Monument in Arizona with the Navajo Nation in 1933, but the objective here was the protection of ancient pueblos in the desert, not wildlife or wilderness conservation on the Prairie. Additionally, while the Navajo Nation continued to own the reservation land for the national monument, they acquiesced to relinquish responsibilities of maintenance and preservation of the pueblos to the National Park Service, which had been the issue of contention with the Salish and Kootenai and the United States government regarding their proposed park site in Montana.[24] Lastly, the Salish and Kootenai are also not the only tribe to manage their own wilderness or park area, as expressed in the Mission Mountain Tribal Wilderness. Of greatest renown to the public, due to its iconic viewshed, is the Navajo Nation's Monument Valley Park in Arizona, which is exclusively managed by the reservation's Park and Recreation Department.

Canyon de Chelly is one of several national monuments located in proximity to a Native American reservation within the United States. First established in 1939 as Badlands National Monument, and later recreated as a national park in 1978, the Badlands of South Dakota are located adjacent to the Oglala Sioux's Pine Ridge Indian Reservation. Shortly after Franklin D. Roosevelt created Badlands

National Monument in 1939, the National Park Service attempted to expand the monument area with the inclusion of adjacent areas on the Pine Ridge Indian Reservation, which the Oglala Sioux successfully blocked. After the United States entered World War II, the Army Air Forces seized these same tribal lands for purposes of developing a practice bombing range.[25] When the land became surplus property during the 1960s, the National Park Service approached the Air Force about acquiring it. Congress brokered an arrangement in which the lands were returned to Pine Ridge Indian Reservation but under National Park Service management. This began a sometimes tumultuous relationship between the Oglala Sioux and the National Park Service, especially due to the lack of sensitivity the Park Service showed in managing the affected lands on the Pine Ridge Indian Reservation, which lasted for nearly four decades.

On November 6, 2000, President William J. Clinton signed Executive Order 13175, which required government agencies "to establish regular and meaningful consultation and collaboration with tribal officials in the development of Federal policies that have tribal implications . . . in government-to-government relationships."[26] In other words, federal agencies like the National Park Service could no longer badger Native American tribes (so long as they were federally recognized). Relations between the Oglala Sioux and the National Park Service began to improve, culminating in a jointly written management plan for Badlands National Park lands on the Pine Ridge Indian Reservation, conducted between 2006 and 2012. One of the objectives outlined in the joint management plan was to create out of the existing overlapping areas between Badlands National Park and Pine Ridge Indian Reservation the first Tribal National Park, which would be tribally administered in coordination with National Park Service management standards, which still (as of this writing) has to be approved by Congress.[27]

The interest of the Oglala Sioux "to bring back the region's native species—including black-footed ferrets, swift foxes and bighorn sheep—has been buoyed by the fact that interest in Native American traditions has surged among Oglala Sioux on the reservation."[28] The central species within this conservation ethic, besides those just mentioned, is the American bison. Part of the traditional heritage of the Oglala Sioux was the relationship they once had with the bison, not only in respect to material culture but also the cultural landscape. For this reason the bison must be brought back to their former numbers within the region.

Within Canada a jointly administered park unit for purposes of environmental conservation, such as Badlands National Park, has yet to be developed, though Canadian First Nations tribes are frequently involved in national park planning decisions, especially in the western and northern provinces and territories where they have land management claims through the Department of Indian Affairs and Northern Development. A site of significance in Canadian government and First Nations partnering is the Head-Smashed-In Buffalo Jump National Historic Site in Alberta, which became a World Heritage Site in 1981. While the historic site was initially established unilaterally in 1968 by Parliament as an important aboriginal archaeological site, contextualizing the heritage of the site as well as interpreting it could not be done appropriately without First Nations involvement. According to the archaeological record, indigenous peoples of the area had been using Head-Smashed-In Buffalo Jump for more than 5,500 years to kill bison for purposes of food and other resources. Here, culture and nature evolved in tandem, as it had throughout the Great Plains. While relations between Jack W. Brink, the government representative and archaeologist for the project, which lasted for much of the 1980s, and the indigenous peoples were not always easy, the Piikani, Siksika, and Kainai tribes of the Blackfoot Nation were able to overcome generations of mistrust from early mistreatments by the Canadian government. Together, they built a world-renowned heritage interpretation center on the history of the buffalo jump as well as the ethno-ecological relationship of native peoples with the American bison.[29]

One last boundary to be crossed, and that by eleven Native American and First Nations tribes of Canada and the United States, has been the Northern Tribes Buffalo Treaty, signed by the Piikani, Siksika, and Kainai as well as the Tsuu T'ina, Assiniboine, Gros Ventre, Yanktonai Sioux, Salish, and Kootenai peoples, among others. Between their respective reservations and reserves, they manage more than 2.5 million acres of grasslands and prairies, for which they have expressed a united interest through cultural heritage towards the restoration of the American bison in its former range.[30] Though not a national park, the Northern Tribes Buffalo Treaty is perhaps the most significant transnational environmental conservation treaty to date of the twenty-first century, and one that commits the signatory native peoples of both the United States and Canada towards an important environmental conservation ethic. Oddly, neither the Canadian nor United States federal governments are signatories, though the respective tribes in each country may have some influence considering their respective rights to have government-to-government relations.

Conclusion: The Prairies as a Commons for All

At the close of the nineteenth century, when national parks in both the United States and Canada were still new, the American humanist and writer Walt Whitman wrote about "America's Characteristic Landscape":

> . . . while I know the standard claim is that Yosemite, Niagara falls, the upper Yellowstone and the like, afford the greatest natural shows, I am not so sure but the Prairies and the Plains, while less stunning at first sight, last longer and fill the esthetic fuller, precede all the rest, and make North America's characteristic landscape. Indeed through the whole of this journey, with all its shows and varieties, what most impress'd me, and will longest remain with me, are these prairies.[31]

Whitman was smitten by the Great Plains just as Catlin had been more than a half century prior, leading to his proposal for some type of preserve for the protection of prairie, bison, and indigenous peoples. Indeed, the seal of the U.S. Department of the Interior (founded 1849) features the American bison on the Great Plains, and the National Park Service (founded 1916) a bison on the Prairie within the foreground, exhibiting the widespread association of the continent's interior with grasslands and bison. The National Park Service's use of an arrowhead as its seal's shape also creates a tie to aboriginal heritage.

While the emphasis of the first established national parks, Yellowstone and Banff in the United States and Canada, respectively, soon refocused on unique geological formations, majestic alpine terrain, and tourism, it was the Great Plains that continued to serve as the catalyst for environmental conservation within a "park" or "preserve" framework in both countries. Nearly simultaneously and politically independently of each other, Congress created National Bison Range (1908) and Parliament created Buffalo National Park (1909), the first wildlife refuges in each country, and used to protect the iconic species of the Prairies, the American bison, becoming an important success story within the wildlife conservation movements of both countries. During the late 1920s and 1930s relations between Canada and the United States bloomed, as made evident from the International Peace Garden and Waterton-Glacier International Peace Park established 1929-32. While Waterton-Glacier is renowned for its mountains, the prairies in the eastern sector of the joint parks' area are significant for American bison habitat. Many other multinational peace parks have since followed, with the most fortuitous perhaps being Białowieża-Belovezhskaya Pushcha International Peace Park, between Poland and Belarus, and the conservation of the European bison.

During the 1970s, with greater interest and respect for aboriginal rights in both countries, relationships between the native tribes of the Great Plains and the American and Canadian governments improved, after generations of mistreatment and distrust. The study of and interpretation of Head-Smashed-In Buffalo Jump became a significant undertaking between the Canadian government and several tribes of the Blackfoot Nation, where understanding the important relationship between indigenous peoples and bison became pivotal. Later, in the United States, the Oglala Sioux and the National Park Service were able to set aside their differences for the common purpose of developing management plans (2006-12) for overlapping areas of the Pine Ridge Indian Reservation and Badlands National Park for the first Tribal National Park (pending congressional approval).

The Great Plains of Canada and the United States have thus proved to be the setting for important national park development and nature conservation in North America, setting precedents for the rest of the continent as well as the world. Indeed, more may be in store when we consider the action taken by eleven tribal governments from both countries to create the Northern Tribes Buffalo Treaty. What this may entail is difficult to say. However, based on the observations from Catlin, Whitman, and Brink, as well the actions of the many tribes and peoples who inhabit the Prairies, future environmental conservation will have to entail a partnership with heritage preservation practices. Indeed, from the UNESCO World

List model, the mixed natural-cultural site structure is something to consider. Multinational partnerships in respect to landscape and ecological conservation, as emulated by the Northern Tribes Buffalo Treaty, provides yet another example of how to address regional threats such as the bi-national Keystone Pipeline System and global climate change.

Notes

[1] Paul Schullery and Lee H. Whittlesey, *Myth and History in the Creation of Yellowstone National Park* (Lincoln: University of Nebraska Press, 2003), 1.

[2] Henry David Thoreau, *Excursions* (Boston: Ticknor and Fields, 1866), 72.

[3] "The Yellowstone National Park," *New York Herald*, 37:32, (1 February 1872), 7; and "A National Park," *Globe* (31 January 1872), 1. Note the printing in the *Globe* was not only front page, but also a day earlier than *The New York Herald*.

[4] *An Act to set apart a certain Tract of Land lying near the Head-waters of the Yellowstone River as a public Park*, Approved March 1, 1872 (17 Stat. 32); also known as the *Yellowstone Act*.

[5] Stan Stevens, "The Legacy of Yellowstone", in *Conservation Through Cultural Survival: Indigenous Peoples and Protected Areas*, Stan Stevens, ed. (Washington, DC: Island Press, 1997), 1-32.

[6] *The Antiquities Act of 1906* (Pub.L. 59-209, 34 Stat. 225, 16 U.S.C. § 431-433).

[7] Ronald F. Lee, "The Origins of the Antiquities Act," in *The Antiquities Act: A Century of American Archaeology, Historic Preservation, and Nature Conservation*, David Harmon, Francis P. McManamon, and Dwight T. Pitcaithley, eds. (Tucson: University of Arizona Press, 2006), 15-34.

[8] See Michael Ann Williams, "'When I Can Read My Title Clear": Anti-Environmentalism and Sense of Place in the Great Smokey Mountains," in *Culture, Environment, and Conservation in the Appalachian South*, Benita J. Howell, ed. (Urbana: University of Illinois Press, 2002), 87-99.

[9] "Yellowstone" *L'Ouest Canadien*, Winnipeg, 1:1, 14 February 1889, 3.

[10] "Banff National Park: Will be increased to 20 times present size," *Globe* (8 February 1902): 22.

[11] R. Gerald Wright, *Wildlife Research and Management in the National Parks* (Urbana: University of Illinois Press, 1992), 46. The Yellowstone Act of 1872 only provided for protection "against the wanton destruction of the fish and game found within said park, and against their capture or destruction for the purposes of merchandise or profit," which thus permitted hunting for purposes of sustenance.

[12] "Wholesale Butchery: Annihilation of the Large Game Animals of the West," *Wheeling Register*, West Virginia, 24:120, (11 November 1886), 3, reprint from the *Cleveland Leader*.

[13] Andrew C. Isenberg, *The Destruction of the Bison: An Environmental History, 1750-1920* (Cambridge: Cambridge University Press, 2000), 165, 183.

[14] Juliet Eilperin, "In the Badlands, a tribe helps buffalo make a comeback," *Washington Post* (23 June 2013), <http://www.washingtonpost.com/national/health-science/in-the-badlands-a-tribe-helps-buffalo-make-a-comeback/2013/06/23/563234ea-d90e-11e2-a016-92547bf094cc_story.html> (25 January 2015).

[15] UNESCO World Heritage Centre, "Wood Buffalo National Park," *World Heritage List*, (1992-2015), <http://whc.unesco.org/en/list/256>, (20 January 2015).

[16] "Uncle Sam Opens Another National Playground," *Appeal* [St. Paul, Minnesota], 28:33, (17 August 1912), 2.

[17] "A Row Over Peace Parks," *Globe* (19 April 1932): 4.

[18] Though the Federal governments of Canada and the United States are involved with border crossing logistics as well as the international commission that manages the site. See Graham MacDonald, *Where the Mountains Meet the Prairies: A History of Waterton Country* (Calgary: University of Calgary Press, 2000), 90.

[19] See П. Козло и А. Буневич, *Зубр в Беларуси* (Москва: ЛитРес, 2011) for a current and authoritative source on the European bison.

[20] Seth Garfield, *Indigenous Struggle at the Heart of Brazil: State Policy, Frontier Expansion, and the Xavante Indians, 1937-1988* (Durham, NC: Duke University Press, 2001), 64-65.

[21] Stan Stevens, "New Alliances for Conservation," in *Conservation through Cultural Survival: Indigenous Peoples and Protected Areas,* Stan Stevens, ed. (Washington, DC: Island Press, 1997), 33-62.

[22] See Grace L. X. Woo, *Ghost Dancing with Colonialism: Decolonization and Indigenous Rights at the Supreme Court of Canada* (Vancouver: University of British Columbia Press, 2011).

[23] Claudia Notzke, *Aboriginal Peoples and Natural Resources in Canada* (Concord, ON: Captus University Publications, 1994), 258-59.

[24] Robert B. Keiter, *To Conserve Unimpaired: The Evolution of the National Park Idea* (Washington, DC: Island Press, 2013), 134-35.

[25] The Army Air Forces was the precursor to the United States Air Force, created in 1947.

[26] William Jefferson Clinton, "Executive Order 13175," *Federal Register,* 65:218 (9 November 2000): 67249-52.

[27] Keiter, *To Conserve Unimpaired,* 134-38.

[28] Eilperin, "In the Badlands, a tribe helps buffalo make a comeback."

[29] See Jack Brink, *Imagining Head-Smashed-in: Aboriginal Buffalo Hunting on the Northern Plains* (Edmonton, AB: Athabasca University Press, 2008).

[30] Rob Alexander, "Historic Intertribal Treaty Works To Restore Bison In Western Canada, U.S., " *The Huffington Post: Canada,* (26 September 2014), <http://www.huffingtonpost.ca/rob-alexander/alberta-montana-bison-treaty_b_5890836.html> (26 January 2015).

[31] Walt Whitman, *Specimen Days & Collect* (Philadelphia: R. Welsh, 1882), 150.

Chapter 6

The War on Wheat:

County Extension Efforts to Stop Wheat Production in Central Montana

Miles D. Lewis

The local response to conservation, most notably toward county extension efforts, in the Upper Musselshell throughout the 1920s and 1930s is telling of both the regional dwellers' attitude toward conservation and, thus, their response to federal programs in general.

Extension services for agriculture have a lengthy history in the United States. In 1887 the Hatch Act created experiment stations joined to every state's land grant university, tasking them to bolster research based in agricultural improvements. Twenty-seven years later, in 1914, the Smith-Lever Act caused experiment stations to focus effort towards cooperative extension, in which the service was to educate rural people about agricultural developments to improve their life-ways via advancing current animal husbandry, farming practices, knowledge, and techniques. Consequently, the service had a profound effect upon improving agriculture. Nevertheless, within the Upper Musselshell Valley of central Montana during the 1930s, actions by extension service agents paint a contrasting picture of the service's methods and goals. Federal conservation policies, the agents enacting such measures, and the local populace all had differing interpretations and responses as to how extension services should be implemented and just what exactly extension goals should encompass in central Montana.

In 1934 the extension agent for Golden Valley County, F. B. Peterson, wrote in his annual report "everything possible" should be done to eradicate dry-land farming from the region. Instead of advocating better irrigation methods, hardier strains of wheat, or improved land management like extension agents in other parts of the Treasure State, Peterson believed Golden Valley should return to a cattle base for its agricultural production and leave wheat in the past. His overall response was untraditional, and very contrary, compared to his colleagues in other counties. It is easy to surmise his recommendations were not well received by county residents, who in the late 1920s had already washed their hands of the extension program due to their belief that it was an un-needed institution, only to have to welcome it back to the county in the mid-1930s.

When Montana State University opened in 1893, it did not excite most Montanans, according to Montana historian Merrill Burlingame, because the general population was more interested in realistic, community-based farming or livestock courses to enhance their own farms, not in formal "degreed" education. Moreover, the university's agricultural academics were more concerned with how their own research could resolve, as Burlingame claimed, "[the] untouched problems confronting agriculture in Montana." Despite these differences, the farmer's institutes taught by academics served both the scientist's purpose and that of the local farmer. Informally, the goals of the fledgling extension service were to provide farmers with access to an agricultural expert prepared to conduct a thorough study of the farmer's lands and crop with the intent of helping the producer enact better farming or livestock raising methods. By 1913 these goals were financially augmented by the state legislative assembly, which granted county commissioners the right to use general funds, one hundred dollars' worth, to defray agent expenses—the only caveat was that fifty-one percent of a county's population had to approve the use of such monetary resources. As a consequence of this and a decade of good crop years, Montana had a strong extension program early in the state's history.[1]

With the passage of the Smith-Lever Act in 1914, Montanans chose to strengthen their extension program: the act not only bolstered the physical presence of cooperative extension, it notably backed the service by providing extension programs with $10,000 the first year the act was in force. The amount, by law, would gradually increase to $40,000. Overall, Merrill Burlingame claimed, in *The Montana Cooperative Extension Service: A History*, the act "provided the most massive program of adult education the world has ever seen [and] brought greater cooperation between various levels of governments and people's organizations than had ever existed before." Additionally, Smith-Lever effectively made the Montana Extension Program's purpose "to aid in the diffusing among people of the United States useful and practical information on subjects relating to agriculture and home economics and encourage the application of the same." Such concepts, and lofty goals, fit well with central

Montana, as nearly fifty percent of people settling within the Upper Musselshell were not really farmers but inexperienced day laborers and shopkeepers with no farming skills or backgrounds, who were merely "anxious to get some land in the last great West."[2] The Upper Musselshell Valley region was first settled by stock producers, attracted through mild winters with chinook winds, who utilized the vast open ranges to graze cattle and sheep. However, when rail lines passed through the valley, the Upper Musselshell was fairly inundated with homesteaders mostly interested in farming, who formed typical T-towns like the small community of Ryegate.

From its very origins, Golden Valley County residents had a strong filial sense in their awareness of being a farm community. The pamphlet "We are Satisfied," published by the *Ryegate Weekly Reporter*, stressed the region could easily be dry-farmed. Charles Snyder, one of the small town's pioneers, stated the valley's "ideal climate and . . . rainfall of more than twenty inches" was perfect for winter wheat and rye. Additionally, land prices were good "ranging up to $40.00 per acre, [with] good land [that could] still be purchased for a considerable sum less" in 1914. Other regional farmers touted corn, extolled the virtues of oats, barley, and massive vegetable gardens—where it "was not a curiosity to see a five pound potato or a forty pound cabbage . . . of the table variety." Alfalfa was praised as well because of claims that it "is easily grown here; is the least expensive crop and is superior to all crops in food content for livestock." Farmer and livestock raiser Loren Lay planted alfalfa, and within one hundred days it had a root system five feet long. To which Lay exclaimed, "this happens to be what they call 'dry farming.'"

Overall, the decades prior to the late 1920s were good to Golden Valley County. It was "Man's Opportunity Land," a region where many claimed "nowhere in the broad expanse of the continent is there better opportunity for those who desire to follow the avocation of farming . . . the soil in the great Musselshell Valley . . . is deep, and farm experts tell us that it will take many years before any deprecation will be noticeable and it will produce large crops as the years go by." Many years did pass since "We Are Satisfied" made that claim, and the so-called "deprecation" hit. With the exception of two drought years, it was a mere twelve years of good farming.[3] Because of drought conditions and poor market values for all agricultural products, Golden Valley County formally requested state and federal relief in 1931. The following year, Wheatland County, the last remaining county in central Montana not on relief, followed suit and requested relief via the Reconstruction Finance Corporation and the American Red Cross.[4] Both counties contained extension programs, but they had been discontinued in the late 1920s due to what amounted to votes of no confidence by the locals. Most likely extension was terminated for three reasons: indifference by agricultural producers, the questionable effectiveness of extension efforts, and county funds being earmarked for other usage. It is well documented that county extension during this era could be a difficult proposition due to funding, and agricultural producer's apathy toward agents, especially to ones who were unknown to the local populace. Taxpayer associations in eleven Montana counties started to cancel extension programs during the early thirties, and the total number of county agents within the state dropped from thirty-three to twenty-eight.[5]

By 1934 Golden Valley County reinstated its extension program, primarily under the Agricultural Adjustment Act (AAA) land and livestock purchase programs. The Livestock Purchase Program bought 3,353 cattle for over $50,000 and 4,674 sheep for just under $30,000.[6] Agent F. B. Peterson then, citing the last nineteen years had yielded only two successful wheat crops, advocated "everything possible should be done toward removing the dry-land wheat farmer and making . . . Golden Valley . . . (into) a livestock" region.[7] One of his main points was that once Deadman's Basin (a local irrigation project that, when finished, could hold up to nearly 73,000 acre feet of water) was complete, its water could help grow more than enough feed for ranches along the Musselshell River and the region's outlying benchlands. Peterson also believed, after the farmer was gone, the number of ranches would have to be reduced, because he found "at the time [meaning the early 1900s] . . . the stockmen were making good returns from their operations . . . [when there] were only about 35 ranches in Golden Valley County . . . [indicating it is] overpopulated."[8] He stressed that under the poor conditions of 1934 at least 3,500 head of cattle needed to be culled from the range. Peterson also acknowledged "after the wheat farmer is removed, it will be a problem of getting these old plowed-up fields back into grass again," signifying there had been significant ecological damage to the region from dry-land farm methods.[9]

By 1935 Peterson softened his rhetoric, but extension program records clearly show his nepotism toward his kinsmen stock raisers as his report for that year greatly downplays farm needs. For example, he pushed for crop standardization; however, his account indicates only two fields, of an unspecified acreage, were seeded in Yogo Wheat while over four-hundred acres were seeded to the primarily hay crop of alfalfa. Accordingly, Peterson wrote, "livestock being the main industry . . . the balance of the projects carried are projects radiating from the livestock industry . . . ." He further stressed, with the exception of a single community within Golden Valley County (referring to Ryegate where "the growing of wheat is encouraged"), that the terrain was more fitted towards stock production. Accordingly, the eleven programs Peterson outlined for the county vastly neglected the region's farm culture and primarily targeted livestock. In the eleven programs, there were nineteen livestock-based sub-projects ranging from livestock marketing projects to turkey marketing. Projects aimed at farms entailed only two major ventures for cropping, comprising five minor sub-projects. Focusing "along the lines of raising the standards of grades and getting a better quality of cattle," Peterson wrote that the 1936 program "should be built principally around the livestock industry, including both cattle and sheep, and leaving the crop program as secondary." To justify his reasoning Peterson wrote that the "Musselshell Valley is the most ideal place to run livestock as less feed is needed in the areas where it is colder and where there is more snowfall . . . ." Additionally, over fifty farm and small ranch families had moved in 1935 enabling "the livestock producers who are left here to have an opportunity to block up areas [meaning those farms and ranches that had been left] for ranging their livestock."[10]

If Peterson softened his rhetoric in 1935, in 1936 and 1937 he almost completely reversed his poor opinion of the region's wheat farmer. Stressing the extension program should still focus on the livestock industry, Peterson admitted "It would be impossible to set up a program of work . . . and make it a straight livestock program as these other projects [referring to farming] play a very important part in the continuation of the livestock industry." Extension efforts in 1936 centered on forage, seeding crested wheat grass for grazing, and crop standardization. Two hundred bushels of a "very good grade" of Marquis Wheat replaced much of the Yogo Wheat seeded the prior year, but it was all lost to grasshoppers. Additionally, hoppers and drought killed Peterson's alfalfa seed project, aimed at making hay for cattle, both for sale and local consumption, as only about 1,100 pounds of seed were produced in Golden Valley County when nearly 15,000 was expected.[11] By the beginning of 1937, Peterson virtually abandoned his quest to return Golden Valley County to being solely a livestock producing region. "Some of the greatest changes in the extension program for . . . Golden Valley County," wrote Peterson in his 1937 annual report, were "that not really as much attention has been paid to the livestock industry as has been in the years past."[12]

Golden Valley County's western neighbor, Wheatland County, faced a much more traditional, and beneficial, extension program. Like that of Golden Valley County, early extension work within the Wheatland County was problematic, according to agent A. D. Anderson because regional dwellers had "a tendency toward clannishness, where people are not in the habit of . . ." relying on outsiders. Thus widespread extension work was difficult and focused mostly within the realm of pest control. As a result county agent work was discontinued by a massive majority vote within Wheatland County. Anderson claimed that "the ballot was evidently not intended to give the county agent work a chance to survive."[13]

Extension work recommenced over a decade later, in late 1934, under the auspices of new agent K. P. Jones, primarily for drought relief in the form of the AAA's Cattle and Sheep Purchase Program.[14] Wheatland County was designated a primary drought region within Montana, and to alleviate stressed feed stores the federal government purchased 1,606 head of cattle valued at just under $24,000 from 145 ranchers. Emergency sheep purchases totaled 15,034 head of sheep from sixty-three producers, totaling $30,000, and over ten thousand of the sheep were killed, being "condemned as unfit for shipment." Even with such large purchases, the county contained eighty-five thousand sheep and fifteen thousand head of cattle, making the locale terribly overstocked and short ten thousand tons of hay for winter feed. [15] Wheatland County landowners listed 162,269 acres for sale to the government. The various federal conservation services, however, only optioned 19,000 acres, and never actually purchased any acreage because the sub-region was designated a secondary area of concern, resulting in discontinuation of the program within Wheatland County.[16] Despite federal aid, according to Jones, 1935 was still "one of the poorest agricultural years . . . ever experienced in the county[;] . . . the drought has been continuous since 1929 . . . (and) many of the ranges have been overgrazed for the past several years."[17] Because the extension program began so late in the year, agent Jones focused his efforts principally toward the livestock purchasing program.

In 1936 Jones began extension work in earnest, concentrating on all agricultural aspects of the county while enhancing his program of work on farm problems. Overall, he created a more holistic approach towards county extension than Peterson did in Golden Valley. Jones outlined fourteen major components for the year. Two programs (crops and rodent control) would benefit both farmers and ranchers; four programs (feed reserves, stock reservoirs, and drought shipments of feed and livestock) focused on ranchers; and five areas aided farmers (weed control, grasshopper control, flood irrigation, the wheat adjustment program, and crop production loans). Jones continued his program for 1937 in a similar vein to that of the previous year, the major addition being more demand in Wheatland County for wheat seed, particularly from the Federal Surplus Commodities Association, caused by the continuing drought.[18] In the conclusion of Jones' yearly report, he believed that Wheatland County was "undergoing considerable change" in terms of agricultural production because "in the past several years there has been a shift from the production of grain and other cash crops into production of livestock."[19]

In a sense, with his regular program of work, Jones achieved in Wheatland County what Peterson wanted to accomplish in Golden Valley County. It was much more natural for Wheatland County to make such a shift. From 1920 to 1935 Wheatland County (150,000 acres larger than Golden Valley County) contained an average of ten to fifty head of cattle per square mile while Golden Valley contained only one to ten head of cattle in a square mile. The two counties did not reach the same livestock levels until after 1935, when both regions claimed ten to fifty head of cattle per square mile. However, by 1940, conditions were so bad in each county there was a marked decrease in livestock as the average number of cattle reached one to ten head per acre in both counties.[20] This suggests, although the two regions are very similar in ecological make-up, that Wheatland County was always more of a livestock region than its eastern neighbor. On the other hand, Golden Valley was settled primarily by practical farmers or those who practiced a hybrid farming/ranching lifestyle. Most farmers there generally practiced a mixed agriculture lifestyle: some solely farmed, while others ran a few head of cattle or sheep, occasional hogs, and various types of fowl but considered their main profession to be that of cropping.

Despite resistance to Peterson's overt efforts to do away with the dry-land farmer, he was right: Golden Valley would probably have been much better off returning to their original stock production base, and leaving mass wheat growing behind, precisely because of the valley's ecosystem and natural weather patterns. Aside from the Musselshell River and its streams providing moisture, the region receives between ten and twenty-two inches of precipitation, with the average being fourteen to eighteen. Temperatures range from minus fifty to over one hundred degrees Fahrenheit, with an average of sixty-seven degrees. The various loams in the Upper Musselshell Valley seem to be perfect for moisture management through dry farming, despite W. B. Hazen describing the Musselshell Country as having only one acre in a hundred being fertile with the remainder being "sterile" and warning that Montana "must not be homesteaded" by a farming culture.[21] After 1915 the valley was blessed by uncommon wetness and great market values for crops. Average recorded rainfall reached twenty-six inches in the years before 1917, ten inches greater than usual. Farmers received eighty-eight cents a bushel for wheat in October of 1913, and some local growers were getting phenomenal wheat yields. One man planted forty acres of wheat, and at harvest time, he averaged sixty-three bushels to the acre. By the end of the homestead boom, around 1917, the valley contained over one thousand farms. At the beginning of the influx, around 1905, there were a mere four hundred.[22] Due to precipitation returning to normal levels, then turning to drought by 1919, homesteader after homesteader faced failure. Crops died at enormous rates, prices fell, and many faced foreclosure. Between 1934 and 1936, precipitation reached only seven inches, less than half the yearly average. The moisture problem was compounded by high temperatures which increased evaporation drastically, and the resulting drought was horrid. Wheat could be grown in the region under its normal weather patterns, but not the vast amounts, on relatively small acreage, with the massive yields considered normal in the teens when there was well above the average amount of rainfall.

What remains is the question of why Peterson showed such large degrees of support towards ranchers and very little toward farmers, while his colleague in Wheatland County illustrated fairly equal treatment to all agricultural producers. The answer may lie with two assumptions: who made up the county board in Golden Valley County and what they were willing to use the county and state money to support and the nature of Peterson's personal background. Peterson's yearly reports never mention who made up the county extension board, or their professions. His records for the early 1930s merely mention the members of several small subcommittees. The County Commissioners for Golden Valley County throughout the 1930s—Glenn A. Reed, J. C. Jensen, and Albert Ice—almost certainly played a role in Peterson's clear approval of ranching. Reed, formerly of Kansas, came to Montana with his spouse in 1918 to manage the Farmers Equity Store in the small town of Rothiemay. By 1919 Reed started to farm wheat with his wife's family. After massive and repeated crop failure throughout the 1920s, Reed ceased farming and started to raise sheep and turkeys. "The only way we could have stayed in the county after so many crop failures," according to Mrs. Margaret Reed, "was because of the sheep." Reed must have been a prodigious sheep man as his land holdings, as Mrs. Reed once wrote, ". . . at one time accommodated 17 families." Reed worked on the county board from 1928 to 1936.[23] Colleague J. C. Jensen served on the county board from 1924 to 1944. Jensen was a butcher by trade, having immigrated to the town of Lavina in Golden Valley County in 1911, where he opened a very successful butcher shop. Jensen eventually purchased a tract of land, and both he and his wife also filed homestead claims to start wheat farming. The terrible climatic conditions of the 1920s made this a short-lived venture, and Jensen switched gears into sheep ranching when he made a large purchase of "a thousand yearlings ewes [sic]."[24] Albert Ice emigrated from Illinois to Washington State, when in 1915 a family member's misfortune called him to Ryegate. Ice decided to stay in Golden Valley and rented land south of Ryegate in Big Coulee to farm wheat. Four years later he was appointed to the county board where he served for nearly twenty years. In addition to his farming venture in Big Coulee, Ice entered into partnership with two other men to form a sheep ranching company. The three men purchased "several sections of land" together. Ice eventually bought out his partner's shares to own the entire company.[25]

The character and aspirations of the three Golden Valley Commissioners is telling. All three farmed wheat until the drought and heat of the 1920s forced them into sheep raising. They all had large land holdings, with the desire to get more land and livestock. Additionally, they all slowly moved into cattle production throughout the 1940s and 1950s. It is easy to surmise that, after failing at farming, something all three had firmly ingrained within their backgrounds and after attaining fairly sizable grazing areas, they were bent on getting more acreage for sheep, while reinforcing regional ranching with federal aid and funds placed at the discretion of county commissioners. Such a powerbase question would explain why the bulk of Peterson's efforts initially went toward stock production rather than cropping. With the board stacked with disgruntled former farmers turned big ranchers, appropriating funds to support cattle and sheep ventures may have been the only route open to a viable form of extension service at the time—a route tainted by regional bias and nepotism toward stockmen.

Peterson's personal background could also possibly explain his initial favoritism. If he had more of a ranch background in his life's development, he may have naturally gravitated towards stock raising due to personal affiliations with that lifestyle. In comparison, Jones's records from Wheatland County are much more complete in terms of county board membership, and it seems there was a fairly even split between ranchers and farmers in terms of who could control appropriations, thus enabling what programs the county agent should focus effort toward. Additionally, Peterson neglected the majority of regional farmers who were not "farmers" in the sense that they specialized in one or two crops. Most practiced a mixed-farming lifestyle like those from Iowa and Ohio: they had very limited acreage for growing so they supplemented their lifestyle with livestock production that ran the gamut from dairying to raising turkeys, beef cattle, wool and mutton. That was only natural as many of them had immigrated to central Montana from the more humid, lowland base regions of the Midwest. As such they were dependent upon help from both perspectives during the turbulent 1930s, while trying to use that region's planting and harvesting techniques, which simply were not possible in central Montana once it returned to its normal ecological levels. Focusing on only one endeavor would have caused their failure just as fast as adverse weather conditions and poor market values. Such ideals effectively hobbled Peterson before he had a chance even to begin focusing solely upon stock production.

The comparison of Golden Valley County and Wheatland County in terms of county extension activities reveals the daunting task faced by local extension agents. Although their main foe was drought and bad market values, they also faced personal and political insurgencies. Appropriating money was a very political concept as the county board, those who were ultimately in control of the purse strings, could virtually force an agent to focus upon an agenda skewed in their or their colleagues' favor or by personal beliefs. At the turn of the century, when cattle was king on the Great Plains, such efforts probably would have been successful at doing "everything possible" to get rid of the dry-land farmer. Peterson encountered a tough task regardless of whether his personal feelings towards ranching or a single-minded county board sponsored his favoritism towards stock raising. Jones faced a less risky situation in Wheatland County, where the board was made up of both stock producer and cropper and was already more of a stock producing county than its neighbor. However, by the 1930s, when the majority of people within Golden Valley practiced mixed farming on small acreages, cattle was no longer king and hybrid croppers had the political power, and numbers, to change the county board's membership, or even do away with the extension service if they wished. However, Peterson's opinions and program of works are certainly a representation of the class interests endemic in early extension programs. As historian Gladys Baker showed in her work *The County Agent,* because county agents were responsible to local political units first and foremost, they were most likely unduly influenced by county boards: "The necessity of pleasing economic and political leaders because of dependence upon county appropriations as well as the natural tendency to conform to social and economic patterns has resulted in service by the county agent primarily for the more prosperous."[26] This almost certainly was the reason for the reactions in the case of Agent Peterson and the Golden Valley County Commissioners.

The local response to conservation, most notably toward county extension efforts, in the Upper Musselshell throughout the 1920s and 1930s is telling of both the regional dwellers' attitude toward conservation and, thus, their response to federal programs in general. Initially, extension agents were mistrusted and treated with indifference by locals, who, in turn, questioned the effectiveness of the agents' program of works and wanted county funds utilized in what they perceived to be more useful manners. Their "clannishness," as one agent remarked, was geared toward halting any type of extension work. Even so, when drought and the Great Depression struck central Montana earlier than many areas in the United States, federal aid via conservation was welcomed, particularly when it came to animal husbandry efforts like the various cattle and sheep purchase programs enacted by the AAA. This tended to skew extension programs, especially in Golden Valley County, toward livestock production and the attempted abolition of the farming culture within that county. It was a response that was not well received by most agricultural producers and was most likely forged as a program of works by the county commissioners, who controlled the proverbial purse strings concerning agent funds and were all serious sheep men. Despite this, most producers in Golden Valley had migrated to central Montana from the humid Midwest to pursue farming in the only way they knew how: diversified cropping where it was rare to specialize in a single crop and where livestock production went hand-in-hand with farming efforts. Communities like Ryegate being steeped in farming culture bear this concept out—that farming communities could indeed control what types of programs were offered by extension agents and, by proxy, federal conservation policy. Seemingly, the response to conservation efforts by regional dwellers in the 1930s suddenly became much more hands-on when compared to that of the 1920s when residents had done away with extension entirely. Consequently, the non-tra-

Wheat crop on the haymaker cap (ca. 1915).

ditional response, manifested in Agent Peterson's attempts to "do everything" possible to halt farmers from farming, was sidelined in favor of creating a holistic program of works similar to the more traditional approach towards conservation through county extension enacted in other central Montana counties.

Notes

[1] Merrill G. Burlingame and Edward J. Bell, Jr., *The Montana Cooperative Extension Service: A History 1893-1974* (Bozeman: Montana State University, 1984), 5-6, 12-13, 20-23.

[2] Burlingame and Bell, *The Montana Cooperative Extension Service*, 34, 42; Montana County Extension Records, 1939, "An Historical Review and Appraisal," by John C. Bower, (Box 79:4, Merrill G. Burlingame Special Collection-Montana State University-Bozeman), 3.

[3] *Ryegate Weekly Reporter*, "We Are Satisfied," (Ryegate: Montana, 1914), passim.

[4] Ibid. 87.

[5] Gladys Baker, *The County Agent* (Chicago: University of Chicago Press, 1939), 59; Merrill G. Burlingame and Edward Bell, Jr., *The Montana Cooperative Extension Service: A History 1893-1974* (Bozeman: Montana State University, 1984), 103.

[6] Montana County Extension Records, 1934, "Annual Report-Golden Valley County," by F. B. Peterson (Box 27:27, Merrill G. Burlingame Special Collection-Montana State University-Bozeman), 25-33. This record contains data for both Golden Valley and Musselshell Counties.

[7] Ibid. 4.

[8] Ibid. 23.

[9] Ibid. 4.

[10] Montana County Extension Records, 1935, "Annual Report-Golden Valley and Musselshell Counties," by F. B. Peterson (Box 27:28, Merrill G. Burlingame Special Collection-Montana State University-Bozeman), 2, 5, 7-9, 10, 45, 50-51.

[11] Montana County Extension Records, 1936, "Annual Report-Golden Valley and Musselshell Counties," by F. B. Peterson (Box 27:29, Merrill G. Burlingame Special Collection-Montana State University-Bozeman), 5-7, 63.

[12] Montana County Extension Records, 1937, "Annual Report-Golden Valley and Musselshell Counties," by F. B. Peterson (Box 27:29, Merrill G. Burlingame Special Collection-Montana State University-Bozeman), 7.

[13] Montana County Extension Records, 1922, "Annual Report-Wheatland County," by A. D. Anderson (Box 66:9, Merrill G. Burlingame Special Collection-Montana State University-Bozeman), 1-2.

[14] Montana County Extension Records, 1934, "Annual Report-Wheatland County," by K. P. Jones (Box 66:10, Merrill G. Burlingame Special Collection-Montana State University-Bozeman), 1-3.

[15] Ibid. 7-10.

[16] Montana County Extension Records, 1935, "Annual Report-Wheatland County," by K .P. Jones (Box 66:10, Merrill G. Burlingame Special Collection-Montana State University-Bozeman), 7.

[17] Ibid. 49.

[18] Montana County Extension Records, 1936,"Annual Report-Wheatland County," by K. P. Jones (Box 66:10, Merrill G. Burlingame Special Collection-Montana State University-Bozeman); Montana County Extension Records, 1937, "Annual Report-Wheatland County," by K. P. Jones (Box 66:10, Merrill G. Burlingame Special Collection-Montana State University-Bozeman), 19.

[19] Montana County Extension Records, 1937, "Annual Report-Wheatland County," by K. P. Jones (Box 66:10, Merrill G. Burlingame Special Collection-Montana State University-Bozeman), 49.

[20] Geoff Cunfer, *On the Great Plains: Agriculture and Environment* (College Station: Texas A&M University Press, 2005), 54-60.

[21] W. B. Hazen, "The Great Middle Region of the United States, and its Limited Space of Arable Land," *North American Review*, 120 (January 1875): 12.

[22] Montana Bureau of Agriculture, Labor and Industry, *Montana: Resources and Opportunities, 1917* (n.p.), 126.

[23] Margaret Reed, "The Fraser-Reed Early Life on the Rothiemay Flat," in Albie Gordon, Margaret Lehfeldt, and Mary Morsanny, comp., from *Dawn in Golden Valley* (Harlowton: Upper Musselshell Museum Archives, 1971), 219-21.

[24] James C. Jensen, "Memoirs of James C. and Anna J. Jensen," in Albie Gordon, Margaret Lehfeldt, and Mary Morsanny, comp., from *Dawn in Golden Valley* (Harlowton: Upper Musselshell Museum Archives, 1971), 162-64.

[25] Madge Ice Vander Voort, "The Ice History," in Albie Gordon, Margaret Lehfeldt, and Mary Morsanny, comp., from *Dawn in Golden Valley* (Harlowton: Upper Musselshell Museum Archives, 1971), 162-64.

[26] Gladys Baker, *The County Agent* (Chicago: University of Chicago Press, 1939) xiv-xv.

Chapter 7

Wild Horses on the Plains:

Conserving a National Symbol

Andrea Glessner

The wind blusters and blows through a dusty canyon. In the distance a rumble shatters the silence and sends vibrations through the hard-packed dusty earth. Suddenly, and without warning, a small herd of mustangs breaks through the opening in the canyon walls. Browns, bays, even a lone gray come into sight, straining into the wind, muscles quivering and powerful, necks stretched towards something in the distance. Their hooves, the source of thunder, strike the ground in fluid and easy rhythms. The staccato beat echoes in the soul.

Some things are inextricably tied to the American West: the cowboy, the range, and certain animals. They carry with them a romantic appeal. Stories, and the people or animals on which they are based, whether factual or mythical, are also a thing of the West. They give people an awareness, somewhat embellished, of life beneath and beyond the Rocky Mountains. Figures, animal and human, often reached legendary status in the pages of books. Few creatures in the history of the American West have gained attention like wild horses. These animals roamed the western states for centuries and they still retain an image of mythic proportion. They have played a role in the romantic notion of the West, becoming icons for a country and cementing their position as underwriters of the imagined West.[1]

The twentieth century was a defining time period for wild horses in American history. People began seeing them in a different way, which in turn promoted a new effort to conserve the wild horse and everything it represented for future generations of Americans. Prior to the mid-twentieth century no one put forth the effort necessary to save them from eradication. Then, in the 1950s, one person did try to save them. Even though that story is essential to the entire wild horse narrative, it is not the only story that should be told. During this time, many voiced their opinions for and against these animals. The wild horse narrative is one of adaptation and resilience, one of survival. Elements of legend and myth still surround wild horses, casting them as untouchable figures, but it is not easy to be a wild horse dependent on public rangelands throughout the western United States. No matter what the tale is, the iconic images of wild horses and the perceptions people have of them have changed continuously.

Between 1934 and 1984 Americans changed their perceptions of wild horses, elevating them into symbolic creatures deserving of protection, rather than treating them as either livestock or feral pests. This crucial fifty-year period, which includes important developments, provides glimpses of wild horse management before, during, and after Congress passed the historic 1971 Wild Free-Roaming Horses and Burros Act. Even though myth, legend, and reality collided during the fifty-year time span, wild horses are, still, only one piece of the story. Humans, too, are important to the narrative of wild horses in the United States. Both sides of the narrative provide perspectives on many areas, including personal and national heritage, range and resource management, animal management practices, and even the legislative process.

Sometimes it is easy to spot a wild horse from the road. This young bachelor stud grazes calmly along the road that traverses Seven Mile Ridge in the Sand Wash Basin of northwestern Colorado. *Photograph by Andrea Glessner.*

Many historians continue to analyze the role the horse played, and continues to play, in the shaping of cultures and regions within the United States. Their contributions to regional history are important because they highlight key concepts, including the environment and adaptation, cultural and economic shifts, and the creation of regional identity. In addition, they provide evidence that the relationship between humankind and horse is one that gives added meaning to life. It shows how humans have adapted to change and how people have had to be innovative and come up with new horse use, trade, training, and capture methods. Beyond that, during the Great Plains' transitory history, people viewed the wild horse as a mythic and symbolic creature, just as many people do now.[2]

Written records provide a good indication of peoples' changing perceptions regarding wild horses. Early literature focuses on their mysticism and the methods of wild horse capture. Later literature and movies focus on the movement to protect them, or show the reasons why people should take an interest in the subject. Government reports, group-published bulletins, and newsletters also provide information in a more specific, and pointed, manner. More recent works discuss the difficulty of managing wild horses merely because they are always in the news in one form or another.

Perceptions regarding wild horses underwent vast changes, reflecting the cultural, economic, political, and social shifts that have taken place in modern American history. These shifts are documented in visual and written media, both of which influence the public perception of wild horses as mythic. Representations of myth occur in visual media. Art, photography, and film all capture perception, sometimes even realistically. Written narratives provide another medium, and physical evidence adds yet an additional element to narratives about wild horses. Simultaneously, varied perceptions based on different media have generated alternative legends connected to the myth and legend of the wild horse. Folklore, combined with research-based knowledge, gives an alternate viewpoint of what life was like in the West and how certain things captured the attention of the public. Combined, all of these have been powerful tools to perpetuate the symbolic and mythic role of wild horses in the United States—and given reason to preserve them.

Stories of the wild horse have been featured in American literature, film, and magazines, elevating the place of the wild horse, particularly its connection with the American West. Wild horses have been romanticized in literature (*Misty of Chincoteague*, *Wild Spirit of the West*, and *The Black Stallion*), movies (*The Misfits*, *Hidalgo*, and *Spirit: Stallion of the Cimarron*), and television documentaries (*Cloud: Wild Stallion of the Rockies* and *Horses of the Wild West: America's Love Story*). These popular stories provided (and still provide) a basis for the mythical treatment of wild horses because they captured the imagination of people everywhere. Folklore was an added element in the spread of these stories. J. Frank Dobie was an early folklorist who focused on horses in the West. His stories about legendary horses are found in *The Mustangs: Valiant, Wild and Free They Roved the Western Plains*. Dobie wove tales, sometimes based on truth, around these animals and their ability to intrigue and captivate an audience without having to do much of anything besides remain aloof and reclusive. In the case of one elusive white stallion, this became true. No man could capture him and therefore every man wanted to capture him. In the latter 1800s this figure became revered in the American Southwest because of his indomitable spirit. Unfortunately, his fame meant that he became a larger target of horse hunters, after which he did not survive long.

The myth and symbolism of the wild horse arise from a long history in America. Those that we recognize today roam freely in social groups of their own making and rarely, if ever, interact with humans. For centuries wild horses have roamed the areas we now recognize as the Great Plains and the American West but they did not always live there. Historical records indicate that they arrived sometime between the late 1400s into the early 1500s on the shores of what is now southern Texas. It was the Spanish explorers who reintroduced domestic horses into the North American environment, where they came to thrive in massive wild herds. This was not the first time that horses are documented as existing in North America. Biologists and archaeologists have determined the true ancestors of modern-day horses, the "dawn horse," existed on the North American continent more than fifty-five million years ago.[3] The dawn horse eventually evolved into the direct ancestor of the modern-day horse. This animal disappeared from the continent during the climate changes that occurred more than 10,000 years ago.[4] Academics have differing opinions on the actual timeline, but most agree that the animal vanished sometime between 8,000 and 11,000 years ago.[5] Evidence shows that horses existed in some fashion on the North American continent prior to that environmental change, but for some combination of reasons (hunting, environment, migration, or resource competitiveness) they disappeared. Nevertheless, whatever the actual reasons for their disappearance, horses evolved and adapted in areas of open land, mostly consisting of deserts and grasslands. As a result, they were built for the harsh environment they eventually were to encounter west of the Mississippi River.

The concept of wild horses roaming the Great Plains and the American West is not new. Many of these animals came from domestic stock, whether directly related to the Spanish horses or from horses in the East. Early peoples, native and Anglo, knew about the existence of these wild herds and many of them utilized the animal in different ways. In the five hundred years since these animals were reintroduced, much has changed. Yet the wild horse has remained a symbolic image in America.

Many have had to adapt to new environments on the Plains. As groups like the Spanish settlers and Native American tribes adapted to new ways, they adopted aspects of horse husbandry, which became an asset to them on the Plains. By the mid-1600s, Indian tribes began to utilize horses in more ways. It was their adaptation to a life with horses that brought about sweeping changes throughout tribes inhabiting the Great Plains and surrounding areas. It gave them ultimate control of their surroundings. They turned even more into nomadic, fierce, and territorial entities, whom eastern settlers feared well into the nineteenth century. The employment of horses in tribal peoples' daily lives shows how they adapted and evolved over time.

In time horses became central assets in the power struggles taking place throughout the central Great Plains. Without them, Native American tribes were unable to maintain territory and influence. With them, they managed to regulate trade and transportation through the Great Plains and into the eastern edge of the Rocky Mountains. This control of trade routes also blocked white settlement patterns from spreading out onto the Great Plains. Native cultures relied on the horse for transportation, protection, and bartering. Horses were viewed as symbols of wealth and status among their people. They built their nomadic lifestyles around the use of the horse. Even so, wild horses contributed less to Native American life than the domesticated animals used by Spanish missions because trained horses were easier to use and steal. The natives, nevertheless, used techniques they learned from the Spanish, as well as those they developed themselves, to capture and train wild ranging horses.

Plains Indian cultures controlled the central region of the United States by the 1600s, mainly because of their adaptation to a life on horseback, but they were not the only people to understand the usefulness of these animals. In the year 1541 the Spanish first came into contact with the Apaches.[6] During ensuing generations, the Apache consistently raided early Spanish settlements for supplies, which often included horses. As a result, they gained some equestrian skills, and by 1700 they began migrating southward, as the Comanche and other tribes (such as the Utes) took dominant positions on the southern and central Plains. In time powerful Comanche controlled the flow of materials, particularly horses, through the Great Plains. During the 1700s these tribes traded large numbers of horses to eastern markets, particularly to French settlers in the southeast.[7] Although the Comanche had access to trained, domesticated horses, they also had access, as Pekka Hämäläinen notes, to nearly "two million feral horses roaming within and near their border."[8] This provided Native Americans with a plethora of what he describes as "exploitable animal wealth."[9] The Comanche adapted their lives to include the horse, and they opened up a new era in Great Plains history, one that they ruled on horseback.

The nineteenth century brought a major shift in settlement, as people in the east began looking for new homes out west. Immense tracts of land throughout the southern and northern plains were already under the control of cattle barons. Then, by the mid- to late 1800s, the Homestead Act of 1862, along with railroad construction, contributed to the vast numbers of white settlers moving into the West, looking for new opportunities and more land. Settlers began fencing off the frontier, creating borders between what did, and did not, belong to them.[10] The fencing of the frontier brought about other changes, including the end of open-range grazing in many areas. As the numbers of settlers rose, so, too, did their need for horses. A horse-powered agricultural and ranching economy could always use more horseflesh.

Horses of all shapes, sizes, colors, and ancestry helped move settlers west. Many of these horses escaped their owners' clutches and began living on their own in the wild. They even induced others to join them. Domestic stock mixed with wild stock. These animals were surefooted, had legendary endurance, and were always aware of their surroundings. Over time, the animals adapted to their environments and became accustomed to little human contact or none at all. As a result, they became even more difficult to round up. At the same time, ranchers liked to use these animals because they knew the land and could work hard.

Because wild horses were a free, and seemingly unlimited, resource at that time, corralling them became a way of life for some. The men who trapped these wild horses, called mustangs, became known as mustangers or wild horse runners, and could be found in most western states, especially Wyoming, Colorado, and Nevada. Cowboys and ranchers controlled the population of wild horses in the western states through hard work, knowledge of the land, and an understanding of horses. Not only did they trap these rogue horses, but they would keep some for ranch work and sell others. Oftentimes they were sold to assist war efforts, supplying mounts during the Civil War and again in World War I through the Army Remount Service.[11] Westerners could make a small profit by catching and selling horses to the government or anyone else willing to pay the right price. Many of the mustangers worked for cattle companies whose main purpose was to remove the horses because they were eating the forage that their cattle or sheep needed. Range use and resource competition played a major role in managing profitable, as well as wild, herds of animals. In some cases, mustangers loaded the animals into railroad cars and shipped them to eastern markets. The more fortunate animals found homes as saddle horses and cavalry mounts, while others ended up in slaughterhouses and rendering works.

The practice of removing wild horses from prime grazing land continued well into the twentieth century. Local wild horse management was common at the time. Land owners often coordinated roundups with one another, family, and hired hands in order to have the extra help. As mechanization became more widely available, the mustangers began incorporating new techniques. Although saddle horses were often used to flush the wild herds out of canyons and desert mountains, twentieth-century horse runners began operating mechanized equipment like trucks, small biplanes, and helicopters. Stories emerged of men running horses with mechanized equipment, resulting in multiple and sometimes fatal injuries, although such incidents were rare, despite media coverage suggesting otherwise.

In some ways the removal of wild horses from rangelands was a direct result of the passage of the Taylor Grazing Act of 1934 (TGA) and its approach to rangeland management. (Rangeland management is defined as the relationship between animals and the land as well as native versus non-native animals.) The act assumed that range utilization needed to be managed in order to prevent a recurrence of the cattle disasters and land abuses of the 1880s, when overstocked range conditions became disastrous and blizzards and drought killed off thousands of animals. Excessive competition and overuse were major issues, as seen in the range wars and land conflicts that took place in western states, such as the Johnson County War of 1892 in Wyoming. It was hoped that the TGA would discourage continued range overuse and abuse. These instances were not the only cases of land or animal abuse. Historian Robert Denhardt described this situation in relation to the plight of the American buffalo, also a western symbol, stating, "The range of the mustang was gradually pre-empted by farmers and cattlemen. Any that hung around were rounded up, sold, or shot. The influence of the wild horse lingered on a little while longer than that of the buffalo."[12] Incoming settlers from the east decimated buffalo herds and pushed wild horses farther into the West, into areas where hospitable landscapes were not the norm, forcing these animals to adapt to new environments. Still, in many parts of the country, the same people who were criticized for their ways of controlling the population of wild horses on public ranges happened to be the individuals who understood the horse better than most of the American population.[13]

Controversy is at the root of the wild horse discussion. It began in the mid-1950s when Velma Bronn Johnston started her campaign to preserve wild horses in the United States. Their inherent symbolism and the mythic representations of the horse were often cited as reasons to save them. Johnston believed that future Americans should have an opportunity to view them in the wild. These animals, it was believed, symbolized the wild, noble, and free spirit of the nation and should be conserved.

Johnston's story, however truthful or embellished, is still persuasive, much like other narratives that celebrate human and equine relationships. Those who read of Johnston's efforts to save wild horses often ask, "Are they worth saving? Why should we, the audience, care about what happens to them?" Johnston, a small woman, a native Nevadan, child polio survivor, wild horse advocate, as well as the daughter of a man who caught and trained mustangs, eventually became nicknamed "Wild Horse Annie" because of her determination to save wild horses in their western habitat. Her crusade began in the early 1950s and did not end until the mid-1970s. Her sensibility to horses can be traced back to one morning in 1950 when she was driving to work and witnessed the transport of wild horses, dripping blood from inhumane capture techniques, to a rendering plant near Sparks, Nevada.[14] She was a pivotal figure whose advocacy formed the basis for initial legislation to protect wild horses in Nevada. She appealed to congressmen, writers, photographers, the media, and children. In her eyes wild horses were integral to the western landscape, indeed the western narrative.

By the mid-1950s Americans began taking an interest in Johnston's campaign, some in opposition, particularly among government officials, cattlemen, horse runners, rendering plants, and slaughterhouse owners. Gus Bundy, however, a well-known Nevada photographer, contributed several photographs to her campaign. Today these are regarded, one of her biographers asserts, as "among the greatest action news photographs of the twentieth century."[15] These images convey the wildness inherent in mustang captures during the 1930s and 1940s. (They also inspired the mustang roundup scene in the Hollywood film *The Misfits*.) They served to provoke concern among the American public, and on September 8, 1959, President Eisenhower signed House Resolution (HR) 2725, which is known as "the Wild Horse Annie Law."[16]

The campaign did not stop in 1959, and neither did the efforts of wild horse runners working under the legal radar. This law was not enough to dissuade all of them, partly because some had personal stock grazing on the open range like the wild horses. As such, a more drastic political action plan was needed. Throughout the 1960s Johnston appealed to the public with newspaper and magazine articles, pamphlets, pictures, and letters, hoping that Congress would pass another law stipulating how wild horses would be federally protected from capture in the United States.[17] Her appeals were not just focused on the protection of horses, but also the care of the range as a renewable resource. She wanted horses to be managed, but in a humane and less intrusive and abusive manner. As the daughter and wife of ranchers, she understood the necessity of controlling populations of wild animals. In time, her efforts prevailed. In 1971 Congress passed the Wild Free-Roaming Horses and Burros Act, which placed the management of wild herds under the authority of the U.S. Bureau of Land Management (BLM) and the Forest Service (FS).[18] These two federal agencies still control the management of wild horses in the United States. Since 1971 several addendums have been made to this law, allowing for modernization of techniques, such as mechanized roundups and animal safety, to name a few, but its overall emphasis on managing wild horses has remained largely unchanged.

At the same time, many other individuals in the West have had experiences with mustangs, and their perceptions have been influenced by the experiences with them. These westerners, like the horses themselves, have been shaped by the land. Clifford Heaverne is one such person who has been shaped by heritage and history. His background has contributed to his understanding of the desired balance among humans, horses, and nature. He is a born-and-raised cowboy as well as a trained helicopter pilot (and Vietnam War veteran) contracted to work roundups for the Bureau of Land Management.[19] His background, like Johnston's, is in Nevada ranch life. His father, Pat Heaverne, was a widely respected Nevada horseman, as well as a man who ran wild horses.[20] From his father Heaverne learned how to work with horses at a young age. As a child he also developed a lifelong fascination with flying. His father's friend Ted Barber, himself a cowboy and a pilot, encouraged Heaverne's interest in the subject.[21] His experience growing up as the son of a renowned horseman, combined with his advanced piloting experience, made him a logical choice when the BLM began managing wild horse herds. His years of rounding up wild herds for the BLM gave him knowledge of government practices. His livelihood depended on wild horse management, a connection clearly influencing his perspective.

Men and women of Wyoming and Colorado have also related their adventures with wild horses. On July 27, 2014, Elmora Vaughan Peterson, a native of Rock Springs, Wyoming, spoke about her father's experience capturing wild horses near the Colorado and Wyoming border.[22] Through photographs, stories, and personal memories, Minford Vaughan, a skilled horseman, tells of rounding up wild horses on the Colorado open range. He often ran horses with his nephew Boyd Walker of Douglas Mountain, Colorado.[23] Peterson's cousin Dawn Walker Nottingham, Boyd's daughter, also spoke of her father's wild horse escapades, which involved her mother, Wanda Walker.[24] She, too, was a skilled horsewoman and mustanger who learned the trade from her own father. Their knowledge of wild horses, the range, and survival speak to the culture of the West and the resilience of the land and its human as well as animal inhabitants. The wild horse narrative includes the adventures of individuals like Minford, Boyd, and Wanda, and the stories they left behind, speak to regional heritage and how elements of western culture are shaped by encounters like these.

Horses are managed daily at the large Palomino Valley National Wild Horse and Burro Center northeast of Reno, Nevada. This facility handles all wild horses captured and managed throughout the western states. *Photograph by Andrea Glessner.*

Government agencies were affected by their complex relationship with the wild horses and the American public. The United States departments of Agriculture and the Interior, in conjunction with the BLM and the FS, manage thousands of wild horses in ten states: Colorado, Wyoming, Montana, Oregon, Nevada, California, Arizona, New Mexico, Idaho, and Utah. This places government officials in the midst of an ever-changing environment, one that mixes and pits horse professionals, ranchers, media, the public, and groups that aim to protect wild horses, against one another. Since the Wild Free-Roaming Horse and Burro Act of 1971, or Public Law 92-195, the BLM and FS have been guided in their managing and protecting wild horses as "living symbols of the historic and pioneer spirit of the West."[25] While this legislation was moving forward the American public gained a better sense of wild horses and their meaning in the West. The wild horses shown in films, or featured in books, are based on folklore, fact, and imagination, and all of these things have contributed to the image of the wild horse as a symbol. It is precisely this "living symbolism" that provides much of the fodder for current debates.

The American public is drawn in by popular media, children and young adult literature, and sensationalist news about current issues and studies on horses in the wild (whether historically accurate or not). Although animals of mythical and legendary proportion, their mere presence on rangelands throughout the country symbolizes much more.

Perceptions regarding wild horses, or at least the horses we believe to be wild even if they are contained within fenced and managed ranges, continued to shift throughout the twentieth century. During the first half of the century, people demonstrated a remarkable lack of knowledge, as well as a lack of interest, concerning horses in the wild. The people who knew them well lived in rural and often remote regions of the West. The second half of the century brought about various forms of legislation, awareness, and opinions from advocacy and activist groups, as well as research, although limited, from scholars and scientists. All of these developments changed perceptions of the mustang.

In less than a century the American public turned what was once an obscure and even mystical animal into one capable of capturing the hearts and minds of people across the United States and beyond. The act of 1959 describes the wild horse as a living historical symbol of the American West.[26] As a result, the public continues to ascribe to wild horses mythic qualities, bestowing on them more than a historical representation of the American frontier. The law itself asserts the symbol's role in the pioneer West, an idea that forms the basis of American historical identity. Such associations with American ideals place added importance on the continued protection and care of wild horse herds in the United States. Changing perceptions and persuasive arguments influence the way the public understands this animal. They represent multiple complex relationships involving people and places as well as a variety of ecological and environmental factors, demonstrating how emotional causes can engineer change where rational arguments cannot.

Symbols often represent ideals, rarely actuality. Much as the American flag symbolizes unity of under one government, the wild horse might represent freedom. In reality, Americans are subject to many governments, and wild horses are not free horses. They are managed, provided with many of the resources they need to survive, including food and water. They are observed, medicated, transported, and researched. They are also protected and cannot roam outside of prescribed areas.

The public's perceptions of individual contributions to this issue are often clouded because of prejudices about who or what an individual, such as Velma Johnston and Clifford Heaverne, represents. Idolized by activists and advocates alike as a symbol for the wild horse protection movement, Johnston is viewed by others as a meddler. Heaverne, on the other hand, has been depicted as a villain because of his role as a contracted roundup pilot for the BLM. Heaverne faced his share of hardships while employed by the federal government, yet he remained a humane individual.[27] The roles of individuals like Johnston and Heaverne, juxtaposed to one another, provide specific historical examples.

Mustangers like Vaughan and the Walkers, and the others like them, are sometimes portrayed negatively, but their roles in the changing West hold importance for the overall narrative. They were called upon to play a role that nature could not since man is the wild horse's number one predator. Without human intervention, herd numbers would quickly rise, resulting in overgrazed rangeland and reduced sustenance for the animals dependent upon it, both wild and domestic. Mustangers utilized the horses on ranches, sold them to the war effort as mounts, and so managed the herds in small enclaves throughout the West. The wild horse is as much a part of regional as it is national heritage.

Another aspect of this often emotional subject is the role of management in conserving wild horse populations in the United States.

What are the struggles and triumphs in managing a so-called living symbol? Although government agencies like the BLM and the FS manage the animals, they are not the only ones involved in the process of removing horses from public rangelands. Conserving wild horses on the public range involves many players. Private contractors control the roundup operations, not-for-profit groups assist in care and adoption events, and scientists analyze range impact and the relationships between native and non-native animals. Horse practitioners examine humane options of working with wild horses, Native American groups seek to preserve certain wild herds for cultural reasons, and ranchers still have a tenuous relationship with groups managing wild horses as well as the horses themselves. Activist groups push to eliminate roundups, because they believe them to be inhumane, while advocacy groups push for awareness. Even today, the plight of wild horses is a subject of debate among legislators, horse practitioners, wild horse managers, and other interest groups.

Wild horses are a part of American national identity. Their history is entwined within the nation's historical threads. In less than a century, the American public turned what was once an obscure animal of the West into one whose existence became symbolic and representative of western myth. It thereby captured the hearts and minds of people all over the United States and beyond.

Popular representations of wild horses, in film and literature, depict stallions rearing on the edge of a cliff or herds galloping off into the distance, leaving a dust cloud in their wake, or convey the ferocity of a stallion defending his herd or a mare protecting her young. Most have witnessed the joy of seeing them run across barren, open spaces looking just as comfortable in desolate environments as they do in lush, green pastures. Most have never seen this anywhere other than in film or in the pages of a book. The rhythmic staccato beats of their hooves moving across the ground are something that must be felt in actuality. Viewing a herd in the wild is similar to examining the social structure, or family tree, of one small group. These animals live on a combination of instinct, intelligence, and stamina. Nature weeds out the weak and nourishes the strong. And it is these images, captured in popular media that resonate with the broader general public. It is what they know about the animals, but it is not the complete truth.

Wild horses have become a part of western culture and myth. Walk into a cafe in a small town in wild horse country and it is possible to overhear stories about catching mustangs on the rugged terrain. Old cowboys with a wealth of experience in the saddle swap stories about the way things were before the government began controlling wild horse populations on federal land. The changes wrought during the 1960s and 1970s regarding federal land and management practices affected, in some way or another, the lives of the men and women who lived there. In areas like these the wild horse was a resource and a nuisance. Whether intentional or not, wild horse conservation has been in place for generations.

The variety of opinions and the complexity of managing a living symbol have kept opposing sides from reaching a viable solution on the issue of wild horse conservation. The animal itself invites people to consider all parties (the range, the land owners, the government, and the animals that need the land for sustenance). Perhaps the horse is not a symbol of just the pioneer West but also of resilience in the face of adversity.

Notes

[1] Much of the material in this chapter comes from my dissertation for North Dakota State University, titled "Running Wild, Running Free: Changing Perceptions of Wild Horses in the American Landscape" (ProQuest LLC, 2014).

[2] J. Frank Dobie, *The Mustangs: Valiant, Wild and Free They Roved the Western Plains*, 4th ed. (New York: Bantam Books, 1952).

[3] Deanne Stillman, *Mustang: The Saga of the Wild Horse in the American West* (Boston: Houghton Mifflin Co., 2008), 37.

[4] Ibid., 40-41.

[5] Joel Berger, *Wild Horses of the Great Basin: Social Competition and Population Size*, Wildlife Behavior and Ecology Series, edited by George B. Schaller (University of Chicago Press: Chicago, 1986), 12; Elliott West, *The Contested Plains: Indians, Goldseekers, & the Rush to Colorado* (Lawrence: University Press of Kansas, 1998), 49. J. Edward de Steiguer, *Wild Horses of the West: History and Politics of America's Mustangs* (Tucson: University of Arizona Press, 2011), 49; For more information on this topic consult Joel Berger, *Wild Horses of the Great Basin* and Robert M. Denhardt's *The Horse of the Americas*. Both consider the adaptability of horses to the North American climate and environment. They also examine the early history of horses on the continent.

[6] Jeffrey D. Carlisle, "Apache Indians," Handbook of Texas Online, Texas State Historical Association, http://www.tshaonline.org/handbook/online/article/bma33.

[7] Dan L. Flores, *Horizontal Yellow: Nature and History in the Near Southwest* (Albuquerque: University of New Mexico Press, 1999).

[8] Pekka Hämäläinen, *The Comanche Empire* (New Haven: Yale University Press, 2008), 240.

[9] Ibid., 240-41.

[10] Walter Prescott Webb, *The Great Plains* (Boston: Ginn and Company, 1931).

[11] Clifford Heaverne, 2011, interviewed by Andrea Mott, digital audio recording, Fallon, Nevada, August 29.

[12] Robert Denhardt, *The Horse of the Americas*, new ed. (Norman: University of Oklahoma Press, 1975), 200.

[13] Heaverne, 2011; Dawn (Walker) Nottingham, 2013, interviewed by Andrea Mott, digital audio recording, Craig, Colorado, July 26; Tom and Elmora (Vaughan) Peterson, 2013, interviewed by Andrea Mott, digital audio recording, Rock Springs, Wyoming, July 27.

[14] David Cruise and Alison Griffiths, *Wild Horse Annie and the Last of the Mustangs: The Life of Velma Johnston* (New York: Scribner, 2010); Heather Smith Thomas, *The Wild Horse Controversy* (South Brunswick, N.J.: A.S. Barnes, 1979); Stillman; Velma Johnston (Wild Horse Annie) Papers, 1949-1977, Western History Collection, Denver Public Library.

[15] Cruise and Griffiths, 120.

[16] Ibid., 137.

[17] Ibid.; Marguerite Henry, *Mustang: Wild Spirit of the West* (Chicago: Rand McNally, 1966).

[18] U.S. Congress, House, Committee on Interior and Insular Affairs, *Testimony of Mrs. Velma B. Johnston Before the Public Lands Subcommittee of the Interior and Insular Affairs Committee of the United States House of Representatives* (Washington, D.C., 1971); U.S. Congress, Senate, Committee on Interior and Insular Affairs, *Wild Free-Roaming Horses and Burros Act of 1971: Hearing Before the Committee on Interior and Insular Affairs*. 93rd Cong., June 26, 1974, 2d sess. (Washington: GPO, 1974).

[19] Heaverne, conversation with author, April 14, 2009.

[20] Paula Morin, *Honest Horses: Wild Horses in the Great Basin* (Reno: University of Nevada Press, 2006).

[21] Ted Barber wrote "The Barnstorming Mustanger," which is an account of his times rounding up horses in different parts of the country. He discusses various methods of horse trapping and piloting.

[22] Peterson.

[23] Ibid., Nottingham.

[24] Nottingham.

[25] U.S. Bureau of Land Management and U.S. Forest Service, *A Report to Congress by the Secretary of the Interior and the Secretary of Agriculture on Administration of the Wild Free-Roaming Horse and Burro Act, Public Law 92-195* (15 December 1971), 1974 Report, Appendix 1:1.

[26] Ibid.; Cruise and Griffiths; Stillman; U.S. Bureau of Land Management and U.S. Forest Service, *A Report to Congress by the Secretary of the Interior*

and the Secretary of Agriculture on Administration of the Wild Free-Roaming Horse and Burro Act, Public Law 92-195 (Washington, D.C.: U.S. Dept. of the Interior, Bureau of Land Management, 1974); U.S. Congress, Senate, Committee on Energy and Natural Resources, Subcommittee on Public Lands and Resources, *Wild Free-Roaming Horses and Burros Act: Hearing before the Subcommittee on Public Lands and Resources of the Committee on Energy and Natural Resources.* 95th Cong., May 23, 1977, 1st sess. (Washington: GPO, 1977); U.S. Congress, Senate, Committee on Interior and Insular Affairs, *Wild Free-Roaming Horses and Burros Act of 1971: Hearing Before the Committee on the Interior and Insular Affairs*. 93rd Cong., June 26, 1974, 2d sess. (Washington: GPO, 1974).

[27] Heaverne.

Chapter 8

Elk Killers, Liberal Politics, and Tourist Magnets:

Outfitter Perceptions of Wolves in Montana

Stephen L. Eliason

While conflict over the use and allocation of natural resources is common, perhaps no wildlife controversy in recent history has been as divisive and acrimonious as the contemporary debate over wolves in different parts of the world.

After being absent from the area for decades,[1] wolves were reintroduced in Yellowstone National Park and in central Idaho in 1995.[2] Since then they have significantly expanded their range in the Northern Plains and moved into parts of Idaho, Montana, and Wyoming. This has generated much concern among those employed in the ranching and livestock industry, which goes back for several generations in Montana and is economically important to the state.[3] It has also generated concern among hunters, who fear that wolves will deplete the state's elk herds.[4] Since many outfitters help clients pursue elk,[5] they hold strong feelings about wolves since wolves have the potential to impact their livelihood.[6]

While conflict over the use and allocation of natural resources is common,[7] perhaps no wildlife controversy in recent history has been as divisive and acrimonious as the contemporary debate over wolves in different parts of the world.[8] Wolves conjure up a variety of images, from a symbol of wildness and the wilderness to a vilified predator.[9] Wolves are simultaneously loved and hated by different segments of the population. Tourists flock to Yellowstone National Park to view wolves.[10] Ranchers and farmers fear economic loss from wolves preying on their livestock.[11] The wolf controversy has been studied in other contexts, such as the perspective of farmers and hunters in Sweden who feel that their heritage is being threatened by the presence of wolves on the landscape.[12] Discussing the wolf recovery controversy in rural areas of Sweden, Sjölander-Lindqvist states in his article published in *Conservation and Society* that "Local residents . . . perceive these ecosystem recovery initiatives as threatening their cherished cultural heritage. By invoking 'heritage,' local residents contribute to the politicisation of the landscape."[13]

The purpose of this chapter is to contribute to our knowledge and understanding of conservation, hunting, and the wolf controversy in contemporary society by analyzing outfitters' attitudes toward wolves. That is, how do outfitters perceive wolves, and what do wolves mean to them? Do outfitters hold positive or negative attitudes about wolves, and why? The objective is to extend and broaden our understanding of the conflict surrounding wolf reintroduction by examining how outfitters socially construct wolves.

The wolf controversy in Montana is part of a broader controversy between two interest groups with vastly different goals, environmentalists and members of the Wise Use movement.[14] Many environmentalists, who are those concerned with biodiversity, sustainability, and ecosystems, favor wolf reintroduction in order to support healthy ecosystems.[15] As McCarthy and Hague note in their article about the cultural politics of "Celtic" identification in the American West, Wise Use advocates favor policy that promotes ". . . one of two broad goals: to continue or increase access to federal lands and resources by primary commodity producers and to reduce governmental regulation of private land and resources."[16]

The controversy over wolf reintroduction in Montana is part of a broader conflict over the appropriation and utilization of natural resources in rural areas. Montana is undergoing social change and experiencing conflict as newcomers buy land and homes in the state and bring values that sometimes conflict with the values of long-term residents.[17] For the most part, outfitting is a rural occupation in an increasingly urban society, a society characterized by rapid social change as well as competing values about the environment. Individuals in rural areas resent outsiders and outside interests making decisions that impinge upon resources and lifestyles that rural residents may cherish and depend upon for their livelihoods. Studies have examined politically divisive conflicts related to the environment, such as the grazing of livestock on public lands,[18] clashes between ranchers and environmentalists over rural landscapes in the western United States,[19] coyote hunting tournaments in Vermont,[20] the hunting of carnivores,[21] conflict over wolves in Sweden and Norway,[22] and wolf recovery policy in Wisconsin.[23]

Hunting is popular throughout Montana, and hunters pursue a variety of big game species such as antelope, mule deer, white-tail deer, elk, moose, bighorn sheep, bison, mountain goats, black bears, and mountain lions.[24] Fishing is also a popular recreational activity in the state. Wildlife issues are important politically and generate much local as well as national attention.[25]

Wildlife in the United States is collectively owned and held in "public trust" for all citizens to enjoy.[26] Individual states are responsible for managing wildlife within their own borders, but the federal government also manages some species.[27] In 1973 an important piece of federal legislation called the Endangered Species Act (ESA) was passed, which allows the federal government to exert control over wildlife species that are endangered or threatened with extinction and to facilitate their recovery.[28] Government control does not end there, however, as a crucial component was added that significantly extended the original provisions of the ESA, as Daniels and Brehm point out in their contribution to *Challenges for Rural America in the Twenty-First Century*:

> An amendment enacted in 1978 provided an important conceptual modification: in addition to conserving individual members of wildlife populations, their critical habitat must also be identified, protected, and potentially expanded. . . . the ESA's habitat requirements have proven to be much more controversial than the prohibition against taking individual organisms.[29]

Outfitters are leisure-service providers who rely on the environment and natural resources but whose livelihoods may be impacted by the wolf reintroduction effort. Outfitting services are found in locations that contain abundant natural resources, including rural areas in North America and Africa.[30] In the United States millions of people spend their leisure time participating in such recreational activities as hunting and fishing, and some of these hunters and anglers hire outfitters and guides to help them with their outdoor recreation experiences.[31] The use of hunting guides has a long history in the United States.[32] Dickson provides a description of guides and outfitters: "*Guides* are licensed individuals who lead the hunts.

Guides work for *outfitters,* who own the business of providing hunting services. Many outfitters are also themselves guides."[33] Outfitters in Montana need to be licensed by the state in order to practice legally (Montana Code Annotated, 2009).[34]

Studies of outfitters and guides are relatively limited.[35] Prior research has examined economic impacts of outfitting activities,[36] hunting issues related to the outfitting industry,[37] and the social psychology of guides.[38]

Theoretical Perspective and Methods

Symbolic interaction provides a theoretical framework from which to examine outfitters' perceptions of wolves.[39] Symbolic interaction is concerned with the meanings that people attribute to their experiences.[40] In their discussion of how this perspective helps us to understand the meaning of work, Shaffir and Pawluch, in their chapter "Occupations and Professions," in *Handbook of Symbolic Interactionism,* state the following:

> . . . symbolic interactionism provides a way to understand, from the perspective of those who do it, the meanings that work has in their lives. It is an approach that concerns itself with the significance we attach to the work we do, the rewards we derive from it, the obstacles and problems we confront in doing it, the goals and ambitions we have for it, and the context that it provides for so any of our social interactions.[41]

Based on social interaction and experiences in specific locales, individuals socially construct phenomena such as the environment, natural resources, and the landscape.[42] In "More than Mere Wolves at the Door: Reconstructing Community amidst a Wildlife Controversy," in *Mad about Wildlife,* Scarce describes how members of different social groups attribute different meanings to things they experience:

> . . . humans imbue all objects and ideas in their societies with meaning, often including nature. . . . There is substantial potential that radically divergent social definitions—

> meanings—will be held by governmental agencies, interest groups, social movements, and citizens whenever environmental issues are on the table.[43]

Jerolmack, for example, writing about the cultural-spatial logic in problem animals, has described divergent meanings attributed to pigeons for opposing sides in the debate over pigeon hunting: ". . . the pigeon or dove is portrayed as a gentle, loving symbol of peace by animal rights activists trying to prevent hunting while their opponents construct it as a useless, vermin-infested rat with wings."[44]

The research for this chapter took a qualitative approach to data collection and examined the attitudes of outfitters in Montana toward wolves. Qualitative studies are especially advantageous when the goal of the research is to provide an understanding of how individuals perceive the world. To accomplish this, it is important to obtain the viewpoints of individuals in their own words.[45] Describing the value of open-ended questions, Neuman states in *Social Research Methods: Qualitative and Quantitative Approaches* that "To learn how a respondent thinks and discover what is important to him or her . . . open questions are best. . . . Open-ended questions are especially valuable in early or exploratory stages of research."[46] In addition, as Henderson observes in *Dimensions of Choice: Qualitative Approaches to Parks, Recreation, Tourism, and Leisure Research,* "The meanings of any symbol (e.g., leisure) have their origins in interactions, which are defined and changed by individuals according to the meanings that are held. The individual studied is the expert and the attempt is to describe their vocabularies, ways of looking, and sense of the important and the unimportant."[47]

The qualitative data in this chapter consist of written outfitter comments from a survey. The survey contained mostly open-ended questions that dealt with the job of an outfitter. A list of licensed outfitters in the state in 2004 was obtained from the Montana Department of Labor and Industry. A mail survey was sent to all licensed outfitters (n=638) in 2005. A total of 156 surveys were returned, for a response rate of twenty-four percent. One of the questions was designed to elicit information from outfitters about their perceptions of wolves: "How do you feel about wolves?" Outfitters were allowed to provide responses in their own words, so the meanings they attributed to wolves could be obtained in rich detail.[48]

The author systematically analyzed data by reading all of the outfitter responses to the question about wolves with the intent of identifying common themes. Common themes that emerged with respect to outfitter perceptions of wolves were given categorical labels, and representative comments that were illustrative of major themes were selected for inclusion in the categories. Summarization and interpretation of the comments is provided by the author.

Threat to Elk, Livestock, and Livelihood

The majority of outfitters in the study held negative attitudes toward wolves for a variety of reasons. Outfitters are leisure-service providers whose continued existence depends to a large extent on access to healthy game populations for their clients to hunt. In general wolves carried a stigma and were perceived as vicious killing machines that took a significant toll on elk herds, thereby threatening the economic well-being of outfitters and the viability of their business. In addition, outfitters viewed wolf reintroduction as an attempt by the federal government to impose not only its will, but the will of environmentalists and liberals, on them and their lifestyle. Consistent themes expressed in outfitter responses were anti-government (especially federal government), anti-liberal, and anti-outsider. Quotes from outfitters are presented in this section.

Wolves were perceived as relentless killers that showed no mercy to their prey. Many outfitters were blunt in their responses and indicated that wolves served no useful purpose and should be killed. Some of the comments suggested these individuals held deep-seated hostility and rage toward these stigmatized predators, which was succinctly, but forcefully and unambiguously, expressed in their remarks:

> *[Wolves] need to be shot on sight. Wolves are the worst thing a taxpayer could have their money spent on. It is sickening the way they kill. They are stealing from every landowner and sportsman statewide.
>
> *Shoot them! They have always been in the upper Madison range and [Yellowstone] Park. I've seen them since 1975. They did not reintroduce the wolf, they added to them!

> *Shoot them.
>
> *[A] dead wolf is a good one.
>
> *Only good wolf is a dead wolf.
>
> *My license plate is "DIE WOLF" enough said.
>
> *The fewer the better.
>
> *Hate them!!!!
>
> *Just like cancer, someday there may be a cure. Until then we will have to learn to live with it.

Wolves are carnivores with a diet that requires them to consume game animals for their survival. This poses a significant problem for outfitters because many of their clients come to the state for the opportunity to hunt elk. Some outfitters hold negative attitudes of wolves because they believe wolves are having a deleterious effect on big game populations, especially elk. If there are limited elk for their hunting clients to pursue, those individuals may elect to go hunting in other states, which could drastically affect the volume of business for the outfitting industry in Montana. This is important to keep in mind because for a significant portion of respondents outfitting was not a very lucrative occupation.[49] Comments from outfitters reflect their concern with the loss of elk:

> *The wolf will cost Montana millions in lost revenue. . . . The wolf eats a lot of elk. F.W.P. just cut permits by Yellowstone from 1,100 to 100. Hunters leaving the old hunting grounds around Yellowstone because the wolves killed the elk, and coming to my hunting area is a bigger concern for me than the wolf.
>
> *They are a direct threat to wildlife populations. History repeats itself and before you

> know it the government will start a bounty, poison program etc.
>
> *I think they are bad for our big game herds.
>
> *I'm plenty mad! They are killing off all of the game.

In comparison to other states in the United States, Montana incomes are low and the state ranks near the bottom in terms of worker earnings.[50] The landscape and natural resources have been identified as important components of the state's tourism industry.[51] Outfitting is an occupation that is found throughout Montana and is important because of its contributions to local economies.[52] Writing about visitor spending data in the *Journal of Travel Research,* Wilton and Nickerson observe that "Outfitters and guides are local entrepreneurs who typically spend their money locally, thereby reducing leakage to outside areas. It is this type of tourism income that most states often encourage because of the local benefit."[53] Outfitting benefits many communities in the state because most of the clients who use outfitters are nonresidents, thus infusing local economies with outside money.[54]

For some outfitters in the study, wolves represented a particularly dire threat to their livelihoods because they were also ranchers who used outfitting earnings to supplement their ranching income.[55] For these individuals, the presence of wolves means not only lost business from hunters seeking big game but also economic losses from livestock that are killed by wolves. Responses from these individuals evoked negative words such as "carnage" and "dread":

> *They are killing off my livelihood, making carnage of a business that has survived three generations but probably won't survive four.
>
> *As a working cattle ranch I dread the over population of wolves. The Yellowstone elk depletion is [a] good example. Neighboring cattle ranches another. We didn't need them.
>
> *They are a shame. They would be okay if they could be managed but they will and are

> hurting a lot of people and nobody cares!! Until it's your ox that is gored!
>
> *[I] hate them! Just a damn predator that kills our livestock and harasses our elk and deer. It's <u>killing</u> our livelihood.
>
> *I feel that wolves will eventually run me out of the outfitting business.
>
> *[I] hate them-lost 3 cows to them last year.
>
> *Leave them alone on public land. On private land they should be fair game.

Native to Montana, wolves were once vilified as useless predators. In their article about wolf and cougar eradication in *Biological Conservation,* Riley et al. states that "By 1930, wolves were eradicated from Montana."[56] The government even became involved in the extermination effort and offered bounties to those who killed wolves.[57] Some outfitters offered a historical perspective and felt that the decision to reintroduce wolves was not right, since wolves had been eliminated for a reason. These claims also reflected animosity toward wolves because of their perceived devastating impact on big game populations:

> *[I] resent them. They lost their place. These wolves aren't native. They like to kill and they have to eat and they aren't going to stay in Yellowstone and eat bison. No doubt they are interesting animals. [The] problem is they were introduced in a large group [which] didn't give prey animals a chance to adapt. They are not native and they are hurting the wildlife populations here. I ride colts in the mountains all summer and I haven't seen a moose for years. [I] used to see them all the time. Wolves are not endangered and should not be treated as such. It is stupid to try to "fix" the fact that we wiped out the native wolves by introducing a larger species that isn't native and that they were not in-

> troduced slowly, giving prey animals time to adapt as mother nature would have done with 1 or 2 wolves. Plus I personally lost 3 horses to wolves and couldn't ever get someone to look at the kills.
>
> *Gut shoot all of them!! They are devastating our elk herds in areas. They have more rights than humans! Man learned long ago it is too difficult to cohabitate with them. Why do you think they tried to eradicate them in the first place?
>
> *The introduction of wolves is the greatest wildlife tragedy to occur since we nearly wiped out the American bison 130 years ago!!!
>
> *Wolves were eliminated for a reason! The state worked hard to build up the herds of game animals, only to have the federal government decrease the game populations.
>
> *Our forefathers spent many years getting rid of them. I don't think they were wrong.

Liberal Political Agendas and the Federal Government

Wolf reintroduction was viewed as a political alliance between wolf conservation interest groups and the federal government. For a large segment of outfitters, wolf reintroduction represented an attempt by environmentalists with liberal political agendas to impose their will on rural America. These outfitters were resentful that a group of "outsiders" (individuals who lived in urban areas outside the state, and didn't have a vested interest in the area) could disrupt their lifestyle and livelihood by reintroducing the wolf. As Scarce states in the journal *Human Dimensions of Wildlife*, "Wolves mean more than potential economic hardship. They are potential lifestyle wreckers and destroyers of years of hard work in a sometimes cruel land."[58]

In a description of tactics used in environmental conflicts by opposing sides to discredit the other, Sheridan states that "Interest groups employ discursive strategies to establish their legitimacy—political, economic, moral, and 'scientific'—while portraying their opponents as villains."[59] The intensity of emotions generated by the wolf conflict in Montana was evident in comments outfitters made to characterize those whom they believed were responsible for the wolf reintroduction:

> *. . . so called, self-proclaimed environmentalists are typically well funded silver spooners that have nothing better to do than spread misinformation about hunting and fishing and the industries that support them! The squeaky wheel gets the grease and I don't have the time or money to outsqueak them! . . . You probably already know I don't want to use profanities! However, one point is that there has always been wolves migrating between Yellowstone and Glacier Parks. This is fact! The "Reintroduction" is a fine example of the silver spoon individuals who don't have to make a living in Montana spreading this misinformation.
>
> *I don't feel they should have been reintroduced! Everything was in balance—good elk herds, moose herds—now the herds are on a fast decline. We'll have to reintroduce elk and moose to Yellowstone. I feel they were forced on us by a small minority of people who don't even live here!
>
> *Government sponsored terrorists!! Lifestyle stealers! Montana economy breakers! Identity thieves. Democrat/liberal pets.
>
> *The same way I feel about dinosaurs, when they're gone then "so be it." Artificial environments are products of bleeding heart liberals. Without it, wolves would not be an issue.

On a related note, some outfitters viewed wolf reintroduction as a blatant attempt by anti-hunting factions to eliminate hunting altogether by significantly reducing the number of game animals available to hunt. The logic of this argument is that if game numbers were sufficiently depleted, the state would be compelled to restrict severely hunting opportunities in a best-case scenario, or to completely curtail hunting in a worst-case scenario, thus accomplishing the objectives of anti-hunting interest groups:

> *Kill them all. The wolf is the worst predator in the U.S. and has no mercy on his prey. [The] wolf is a neat animal doing what they do. We always had a few which was OK. If anything stops hunting or forces a permit system the wolf will create that faster than any other predators. The anti-hunters will win.
>
> *The wolves are intended to eliminate big game hunting and the U.S. government is behind anti-hunting legislation. . . . [I] hope the season opens soon.
>
> *It is the anti-hunter weapon of choice!
>
> *. . . the wolves are the anti-hunters way of getting rid of us.

In general, Montana outfitters may be characterized as individuals who cherish their independence, subscribe to the value of rugged individualism, and espouse a laissez-faire approach with respect to government regulation of business enterprises and intrusion into local affairs. Some outfitters expressed hostile attitudes toward wolves because they felt the reintroduction effort was imposed on them by the federal government:

> *The feds have created great resistance by forcing the wolf on us. This is one of the problems with our system. The outside majority can force its will on the local minority. Montanans were eighty-five percent against.

> *Federal tax dollars were used to sell the idea that we needed wolves to reinstate the food chain. This is not 1850. Wolves are a property taken by the federal government. No different than saying welfare recipients can kill your livestock because they are hungry. Ongoing expenditures to manage and initial introduction are [a] total waste of money!
>
> *I don't approve of their depletion of our elk herds! I do approve of state management—not federal!
>
> *Nothing against the wolves but something against the people who put them there! A few wolves weren't bad. We always had some wolves in our area prior to the reintroduction. They didn't hurt anything and most people didn't bother them. Now it's out of control. The feds and the "do-gooders" shouldn't have interfered. The wolves populated faster than anticipated, wildlife and livestock are affected and the wolves get shot.

Much of the outfitter resistance to wolves was not directed to the wolf per se, but to the extensive control the federal government exerted over environmental policy and the management of wolves. In a description of how environmentalists can exert pressure on the government, Sheridan states, "The ESA and the National Environmental Policy Act (NEPA) have given environmentalists powerful legal tools to add to their arsenal of moral suasion and political pressure. Environmental groups can now sue federal agencies for noncompliance with the ESA, NEPA, and other legislation."[60] Comments from outfitters suggested they might be supportive of wolves if they were delisted from the Endangered Species Act so that the state, not the federal government, could manage them:

> *[I'm] not happy with the reintroduction of wolves in Yellowstone, Montana, Wyoming and Idaho. Too many easterners are anti-hunting and anti-guns. Our government

> has too much power and control and keeps taking some [of] our rights away. [I'm] not happy that we have them but the fact is they are here. [I] want to see them delisted so we can manage them.
>
> *I wish they'd let them come back on their own. Now I wish they'd turn management of them to the state so they could be managed more as wildlife than HOLY animals.

It is important to note that the survey was conducted in 2005, and wolf hunting seasons have been established since that time, as Eliason states in his article in *Wildlife Biology in Practice:* ". . . wolves were protected because of their status as an endangered species and wolf hunting was not allowed in Montana. In an effort to help control the rapidly expanding wolf population, Montana Fish, Wildlife and Parks established a wolf hunt and now issues unlimited tags to residents and nonresidents. . . . Wolf hunts were held in 2009, 2011, 2012, and 2013."[61] A wolf hunt also occurred during the 2014-15 hunting season.

Healthy Ecosystems and Tourism

A minority of outfitters had positive attitudes toward wolves. Some expressed a fondness for the animals and believed they were an integral component of a healthy ecosystem. Some of these individuals also felt that wolves should be hunted at some point when their numbers were sufficient to maintain a viable population. Some outfitting operations were restricted to fishing only, and for these outfitters game depredation due to wolves had no bearing on their business:

> *I believe wolves are an integral part of the greater western ecosystems and enjoy seeing and hearing them and have great appreciation for what they stand for. I also believe after a certain point they should be managed as well so as to keep a balance with present day deer and elk herds.

*I have no problem with wolves. They are part of the ecosystem. They actually help promote healthier game herds over time.

*They are a benefit to us and the ecosystem.

*They are components of the Yellowstone Ecosystem but they shouldn't be allowed to spread all over the mountain West.

*I like them. Hunters would love to have an excess of game because that makes it easier to kill, but game numbers should match the range available. If you build houses where elk winter or calve you can't and shouldn't have as many elk. Hunting is a management tool, not a free ride. If wolves get plentiful, hunting could control them too.

*Neutral. Wolves are okay but must be controlled. Transplanted wolves are wrong and [they] need to be shot.

*A small managed population is beneficial. Today's pack size is far too big.

*I feel sorry for the wolf they didn't ask to be brought down here. We need to have the ability to keep them at bay by managing the populations.

*What's to say? I saw one the other day from my car on I-90 north of the Beartooths but a long way from the safety of the mountains. He was in dangerous terrain and I mentally wished him well.

*I like wolves. It is too bad that things were done in such a foolish manner.

*They are okay to a degree but have no food value or money value as hoofed animals. They are predators.

For some outfitters the wolf is viewed as an asset because of the business it brings to the state. Wildlife watching is a growing activity worldwide, and one that some outfitters can capitalize on, either directly or indirectly.[62] Wolves attract tourists, and some will hire outfitters to take them on excursions to view wolves. In other instances, the potential for a glimpse of a wolf was an added bonus that could be used to induce clients to book their services:

> *I make lots of money guiding trips to view them.
>
> *I love wolves and would help promote them at all opportunities. [It is] very wonderful to be with clients in the back country and see wolves—it's one reason people come here.
>
> *I have no problem with them. They help the tourist business.

Conclusion

This chapter extends our understanding of conservation by analyzing attitudes held by outfitters toward a controversial predator and symbolic icon: the wolf. Wolves mean different things to different people, including those who work in the same occupation. As with nature, landscape, and the environment, the meaning of wolves is socially constructed and closely aligned with the respective positions of interest groups vying for control of land and natural resources.[63] Daniels and Brehm state that ". . . attitudes toward wildlife . . . are socially constructed on the basis of direct experience, and they are both reinforced and mediated by a person's immediate social milieu and broader cultural context."[64] In his article detailing the various ways wolves have been portrayed, published in the journal *Society and Animals*, Lynn remarks:

> . . . the wolf has been interpreted as a teacher of hunting skills; an attentive parent; an exemplar of courage; a loyal pack member; a fellow creature; a spirit guide; a competitor for game; a depredator of herd animals; a symbol of strength, cunning, and power; a fool driven by gluttony; a cowardly op-

> portunist; a villain, varmint, and vermin; an agent of the devil; the Devil himself; a threat to the safety of other wildlife; a parasite; a stalker of children and the elderly; a paragon of wildness; and the irrepressible spirit of women, to name a few.[65]

The majority of outfitters in the study were unhappy with wolf reintroduction and viewed the predators as dire threats to their economic livelihoods. In addition to the reintroduction effort, which they believe was motivated by a political alliance of environmentalists and the federal government, many outfitters expressed a strong dislike of wolves and felt wolves should be killed. Wolves were also viewed negatively because they kill elk as well as livestock and represent a serious threat to the livelihood of outfitters. Many outfitters were resentful and felt that wolves were imposed on the state by outside interests including anti-hunting factions as well as those with liberal political agendas. In particular, they believed that the reintroduction of wolves would culminate with the abolishment of hunting. Resentment toward the federal government was also evident in the responses.

Outfitters believed that environmentalists and the federal government were more concerned with restoring wolves to the landscape than with saving jobs in economically depressed rural regions or preserving rural lifestyles. For outfitters, wolves represent the encroachment of urban values into rural society. Comments clearly reflected antagonism between locals and outsiders. For many outfitters wolves were symbolic of the federal government overstepping its bounds and interfering with the lives of rural citizens. This is consistent with the work of Heberlein and Ericsson, who describe cultural conflict associated with wolves in their article about urbanites attitudes toward wildlife: "In rural areas wolves are sometimes seen as a symbol of urban dominance over the less populated countryside, or over rural minorities with strong ties to nature. In the United States and Europe, pro-wolf urban attitudes have influenced wolf restoration in rural areas and led to strong local opposition."[66] As Brogden and Greenberg note in their study of the political ecology of land use conflicts, "Economic systems evolve logics of interaction and production . . . that are quite different from those governing ecological systems. The problem for policy makers is how to reconcile these very different rationalities."[67]

A minority of outfitters viewed the wolf in a positive manner. Some of these individuals expressed an awareness of the need for biological diversity and recognized the role wolves played in terms of maintaining a healthy ecosystem. Others were influenced by financial motives and suggested wolves would help outfitting businesses as well as the general economy by attracting tourists to the state.

The findings presented in this chapter contribute to our understanding of the complexities associated with conflict involving access to and allocation of natural resources in the context of a leisure occupation in contemporary society. It is hoped that the findings will provide insight for policymakers and generate interest in the outfitting industry and stimulate additional research about outfitters and the clients they serve as well as research into hunting, animals, and conservation.

Notes

[1] Riley, Nesslage, and Maurer (2004).

[2] Fischer (1995); Rinfret (2009); Robbins (2006); Scarce (1998); Wilson (2006).

[3] Fletcher (1929); Fritz (2002); Malone, Roeder, and Lang (1991).

[4] Palamar (2007); Robbins and Luginbuhl (2005).

[5] Eliason (2008).

[6] Scarce (1998).

[7] Bruckmeier (2005).

[8] Anahita and Mix (2006); Dajani (2013); Houston, Bruskotter, and Fan (2010); Lynn (2010); Nie (2002); Palamar (2007); Scarce (2005); Sjölander-Lindqvist (2009); Skogen and Thrane (2008); Skopek and Schuhmann (2005); Treves (2008); Wilson (1997); Wilson (2006).

[9] Hunt (2008); Lynn (2010); Scarce (1998); Wilson and Heberlein (1996).

[10] Montag, Patterson, and Freimund (2005); Rolston (2008).

[11] Scarce (1998); Sjölander-Lindqvist (2009).

[12] Sjölander-Lindqvist (2009).

[13] Ibid., 137-38.

[14] Black (2006); Kline (2007); McCarthy and Hague (2004); Wilson (1997).

[15] Brogden and Greenberg (2003).

[16] McCarthy and Hague (2004), 393.

[17] Robbins (2006); Robbins, Meehan, Gosnell, and Gilbertz (2009); Scarce (1998); Sheridan (2007).

[18] Brogden and Greenberg (2003).

[19] Sheridan (2007).

[20] Boglioli (2009a); Boglioli (2009b).

[21] Treves (2009).

[22] Sjölander-Lindqvist (2009); Skogen and Krange (2003).

[23] Treves (2008).

[24] Eliason (2008); Koch (1941); U.S. Department of the Interior (2006b).

[25] Bidwell (2010); Brownell (1987); Kelley (2001); Robbins (2006); Shanahan, McBeth, Tigert, and Hathaway (2010).

[26] Condy (2008); Fitzgerald (2009); Mahoney, Vahldiek, and Soulliere (2015); Posewitz (1999); Posewitz (2004).

[27] Freyfogle and Goble (2009).

[28] Black (2006); Daniels and Brehm (2003); Freyfogle and Goble (2009); Kline (2007).

[29] Daniels and Brehm (2003), 334.

[30] Eliason (2011); Eliason (2012); Eliason (1997); Bryant (2004); Bryant and Forsyth (2005); Dowsley (2009); Dunk (2002); Garland (2008); McGrath (1996).

[31] Arnett and Southwick (2015); Hendee (1969); Palmer and Bryant (1985); U.S. Department of the Interior (2006a).

[32] Herman (2005); Johnston (2007); Jones (2010); Lowrey (1986); Rattenbury (2008).

[33] Dickson (2010), 23.

[34] Montana Code Annotated (2009).

[35] Adams (2000); Green, Miller, and Yeager (1999).

[36] Adams (2000); Hjerpe and Kim (2007); Hussain, Munn, Grado, and Henderson (2008); Janecek (2006).

[37] Baker (1997); Little and Berrens (2008); Miller (2003); Nicolaysen (1997).

[38] Holyfield and Jonas (2003); Sharpe (2005).

[39] Capek (2006); Granfield and Colomy (2005); Lawson, Lawson, and Leck (2005); Leong (2010); Scarce (1998); Shaffir and Pawluch (2003).

[40] Blumer (1969); Shaffir and Pawluch (2003).

[41] Shaffir and Pawluch (2003), 906.

[42] Daniels and Brehm (2003); Granfield and Colomy (2005); Greider and Garkovich (1994); Scarce (1998); Sheridan (2007); Wilson (1997).

[43] Scarce (1998), 28, 43.

[44] Jerolmack (2008), 75.

[45] Henderson (2006); Neuman (2011).

[46] Neuman (2011), 324-25.

[47] Henderson (2006), 48.

[48] Fowler (1993); Henderson (2006); Neuman (2011).

[49] Eliason (2011).

[50] Yung, Patterson, and Freimund (2010); Fritz (2002); Malone et al. (1991).

[51] Ellard, Nickerson, and Dvorak (2009); Wilton and Nickerson (2006).

[52] Nickerson and Dubois (2008).

[53] Wilton and Nickerson (2006), 21.

[54] Adams (2000); Wright and Sanyal (1998).

[55] Eliason (2011).

[56] Riley et al. (2004), 575.

[57] Ibid.

[58] Scarce (1998), 35.

[59] Sheridan (2007), 131.

[60] Ibid., 129

[61] Eliason (2014), 137.

[62] Knight (2009).

[63] Daniels and Brehm (2003); Granfield and Colomy (2005); Greider and Garkovich (1994); Sheridan (2007); Wilson (1997).

[64] Daniels and Brehm (2003), 330.

[65] Lynn (2010), 82.

[66] Heberlein and Ericsson (2005), 215.

[67] Brogden and Greenberg (2003), 289.

References

Adams, J. (2000). *Wildland Outfitters: Contributions to Montana's Economy.* Helena, MT: Montana Wilderness Association.

Anahita, S., and Mix, T. L. (2006). "Retrofitting Frontier Masculinity for Alaska's War against Wolves." *Gender and Society* 20(3): 332-53.

Arnett, E. B., & Southwick, R. (2015). "Economic and Social Benefits of Hunting in North America." *International Journal of Environmental Studies* 72(5): 734-45.

Baker, J. E. (1997). "Development of a Model System for Touristic Hunting Revenue Collection and Allocation." *Tourism Management,* 18(5): 273-86.

Bidwell, D. (2010). "Bison, Boundaries, and Brucellosis: Risk Perception and Political Ecology at Yellowstone." *Society and Natural Resources* 23(1): 14-30.

Black, B. (1996). *Nature and the Environment in Twentieth-century American Life.* Westport, CT: Greenwood Press.

Blumer, H. (1969). *Symbolic Interactionism: Perspective and Method.* University of California Press: Berkeley.

Boglioli, M. (2009a). *A Matter of Life and Death: Hunting in Contemporary Vermont.* Amherst: University of Massachusetts Press.

Boglioli, M. A. (2009b). "Illegitimate Killers: The Symbolic Ecology and Cultural Politics of Coyote-hunting Tournaments in Addison County, Vermont." *Anthropology and Humanism* 34(2): 203-18.

Brogden, M. J., and Greenberg, J. B. (2003). "The Fight for the West: A Political Ecology of Land Use Conflicts in Arizona." *Human Organization* 62(3): 289-98.

Brownell, J. L. (1987). *The Genesis of Wildlife Conservation in Montana.* Unpublished Master's Thesis. Montana State University, Bozeman, MT.

Bruckmeier, K. (2005). "Interdisciplinary Conflict Analysis and Conflict Mitigation in Local Resource Management." *Ambio* 34(2): 65-73.

Bryant, C. D. (2004). "The Quest for Dead Animals on the Wall: The African Safari as Phantasmagorical Experience." Paper presented at the annual meeting of the American Sociological Association. San Francisco, CA, August.

Bryant, C. D., and Forsyth, C. J. (2005). "The Fun God: Sports, Recreation, Leisure, and Amusement in the United States." *Sociological Spectrum* 25(2): 197-211.

Capek, S. M. (2006). "Surface Tension: Boundary Negotiations around Self, Society, and Nature in a Community Debate over Wildlife." *Symbolic Interaction* 29(2): 157-81.

Condy, P. R. (2008). "Conservation—Public or Private, Socialism or Capitalism?" *The Wildlife Professional* 2(2): 52-53.

Dajani, K. F. (2013). "Wolf Wars: Online Information about Wolves in the Northern Rocky Mountains." *Applied Environmental Education and Communication* 12(1): 46-54.

Daniels, S. E., and Brehm, J. M. (2003). "Fur, Fins, and Feathers: Whose Home Is It Anyway?" In D. L. Brown and L. E. Swanson (eds.), *Challenges for Rural America in the Twenty-First Century* (329-39). University Park, PA: The Pennsylvania State University Press.

Dickson, T. (2010). "Welcome to Montana Elk Hunting." *Montana Outdoors* 41(6): 20-27.

Dizard, J. E. (2003). *Mortal Stakes: Hunters and Hunting in Contemporary America*. Amherst, MA: University of Massachusetts Press.

Donihee, J. (1996). "Wildlife Outfitting Rules Tested in the Territorial Court." *Journal of Environmental Law and Practice* 6(1): 67-79.

Dowsley, M. (2009). "Inuit-organised Polar Bear Sport Hunting in Nunavut Territory, Canada." *Journal of Ecotourism* 8(2): 161-75.

Dunk, T. (2002). "Hunting and the Politics of Identity in Ontario." *Capitalism, Nature, Socialism* 13(1): 36-66.

Eliason, S. L. (2008). "A Statewide Examination of Hunting and Trophy Nonhuman Animals: Perspectives of Montana Hunters." *Society and Animals* 16(3): 256-78.

Eliason, S. L. (2011). "Motivations for Becoming an Outfitter in Big Sky Country." *Human Dimensions of Wildlife* 16(5): 299-310.

Eliason, S. L. (2012). "Crowding, Public Image, and Bureaucracy: Issues in the Montana Outfitting Industry." *Journal of Rural and Community Development* 7(2): 57-71.

Eliason, S. L. (2014). "Hunting Issues in Contemporary Society: Perspectives of Resident Hunters in Montana (USA)." *Wildlife Biology in Practice* 10(2): 132-48.

Ellard, A., Nickerson, N. P., and Dvorak, R. (2009). "The Spiritual Dimension of the Montana Vacation Experience." *Leisure/Loisir* 33(1): 269-89.

Fischer, H. (1995). *Wolf Wars: The Remarkable inside Story of the Restoration of Wolves toYellowstone*. Helena and Billings, MT: Falcon.

Fitzgerald, E. A. (2009). "The Alaskan Wolf War: The Public Trust Doctrine Missing in Action." *Animal Law Review* 15(2): 193-235.

Fletcher, R. S. (1929). "The End of the Open Range in Eastern Montana." *Mississippi Valley Historical Review* 16(2): 188-211.

Fowler, F. J., Jr. (1993). *Survey Research Methods*. Newbury Park, CA: Sage.

Freyfogle, E. T., and Goble, D. D. (2009). *Wildlife Law: A Primer*. Washington, DC: Island Press.

Fritz, H. W. (2002). "Montana in the Twenty-first Century." In H. W. Fritz, M. Murphy, and R. R. Swartout, Jr. (eds.), *Montana Legacy: Essays on History, People, and Place* (341-58). Helena, MT: Montana Historical Society Press.

Garland, E. (2008). "The Elephant in the Room: Confronting the Colonial Character of Wildlife Conservation in Africa." *African Studies Review* 51(3): 51-74.

Granfield, R., and Colomy, P. (2005). "Paradise Lost: The Transformation of Wildlife Law in the Vanishing Wilderness." In A. Herda-Rapp and T. L. Goedeke (eds.), *Mad about Wildlife* (147-69). Leiden, The Netherlands: Brill.

Greer, J., Miller, C., and Yeager, S. (1999). *Riding West: An Outfitter's Life*. Niwot, CO: University Press of Colorado.

Greider, T., and Garkovich, L. 1994. "Landscapes: The Social Construction of Nature and the Environment." *Rural Sociology* 59(1): 1-24.

Heberlein, T. A., and Ericsson, G. (2005). "Ties to the Countryside: Accounting for Urbanites Attitudes toward Hunting, Wolves, and Wildlife." *Human Dimensions of Wildlife* 10(3): 213-27.

Hendee, J. C. (1969). "Rural-urban Differences Reflected in Outdoor Recreation Participation." *Journal of Leisure Research* 1: 333-41.

Henderson, K. A. (2006). *Dimensions of Choice: Qualitative Approaches to Parks, Recreation, Tourism, and Leisure Research*. State College, PA: Venture Publishing.

Herman, D. J. (2005). "Hunting Democracy." *Montana: The Magazine of Western History* 55(3): 22-33.

Hjerpe, E. E., and Kim, Y. (2007). "Regional Economic Impacts of Grand Canyon River Runners." *Journal of Environmental Management* 85(1): 137-49.

Holyfield, L., and Jonas, L. (2003). "From River God to Research Grunt: Identity, Emotions, and the River Guide." *Symbolic Interaction* 26(2): 285-306.

Houston, M. J., Bruskotter, J.T., and Fan, D. (2010). "Attitudes toward Wolves in the United States and Canada: A Content Analysis of the Print News Media, 1999-2008." *Human Dimensions of Wildlife*, 15(5): 389-403.

Hunt, D. (2008). "The Face of the Wolf Is Blessed, or Is It? Diverging Perceptions of the Wolf." *Folklore* 119(3): 319-34.

Hussain, A., Munn, I. A., Grado, S. C., and Henderson, J. E. (2008). "Economic Impacts of Mississippi Wildlife-associated Outfitters and their Clientele." *Human Dimensions of Wildlife* 13(4): 243-51.

Janecek, J. A. (2006). "Hunter v. Hunter: The Case for Discriminatory Nonresident Hunting Regulations." *Marquette Law Review* 90(2): 355-81.

Jerolmack, C. (2008). "How Pigeons Became Rats: The Cultural-spatial Logic of Problem Animals." *Social Problems* 55(1): 72-94.

Johnston, J. (2007). "Theodore Roosevelt's Hunting Guide: John B. Goff." *Annals of Wyoming* 79(2): 12-28.

Jones, K. (2010). "'My Winchester Spoke to Her': Crafting the Northern Rockies as a Hunter's Paradise, c.1870-1910." *American Nineteenth Century History* 11(2): 183-203.

Kelley, J. M. (2001). "Implications of a Montana Voter Initiative that Reduces Chronic Wasting Disease Risk, Bans Canned Shooting, and Protects a Public Trust." *Great Plains Natural Resources Journal* 6: 89-109.

Kline, B. (2007). *First along the River: A Brief History of the U.S. Environmental Movement*. Lanham, MD: Rowman and Littlefield.

Knight, J. (2009). "Making Wildlife Viewable: Habituation and Attraction." *Society and Animals* 17(2): 167-84.

Koch, E. (1941). "Big game in Montana from early historical records." *Journal of Wildlife Management* 5(4): 357-70.

Lawson, H. M., Lawson, L. R., and Leck, K. (2005). "The Meaning of Animals." *Sociological Viewpoints* 21: 35-52.

Leong, K. M. (2010). "The Tragedy of Becoming Common: Landscape Change and Perceptions of Wildlife." *Society and Natural Resources* 23(2): 111-27.

Little, J. M., and Berrens, R. P. (2008). The Southwestern Market for Big-game Hunting Permits and Services: A Hedonic Pricing Analysis." *Human Dimensions of Wildlife* 13(3): 143-57.

Lowrey, N. S. (1986). "A Historical Perspective on the Northern Maine Guide." *Maine Historical Society Quarterly* 26(1): 2-21.

Lynn, W. S. (2010). "Discourse and Wolves: Science, Society, and Ethics." *Society and Animals* 18(1): 75-92.

Mahoney, S. P., Vahldiek, P., & Soulliere, C. A. (2015). "Private Land: Conservation's New Frontier in America." *International Journal of Environmental Studies* 72(5): 869-78.

Malone, M. P., Roeder, R. B., and Lang, W. L. (1991). *Montana: A History of Two Centuries*. Seattle: University of Washington Press.

McCarthy, J., and Hague, E. (2004). "Race, Nation, and Nature: The Cultural Politics of 'Celtic' Identification in the American West." *Annals of the Association of American Geographers* 94(2): 387-408.

McGrath, D. M. (1996). "Poaching in Newfoundland and Labrador: The Creation of an Issue." *Newfoundland Studies* 12(2): 79-104.

Miller, M. (2003). "Casenote: Conservation Force, Inc. v. Manning: When Hunting Means Business." *Great Plains Natural Resources Journal* 7: 71-78.

Montag, J. M., Patterson, M. E., and Freimund, W. A. (2005). "The Wolf Viewing Experience in the Lamar Valley of Yellowstone National Park." *Human Dimensions of Wildlife* 10(4): 273-84.

Montana Code Annotated. (2009). *Title 37. Professions and Occupations, Chapter 47. Outfitters and Guides, Part 3. Licensing, 37-47-301. License Required—Services Performed—Standards.* Retrieved on May 10, 2011, from <http://data.opi.mt.gov/bills/mca/37/47/37-47-301.htm>.

Neuman, W. L. (2011). *Social Research Methods: Qualitative and Quantitative Approaches*. Boston: Allyn and Bacon.

Nickerson, N. P., and Dubois, M. (2008). "Outlook and Trends 2008: Montana Travel and Recreation." *Montana Business Quarterly* 46(1): 18-21.

Nicolaysen, P. C. (1997). "Comment: Reserving Wildlife for Resident Consumption: Is the Dormant Commerce Clause the Outfitters' White Knight?" *Land and Water Law Review* 32: 125-53.

Nie, M. A. (2002). "Wolf Recovery and Management as Value-based Political Conflict." *Ethics, Place and Environment* 5(1): 65-71.

Palamar, C. R. (2007). "Wild, Women, and Wolves: An Ecological Feminist Examination of Wolf Reintroduction." *Environmental Ethics* 29(1): 63-75.

Palmer, C. E., and Bryant, C. D. (1985). "Keeper's of the King's deer: Game Wardens and the Enforcement of Fish and Wildlife Law." In C. D. Bryant, D. W. Shoemaker, J. K. Skipper, Jr., and W. E. Snizek (eds.), *The Rural Workforce: Non-agricultural Occupations in America* (111-37). South Hadley, MA: Bergin and Harvey.

Posewitz, J. (1999). *Inherit the Hunt: A Journey into the Heart of American Hunting*. Helena, MT: Falcon.

Posewitz, J. (2004). *Rifle in Hand: How Wild America Was Saved*. Helena, MT: Riverbend.

Rattenbury, R. C. (2008). *Hunting the American West: The Pursuit of Big Game for Life, Profit, and Sport, 1800-1900*. Missoula, MT: Boone and Crockett Club.

Riley, S. J., Nesslage, G. M., and Maurer, B. A. (2004). "Dynamics of Early Wolf and Cougar Eradication Efforts in Montana: Implications for Conservation." *Biological Conservation* 119: 575-79.

Rinfret, S. (2009). "Controlling Animals: Power, Foucault, and Species Management." *Society and Natural Resources* 22(6): 571-78.

Robbins, P. (2006). The Politics of Barstool Biology: Environmental Knowledge and Power in Greater Northern Yellowstone. *Geoforum* 37(2): 185-99.

Robbins, P., and Luginbuhl, A. (2005). "The Last Enclosure: Resisting Privatization of Wildlife in the Western United States." *Capitalism, Nature, Socialism* 16(1): 45-61.

Robbins, P., Meehan, K., Gosnell, H., and Gilbertz, S. J. (2009). "Writing the New West: A Critical Review." *Rural Sociology* 74(3): 356-82.

Rolston, H. III. (2008). "Mountain Majesties above Fruited Plains: Culture, Nature, and Rocky Mountain Aesthetics." *Environmental Ethics* 30(1): 3-20.

Scarce, R. (1998). "What Do Wolves Mean? Conflicting Social Constructions of *Canis Lupus* in 'Bordertown.'" *Human Dimensions of Wildlife* 3(3): 26-45.

Scarce, R. (2005). More than Mere Wolves at the Door: Reconstructing Community Amidst a Wildlife Controversy. In A. Herda-Rapp and T. L. Goedeke (eds.), *Mad about Wildlife* (123-46). Leiden, The Netherlands: Brill.

Shaffir, W, and Pawluch, D. (2003). Occupations and Professions. In L. T. Reynolds and N. J. Herman-Kinney (eds.), *Handbook of Symbolic Interactionism* (893-913). Walnut Creek, CA: AltaMira Press.

Shanahan, E. A., McBeth, M. K., Tigert, L. E., and Hathaway, P. L. (2010). "From Protests to Litigation to *YouTube*: A Longitudinal Case Study of Strategic Lobby Tactic Choice for the Buffalo Field Campaign." *Social Science Journal* 47(1): 137-50.

Sharpe, E. K. (2005). "'Going above and beyond:'" The Emotional Labor of Adventure Guides." *Journal of Leisure Research* 37(1): 29-50.

Sheridan, T. E. (2007). "Embattled Ranchers, Endangered Species, and Urban Sprawl: The Political Ecology of the New American West." *Annual Review of Anthropology* 36(1): 121-38.

Sjölander-Lindqvist, A. (2009). "Social-natural Landscape Reorganised: Swedish Forest-edge Farmers and Wolf Recovery." *Conservation and Society* 7(2): 130-40.

Skogen, K., and Krange, O. (2003). "A Wolf at the Gate: The Anti-carnivore Alliance and the Symbolic Construction of Community." *Sociologia Ruralis* 43(3): 309-25.

Skogen, K., and Thrane, C. (2008). "Wolves in Context: Using Survey Data to Situate Attitudes within a Wider Cultural Framework." *Society and Natural Resources* 21(1): 17-33.

Skopek, T. A., and Schuhmann, R. (2005). "Wolf in Sheep's Clothing? State Implementation of the Gray Wolf Recovery Plan under the Endangered Species Act." *Green Theory and Praxis* (1): 1-24.

Treves, A. (2008). "Beyond Recovery: Wisconsin's Wolf Policy 1980-2008." *Human Dimensions of Wildlife* 13(5): 329-38.

Treves, A. (2009). "Hunting for Large Carnivore Conservation." *Journal of Applied Ecology* 46 (6): 1350-56.

U.S. Department of the Interior. (2006a). *2006 National Survey of Fishing, Hunting, and Wildlife-associated Recreation*. U.S. Department of the Interior, Fish and Wildlife Service, and U.S. Department of Commerce, U.S. Census Bureau. Retrieved on January 6, 2010, from: <http://wsfrprograms.fws.gov/Subpages/NationalSurvey/nat_survey2006_final.pdf>.

U.S. Department of the Interior. (2006b). *2006 National Survey of Fishing, Hunting, and Wildlife-associated Recreation: Montana*. U.S. Department of the Interior, Fish and Wildlife Service, and U.S. Department of Commerce, U.S. Census Bureau. Retrieved on January 6, 2010, from: <http://www.census.gov/prod/2008pubs/fhw06-mt.pdf>.

Wilson, M. A. (1997). "The Wolf in Yellowstone: Science, Symbol, or Politics? Deconstructing the Conflict between Environmentalism and Wise Use." *Society and Natural Resources* 10(5): 453-68.

Wilson, M. A., and Heberlein, T. A. (1996). "The Wolf, the Tourist, and the Recreational Context: New opportunity or uncommon circumstance?" *Human Dimensions of Wildlife* 1(4): 38-53.

Wilson, P. I. (2006). "Forward to the Past: Wolves in the Northern Rockies and the Future of ESA Politics." *Society and Natural Resources* 19(9): 863-70.

Wilton, J. J., and Nickerson, N. P. (2006). "Collecting and Using Visitor Spending Data." *Journal of Travel Research* 45(1): 17-25.
Wright, M. V., and Sanyal, N. (1998). "Differentiating Motivations of Guided Versus Unguided Fly Anglers." *Human Dimensions of Wildlife* 3(1): 34-46.
Yung, L., Patterson, M. E., and Freimund, W. A. (2010). "Rural Community Views on the Role of Local and Extralocal Interests in Public Lands Governance." *Society and Natural Resources* 23(12): 1170-86.

Chapter 9

Saving Up on the Prairie:

The Honeybee, the Pheasant, Lake Politics, and Ethanol

Anthony J. Amato

Conservation is about imaginings and the actions taken based on these imaginings.

Conservation evokes many images, all of which share an aura of measure and care. Seeing conservation in this light, many have assumed that the movement and the concept have marched in step with scientific discovery and rising prosperity toward the single goal of greater wealth and harmony with nature. Nevertheless, actual conservation has often departed from the narrative arc of the story of increasing concern for non-human elements of the environment over time. In reality, conservation on the Plains and elsewhere was (and is) a jumble of modernity or an "alphabet soup" of agencies, laws, studies, and even places. In the vast grasslands, resource-saving and nature-preserving projects ran up against limits and scarcity, sometimes natural and sometimes cultural, yet rarely as expected. Endeavors to save the Prairie (or objects in or on it) suffered from the conflicting impulses and visions coming from the people living there. The stories of these endeavors featured frequent reversals and inversions and only sometimes picked up where they left off. As much as it has followed scientific progress and progressive politics, conservation on the Northern Plains has been about redefinition, compromise, conflict, and concealment.[1] Four areas offer illustrations of the dynamic rhetoric and shifting practices on the Plains. These areas are ecological theory, ethanol, water and lake projects management, and the histories of two imported species in southern Minnesota. Turned into a program of action on land, conservation has relied on local translations in each area.

The concept of conservation has rested on two elements: maximum efficiency in use of natural resources and concern for the environment's non-human elements. From the United Nations to U.S.

counties, official statements of conservation espoused rational use. Use and cost-benefit analysis based on people became guidelines in policy, but, from the outset, the implementation of policies lagged behind the latest science and sentiments. While rational-use was taking hold in policy, conservation had been losing its attractiveness to those who did the science for decades. Although the words "maximize" and "maximization" appeared in one publication as late as the 1960s, the words "minimize" and "minimization" appeared as often.[2] Some had begun to look beyond conservation based on rational use and production.[3] They came to settle on a definition of conservation put forward by Aldo Leopold as "a state of harmony between men and land," which shunned calculation and "show pieces."[4] As the twentieth century wore on and ecology advanced from prejudice to science, students of nature and politics began to abandon the term conservation altogether in favor of concepts that captured larger wholes and specific objects of concern.[5]

Despite its contradictions, conservation retains value both as an approach for understanding and a shaper of realities. The applications and utility of conservation in science and policy are most apparent in cultured-nature areas, and some rural areas on the Northern Plains are the best places to see the concept's applications for yields and harvests, predator-prey interaction, and invasive species. Recent concepts, such as Ian Rotherham's eco-history, break with established understandings of nature, forming the basis for future productive arrangements between people and nature on the Northern Plains.

Nature itself has been the subject of controversy. The century-old debate between preservationists and their technocratic conservationist counterparts offers insight into nature and its uses. The late-nineteenth and early-twentieth-century conservationist technocrats took a surprising view of conservation. In contrast to images of the conservationists as the preventative guards of stores of nature, the technocrats actually aimed for maximum use of resources and favored conservation only to maximize use. Efficiency, for them, was merely a way to ensure maximum use, and it was only at maximum output that efficiency could be achieved.[6] With its true face revealed, this technocratic view offers insights into conservation's role in nature. Technocrats insisted that land and natural features had maximum levels of output, and these levels of output were not always present under existing arrangements among human and natural elements. For the early-twentieth-century mind, the movement of energy and materials out of and within ecosystems varied and was a mystery, but exploitation by people was knowable and calculable. Because neither theory nor instruments could capture nature, they focused on people's overuse and left nature as a constant force.[7]

Maximum use remained a foundation of conservation, and the notion of maximums and efficiency found their proper place in the science of nature. In the 1940s, scientists had both the theory and measurements to understand energy and materials in ecosystems. As the twentieth century progressed, more attention in the sciences fell to the global scale and to the variations at the level of individual organisms even at the microscopic level.[8] Conservation's foundations were buried in understandings of use and natural resources, and did not rise to the level of the emerging science of ecology.

Although mid-twentieth-century calculations of ecosystems' maximum capacities strike twenty-first century minds as antique, efficiency, productivity, and maxima have great utility in explaining nature's departures from expected patterns of succession and composition. Species' and nutrient cycling's ability to operate at a number of "different gears," so to speak, has commanded the attention of contemporary students of nature.[9]

Maxima have a foundation in biology. Into, within, and from ecosystems, energy, materials, and information flow, and the organisms within ecosystems are packets of these three. As an organism can perform at a maximum metabolic rate beyond the point of efficiency, ecosystems and socio-metabolisms that manage them can function at rates above efficiency, and these performances are the bases for a revised understanding of conservation. Long thought to be set, the energy flow in ecosystems in the food chains' trophic levels has shown great variations depending on the age of the species, nutrients present, and even some unknowns.[10] Individual species can provide a guide to some of the variability inherent in ecosystems, as the energy use of individual species (e.g., horses) can be isolated and ascertained with more ease than that of areas (e.g. swamps). Species are not merely placeholders in a hierarchy of trophic levels. The variety of species' specific maximum metabolic rates (MMRs) conforms to a scale based on mass, not on food chain location or other external ecological variables.[11] Similar departures and variety can account for some of the species variation in ecosystems at a given moment.

More precise understandings of maxima, efficiency, and outcomes create problems for the concept of perpetuation integral in conservation and sustainability. Starts and restarts are the issues in rural ecosystems and agro-ecosystems, both of which are always running on momentum. One-time outlays of sufficient transformational energy (e.g., sod-busting and swamp-draining) rewrite the land and even become a force against which subsequent rewrites must contend.

Ecosystems carry with them complexity, which is the foundation of all ecological functions. Given the power of origins and complexity, some ecologists have chalked up natural outcomes that are odd in sequence and scale to chaos theory. Others have argued that these outcomes are simply different levels of efficiency determined by maxima sustained or unachieved. Yet others have contended that chaos theory itself is just a chart of the variability in nature from its smallest elements' inherent variations.[12] Whichever is the case, the assessment of complicated outcomes and courses of action themselves bedevil ecology and rural conservation. Perhaps the ecological eye of conservation, which is keen to maxima, can see parameters better, making it better than the eye of management, which is keen to balance.

The failure of species to come back as well as many indicators of less healthy productivity areas has caught the attention of countless scientists who have sought to restore or re-nature areas. Findings indicate that some places, left without man-made disturbances and introductions, accumulate material and energy in certain forms and locations at the expense of other forms and locations. This in part accounts for the cases when ecosystems do not contain species and processes as predicted and even for those cases when ecosystems seem to fare worse when human activity is removed. Abandoned areas, most have concluded, do not re-wild. Instead, they collect, amass, and store material and energy. Some insist that natural agents and processes are insufficient to stop this perpetual accumulation and intervention by people is the only way.[13] Conservation has begun to consider legacies, not just limits, when making determinations about use.[14]

Conservation that includes extremes in its understanding of efficiency can also apply to people's use. Charting a course for use involves awareness of the feedback from existing uses, and maximum sustainable yield, once thought to be fixed and constant but seemingly inconstant to the point of excessiveness at times or non-existent at others. Harvests mimicking a boom-and-bust cycle, some contend, are the solution for an inconstant nature, and extreme maxima are stressed rather than those that are just above average.[15] Non-equilibrium-based concepts such as ecosystem momentum, inherent uncertainty, and quantum ecology also appear to be coming down the pike. Although the Northern Plains exist in an apparent timelessness, their fields, woods, and waters are defined by extremes and frenzy.

Conservation done properly has become more than the management of equilibria. Management for both areas and animals has put a difficult twist and double burden on conservation. Its practice ranges from an art to a hunch, and its practitioners must account for stages in plant community succession, climate changes, and the geologic processes of erosion and deposition. For instance, upstream pollution and silt sources have threatened downstream wildlife areas.[16] Based on people's informed judgment, conservation is as much about creation as it is about preservation. It is bringing a place into being not just saving a place and its inhabitants.

Across the Plains, conservation efforts have organized themselves around re-creation for recreation. Hunters, visitors, and officials encountered places that had been damaged, depleted, or desolated. Out of these places and with great effort, they improved and created places they deemed restored.[17] In the 1930s the Civilian Conservation Corps (CCC) and its lesser-known wing, the Veterans' Conservation Corps, re-purposed land, creating useable places for recreation. One of these places was Minnesota's Camden State Park, a wooded cove on an ocean of open plains soil.[18] The legacy of the CCC testifies to conservation's goal of seeking greater use than that which nature would allow on its own.

Conservation is about imaginings and the actions taken based on these imaginings. Two species have captured the rural imagination in Minnesota, South Dakota, and North Dakota. One, the honeybee, is the focus of the observers who behold the countryside from afar. The other is the pheasant, the birthright of everyone who has hunted the Prairie—if only vicariously in a Terry Redlin painting. Both creatures reveal a world shaped by use and past action.

For almost a decade, the mystery of vanishing honeybees has kept specialists and casual audiences on edge. The latest chapter in the apian whodunit has focused on neonicotinoids and other systemic pesticides.[19] Lost in this "CSI" story is the history of the bee. The insects are local species and have depended on specific acts in the past and the characteristics of places. The introduction of the honeybee (*Apis mellifera)* entailed energy of activation and inputs of energy for decades. A great leap forward for the exotic species in Minnesota came from an army of beekeepers trained at the University of Minnesota and unleashed on the countryside. Men like the late Ray Klein of Marshall took classes and took over beekeeping operations in the 1930s. Klein's honey farm, which once included several thousand hives, came to an end in the 1990s when big beekeeping forced the issue of scaling up even larger. [20] The conservation of this insect might invoke a concept similar to critical mass, especially in a country where beekeeping is perceived as a hobby.[21]

Saving bees holds itself out as a simple goal, but bug, habitat, and farm economy blend together in this endeavor as they do in a cheap blended honey. Beekeeper Steve Klein, who has drawn on the experience of his centenarian father, the late Ray Klein, once described the changes as "unbelievable," intending no pun. Growing up in apiculture, Steve was one of nine fulltime beekeepers in Lyon County just as it took leadership in honey production in Minnesota, surpassing Iowa. At present there is only one working beekeeper in the southwest corner of the state. Klein attributed the decline to complex ecology and economics on the Plains and elsewhere. When he started as a boy, the weather was perfect, in his words. Ample spring rains and dry summers allowed three cuttings of hay (one after the aftermath). Many farmers cut only twice, though, and from August there were standing flowers. Since the 1950s, the weather has not been as favorable. Klein stresses that if the present state of affairs forms a point on the downslope for southern Minnesota, then it forms a point on the upslope for areas just to the west: the Dakotas, "God's country" for the bees. When they get rain, Klein insists, there is no better place for apiculture. The clover-covered meadows of pasture and hayfields, together with fields of sunflower and rapeseed plant, form one vast apiary.[22] Rain doesn't follow the plow on the Plains, but bees follow the cow.

Klein has noted that the small things have added up. Biological and economic changes have entered the scene. The switch from pasture to feedlot and cattle to corn, soybeans, and pigs has eliminated fields of forage plants. Dietary supplements have supplanted the need for clover and alfalfa for cattle, so the insects have less forage. Pesticides are a known threat that people fear, but herbicides and farmers with spare time have created cleaner ditches and fields than ever before, eliminating much of the wild forage. In the 1990s the Conservation Reserve Program and the Conservation Reserve Enhancement Program switched to native grasses, which offer no sustenance for *Apis*. Long after start-up, energy in the form of labor is still necessary to sustain apiculture, and the necessary labor inputs have remained great and difficult to find in a country that has become physical-labor-averse, highly paid, and professional. Beekeepers, once honey producers, have come to depend on pay for their insects' pollination. California's booms, manias, and mass expansions (most recently with almond trees) have pulled billions of bees there for seasonal pollination. In three decades since the age of bigtime pollination, the concentration and transcontinental shipping of bees has resulted in mites and viruses spreading like wildfire in apian populations.[23]

The honeybee as a habitat predicament dates back several decades. As two authors in another Northern Plains on the other side of the planet pointed out, too much cultivation means fewer bees, but specific cultivars (e.g. buckwheat) could mean many more bees.[24] The fates of the hives have rested on agriculture. As the eastern Northern Plains have lost habitat, areas to their west have become the resting place for the industry, and, as apiculture has become an activity involving scale, areas with open space and vast fields of plants accommodate big beekeeping. Beekeeping's shift in the Plains reveals the difficulties of conservation even with approaches sensitive to the nuances of nature and the past.

The common pheasant (*Phasianus colchicus*) and its former farm habitat touch off riots of biophilia in many plainspeople. Wildlife stamps, prints, and paintings have created careers for more than a few artists of the Plains. The iconic ring-necked pheasant and its landscape find their greatest celebration perhaps, not in the works of Terry Redlin, but in the work of John Green, whose painting entitled *Reunion Hunt* at the Sioux Falls Regional Airport has welcomed air travelers to Sioux Falls.[25] It is Redlin, however, who is most identified with the bird and the open farm and country landscape. The official site of Terry Redlin even posted an article on the 2012 pheasant count in South Dakota.[26] So critical is the actual conservation of the bird that even the sublime has wound up adorned with prosaic wildlife biology.

The pheasant has a storied past. The bird arrived in the Midwest almost one hundred years ago. Introduced to replace the passenger pigeon and the invasive prairie chicken, it thrived for several decades. In the 1980s, the bird's numbers entered a steep decline, which has continued after brief turnarounds.[27] The plight of the ring-neck is so significant for the landscape in which rural conservation operates that over two hundred people turned out in December 2014 for a Minnesota Democratic-Farmer-Labor governor's event. Held in Marshall, the "red" star in the "reddest" (that is, Republican) corner of the state, the first-ever Pheasant Summit addressed the bird and its fate.[28] The loss of habitat is the common explanation for the bird's dwindling numbers, but the fluctuations in numbers, especially when population patterns that depart from Alfred Lotka's oscillations, have remained almost as mysterious as they were for Aldo Leopold eight decades ago.[29] One journalist described the times as a "perfect storm" on the Plains due to "high commodities, prices, dubious energy policy [i.e., ethanol], and weather."[30] Some have gone so far as to declare that climate change, which would reduce winterkills, might be a boon for the bird.[31] Like the bee, the pheasant has moved west and continues "to go west" as the Corn Belt expands.[32] Thousands stand at the ready to conserve and perpetuate, but conditions do not accommodate, and bird, habitat, and farm economy do not blend as they do in a Terry Redlin painting.

The pheasant's short past on the Plains has made its current difficulties all the more ominous. Much of the bird's notoriety came in the two decades after World War II. In fact, so minor and tenuous was this Chinese import's place in 1939 (two decades after its introduction) that the bird warranted only one short mention in a history of Minnesota's game, which dwelled on the grouse, quail, and prairie chicken, the fowl of earlier times.[33] By the 1960s, however, the bird had risen from a novel introduction to a regional icon, all in fewer than five decades. Since the 1980s, population cycles, subject to knowns, unknowns, and "unknown unknowns," have been foretelling a bust as big as this boom.[34]

In the far east of the Northern Plains, the pheasant and the bee took hold and prospered on land that was "country" in the definition of Aldo Leopold. The two grew up with and in this country. Not fully converted to "land" for maximum profit, plains country had freedom in flora and fauna.[35] Grass stands stood and water flowed just enough so that birds and bees could multiply. As the law of the land became maximizing profit, though, order and cleanliness became worthy goals in and of themselves. Both bee and bird have been called "a canary in a coal mine," and their advocates have cast their stories as part of a larger environmental destruction—from nitrate pollution in streams to milkweed and monarchs.[36]

Hunting defines the conservation of many species. This approach, although utilitarian, places a value on species and their perpetuation. This form of use became and has remained a strong stimulus for conservation of habitat. To the ire of some, game has remained the strongest force behind many efforts around wildlife.[37] Critics might be correct in asserting that game-management mentality has advanced little beyond its century-old roots, but the underlying approach in game management continues to make century-old conservationism an active force in shaping places today. *Field and Stream* conferred the title of "hero of conservation" and "prairies protector" on one Minnesota financial adviser who effected successful land acquisitions for pheasant habitat.[38]

For their part, farmers on the Plains have asserted that theirs is the most efficient use of land as a resource. Aside from those who have argued about the need for productivity, there are those who have been making cases for specific forms of agriculture as conservation. Conservationist agriculturists have been quick to cite the benefits of grazing in making their case.[39] The perpetuation of the genetic and habitat legacies of different breeds of domestic animals, they have argued, can be a focus of natural conservation, with wild species serving as a model for the conservation of domestic species.[40] Some have already made a case for "resilience," claiming that a green-year-round landscape is the way to save soil, water, and farms.[41] From the Seed Savers Exchange, of Decorah, Iowa, to the preference for perennial polycultures of the Land Institute, in Salina, Kansas, there is a range of competing conservations on the Prairie.

Rural areas are often the places of leftovers, holdovers, and holdouts. There are few better illustrations of the contradictions of understandings and legacies of yesteryear's conservation than the case of lake politics in southern Minnesota. On the surface, Currant

Lake in Murray County is just one of 10,000 other lakes in Minnesota. Held at a minimum level by a state law passed at the turn of the millennium, this shallow lake has been the object of fierce disputes. The lake includes several sources of inflow and one source of outflow. Local farmers, concerned about erosion, sided with waterfowl advocates (who wanted duck habitat) in opposing the continued maintenance of a diversion structure that kept water levels high by diverting water to the lake. The DNR and fishing advocates sought to keep levels high to support fish in a fishable lake. To add confusion to the controversy, there was uncertainty as to responsibility for the structures on the lake, and people have referred to the lake by two names: "Current" and "Currant."[42]

After decades of confusion and dispute, flooding in the 1990s made the lake a state issue. In 2001, siding with the fishing people, Minnesota enacted legislation that stated, "The Commissioner of Natural Resources must not abandon the diversion system at Currant Lake in Murray County. The commissioner may develop a management plan to operate the diversion in a manner to maintain the water level and fish habitat in Currant Lake and to maintain the aquatic vegetation and waterfowl habitat in Hjermstad State Wildlife Management Area."[43] The legislation guaranteed fish and plans for both sides, but weather and silt ensured that neither side received full satisfaction and that farmers would remain angry over an infringement of recreationalists and state officials on livelihood. The county has developed a ten-acre park on the east side of the lake, and to ensure the good fishing that wild fisheries rarely permit, the DNR has been stocking the lake with walleye, the prince of fish in Minnesota.[44]

Neighboring Lake Maria was diverted into a different conservation channel. Prodded by a massive rally for wetlands, organized by Ducks Unlimited in 2006, and giddy over the passage of an additional sales tax earmarked partially for the environment in 2006, the state of Minnesota undertook a sizable project to create waterfowl habitat out of Lake Maria a few years thereafter. It targeted "problem fish" (i.e., carp, bullheads, and minnows) that destroyed vegetation that ducks needed. To do so, the DNR installed an electric fish barrier and a pump at the outlet in order to ensure that the lake levels reached nadirs for effective fish winterkills.[45] Works such as the film *The Cry of Marsh* have portrayed ducks in the prairie's potholes as the victims of expansionist farmers, but a minor quack attack on the State Capitol bullied officials into launching an attack on bullheads and other agents of nature. Both Lake Maria and Currant Lake illustrate how ecological knowledge and deliberate programs of re-naturing create conflict and entail denaturing.

The two lakes are intersections of policies, worldviews, and pasts. Although the details of each differ, neither falls outside the pale of prairie lakes and marshes. Throughout the Prairie Pothole Region in the post-World War II era, the Fish and Wildlife Service initiated Waterfowl Protection Areas (WPAs). It leased and purchased potholes and managed them (especially their hydrologic aspects) for waterfowl. The program slowed in its expansion in the 1980s when concerns arose over the WPAs' impact on local tax bases, land title encumbrances, and federal expansion.[46] It was in this environment of expansion, contraction, and conflict that the conservation disputes over two shallow lakes took place.

Prairie Pothole Region. United States Geological Survey and the Northern Prairie Wildlife Research Center via the Wikipedia Commons.

Wetlands policies have continued to shape the wet prairies of the Plains. In the United States, wetland mitigation has required that wetland areas lost to development be replaced on a one-to-one basis in terms of area, but this has not taken into account the vast differences between types of wetlands lost.[47] Pasts of inundation (water levels) and muskrat action (herbivores' vegetation consumption) have determined the state of a marsh at a given moment. Moreover, species make marshes habitat for well-timed migration and lifecycle processes, and at this moment the wetlands must suit them.[48] All of these conditions and processes have put wetlands and shallows lakes on different historical channels.

Markets and money have managed the Prairie's potholes. At the turn of the millennium, with land and commodities prices low, farmers flocked to accept federal and state paid conservation easements. A few even created hunting habitat for free and then sought easements.[49] When the pendulum swung back in the other direction in the first decade of the twenty-first century, many turned to sodbusting, de-groving, and windbreak-cutting in order to return land to crops. The forces behind the swings, which some have noted, reveal that the Prairie's land and conservation are all policy and economy, and no spontaneity.[50] With no unmanaged space, it is difficult to have the wildness necessary for wildlife.

The expansion of corn ethanol production on the Prairie provides another instance where conservation's proprietary concepts offer insight. This biofuel suffers from the tangle of issues intertwined in all crops: energy loss versus energy gain, carbon budgets, ethanol's pollutants versus petroleum's pollution, fields for fuel versus fields for habitat, food versus fuel fields, the question of scale, the question of renewability, the placement of effects, and the placement of demands (e.g., local resource demands of water versus global resource demands). The target of scrutiny in each area, corn ethanol has not fared well. Its advocates, however, have adopted a position beyond traditional conservation, one that is in step with newer maximum-use conservation. They argue that distillation from corn is by definition inefficient and demanding, but the inefficiency is the price that must be paid for the development of future renewable resources, which will come from other crops, plants, and processes. Corn-based production, they suggest, is a temporary environmental and economic debt that must be incurred in order to attain the higher level of efficiency and use that other processes and crops will permit. For now there are two conservation certainties, one tangible, one abstract: the land and water of the endless Prairie are finite, and a narrow focus on efficiency often leads to a catabolic path.

Water consumption on the Plains has often been the focus of conservation. Water use has not been as straightforward as it might seem, and, in fact, much about use and conservation might be the opposite of what it seems on the surface. The late Marc Reisner captured the distinction between water conservation in the East and in the West: "In the East 'to waste' water is to consume it needlessly or excessively. In the West 'to waste' water is *not* to consume it—to let it flow unimpeded and undiverted down rivers."[51] Use as necessary for conservation came from even older understandings of waste and use. Not to use at all was the highest form of waste. Water law and use in the West reflected this older understanding from the territorial periods. Throughout the West but in different forms, the Western water legal doctrine of prior appropriation, which has conferred use rights on first users, has rested on usufruct and priority. The South Dakota Department of Environment and Natural Resources even features a didactic section on its website entitled "Historical background of water rights in South Dakota." It explains the state's prior appropriation system as an adaptation to deal with scarcity and aridity.[52]

The waters on and beneath the Plains have concealed the deeply contested definitions of conservation and equally deep opposing natural processes. The Northern Plains are home to one of the last great Western water projects: the still-unfinished Lewis and Clark Regional Water System. Designed to deliver water to the booming metropolis of Sioux Falls and its far-flung hinterlands in South Dakota, Minnesota, and Iowa, the project draws water from wells fed by Missouri river-water infiltration and aims to pipe it over hundreds of miles to slake rural industry and residences. The project opened in 2003, but it has come to a halt as state and local matches, such as Minnesota's dollar-for-dollar, were held up because the federal government failed to fund it. Sioux Falls has footed the lion's share of the bill, and a town in southwestern Minnesota prepaid two million dollars and then had to invest hundreds of dollars developing its own wells when the water did not flow.[53] Supporters and state officials have recently succeeded in prying funds out of the federal government, and the final chapter in one of the West's great water stories is coming to a close. Nevertheless, the story of the project is less *Chinatown* and more *Field of Dreams*—if you build it, capricious executives and legislators will fund it, but only if they can get in step. Here and elsewhere on the Plains, there is no story-worthy intrigue or scandal, only boosterism and the region's tired refrain of blaming government, especially "the Feds."

The project ties in with older stories of Plains' water conservation: the Missouri River and the Ogallala Aquifer. Drawing water from under the semi-arid Plains, the Lewis and Clark Project invites associations with the father of Plains groundwater, the nearby Ogallala Aquifer. The groundwater sources from which the project draws depend on the Missouri River's water levels, and this connects the project to a resource whose use is contested by those upstream and downstream on the river.[54] Aquifers throughout the Plains are coming up dry. As the controversy in 2014 revealed, even beneath Minnesota, the Land of 10,000 Lakes, groundwater has very limited limits.[55] Surface waters hold out even less hope—they are imperiled and in peril. A conservation effort to maximize available water and save other waters, the Lewis and Clark project reveals maximizing use as the guiding principle of conservation, which, according to some abstract economic theory, might entail the users "betting on the come." On the real Prairie, the interstate waterworks marks the U.S. Bureau Reclamation's crossing into and dispensing groundwater to the humid East.

As much as it has been the result of trends, conservation on the Prairie has arisen from events and places. Like the nature that it seeks to mimic and like the towns in its western extreme, it is less about saving up and spending down—and more about booms and busts.

Notes

[1] For a discussion of this variance, see Keith Thomas, *Man and the Natural World: Changing Attitudes in England 1500-1800* (Oxford: Oxford University Press, 1983), 302-03; and Joachim Radkau, *The Age of Ecology: A Global History*, Patrick Camiller, trans. (London: Polity, 2014), viii, 5. For a reconsideration of the Great Plains and environmental compromise, see Geoff Cunfer, *On the Great Plains: Agriculture and Environment* (College Station, Texas: Texas A&M University Press, 2005).

[2] Richard J. Highsmith Jr., J. Granville Jensen, and Robert D. Rudd, *Conservation in the United States* (Chicago: Rand McNally and Company, 1969), 4-7.

[3] William Souder, *On a Farther Shore: The Life and Legacy of Rachel Carson* (New York: Broadway Books, 2012), 123-26.

[4] Aldo Leopold, *A Sand County Almanac, with Essays on Conservation from Round River* (New York: Ballantine Books, 1980), 189, 193.

[5] Ecology's separate early roots and its differences from conservation are well covered in the pages of Carl H. Moneyhon, "The Environmental Crisis and American Politics, 1860-1920," in *Historical Ecology: Essays on Environmental and Social Change*, Lester J. Bilsky, ed. (Port Washington, MY: Kemikat Press, 1980), 143-55. The transition in the middle of the twentieth century is covered by Stephen Fox, *The American Conservation Movement: John Muir and his Legacy* (Madison: University of Wisconsin Press, 1985), especially 355-57.

[6] Samuel P. Hays's *Conservation and the Gospel of Efficiency: The Progressive Conservation Movement, 1890-1920* (Cambridge, MA: Harvard University Press, 1959, reprinted by University of Pittsburgh Press, 1999), 122-27.

[7] See Donald Worster, *Nature's Economy: A History of Ecological Ideas*, 2nd ed. (Cambridge: Cambridge University Press, 1994), 303.

[8] See William Hoffman's chapter on Raymond Lindeman in this volume.

[9] Ibid.

[10] See Worster, 304-15.

[11] For example, horses, although with MMRs two times higher than other grazers, do not match rates achieved by smaller mammals such as field mice. These and other insights come from Paige Painter, "Allometric scaling of the maximum metabolic rate of mammals: oxygen transport from the lungs to the heart is a limiting step," *Theoretical Biology Med Model*, 2005; 2: 31. Published online 1 August 2005, and posted at Metabolism http://www.ncbi.nlm.nih.gov/pmc/articles/PMC1236962/ accessed March 27, 2015.

[12] See Worster, 405-14.

[13] Ian D. Rotherham, *Eco-history: An Introduction to Biodiversity and Conservation* (Cambridge: White Horse Press, 2014), 59-61, 115-116.

[14] See Della Hooke, "Re-wilding the landscape: Some observations on landscape," in *Trees, Forested Landscapes, and Grazing Animals: A European Perspective on Woodlands and Grazed Treescapes*, Ian D. Rotherham, ed. (London: Routledge, 2013), 35.

[15] See Paul Raebaum, "Using Chaos Theory to Revitalize Fisheries," *Scientific American*, 19 January 2009 posted at http://www.scientificamerican.com/article/using-chaos-theory-to-revitalize-fisheries/ accessed 17 April 2015.

[16] "Awash in Water and Politics," *Star Tribune* (Minneapolis) 29 June 2014, C10.

[17] These groups heeded the early call of George Perkins Marsh.

[18] http://www.mnhs.org/places/nationalregister/stateparks/Camden.php accessed 21 April 2015.

[19] Morgan Spurlock's "Inside Man" broadcast on CNN in March 2015.

[20] "Raymond Klein, age 101 of Marshall," 9 October 2013, *Marshall Independent*, posted at marshallindependent.com and accessed 9 October

2013; and "A Honey of a Business," *The Independent* (Marshall, Minn.) 14-15 January 2012, 1C, 6C.

[21] Morgan Spurlock's "Inside Man" broadcast on CNN in March 2015.

[22] Interview with Steven Klein 4 April 2007 (notes in the author's possession); and "A Honey of a Business," *The Independent* (Marshall, Minn.) 14-15 January 2012, 1C, 6C.

[23] Interview with Klein.

[24] V.V. Rodionov and I.A. Shabarshov, *IAkshcho vy maiete bzhil* (Kyïv: Urozhai, 1984), 184.

[25] For a posting of the painting, see the page http://www.johngreenartgallery.com/wildlife-art-prints.html accessed 15 April 2015.

[26] http://www.redlinart.com/pheasants_trcountry/ accessed 15 April 2015.

[27] "For pheasant hunters, let the good times roll," *StarTribune* (Minneapolis) 10 September 2006, C22. For a deeper, earlier local study of the bird, see Janet Timmerman, "Birds," in *Draining the Great Oasis: An Environmental History of Murray County, Minnesota*, Anthony J. Amato et al., eds. (Marshall, Minn: Crossings Press, 2001), 92-96. On the economic impact of the pheasant in South Dakota, see Robert E. Wright, *Little Business on the Prairie: Entrepreneurship, Prosperity, and Challenge in South Dakota* (Sioux Falls, SD: Center for Western Studies, 2015), 171-81.

[28] The http://minnesota.cbslocal.com/2014/12/13/gov-dayton-talks-hunting-at-pheasant-summit/ accessed March 30, 2015.

[29] See Leopold's comments in Evadene Burris Swanson, *The Use and Conservation of Minnesota Wildlife, 1850-1900*, Foreword by Aldo Leopold (St. Paul, MN: Department of Natural Resources, 2007).

[30] "Field Report" *Field and Stream*, October 2014, 14.

[31] "Dennis Anderson: Staying optimistic about the future of pheasants" posted at http://www.startribune.com/sports/outdoors/226600061.html?page=1&c=y accessed 20 April 2015.

[32] "The Great American Bird," *Field & Stream*, October 2014, 66.

[33] Swanson, 95.

[34] One should note all of the different causes and scenarios proposed at "Dennis Anderson: Staying optimistic about the future of pheasants" posted at http://www.startribune.com/sports/outdoors/226600061.html?page=1&c=y accessed 20 April 2015.

[35] Leopold, *A Sand County Almanac*, 177.

[36] "Field Report," *Field & Stream*, October 2014, 15.

[37] For a note on selfishness in hunting, see Stephen Fox, *The American Conservation Movement: John Muir and his Legacy* (Madison: University of Wisconsin Press, 185), 335-36.

[38] "The 2014 Heroes of Conservation," *Field and Stream*, October 2014, 57.

[39] Brian DeVore, "Grazing as a Public Good: When it comes to Grass, Farmers & Conservationists are sharing a Mutual Goal," *The Land Stewardship Letter* (Minneapolis) 32:1 (2014) 24–25.

[40] Stephen J. G. Hall, "Integrated conservation of a park and its domestic cattle herd," in *Trees, Forested Landscapes, and Grazing Animals: A European*

Perspective on Woodlands and Grazed Treescapes, Ian D. Rotherham, ed. (London: Routledge, 2013), 249-51.

[41] DeVore.

[42] For a fictionalization of the full case, see Janet Timmerman and Anthony J. Amato, "A Shallow Lake and Deep Conflicts," in *Environmental Policy: Cases in Managerial Role-Playing*, Robert Watson et al., eds. (Malabar, Florida: Krieger Press, 2004), 57-61.

[43] http://files.dnr.state.mn.us/aboutdnr/laws_treaties/leg_summaries/legis2001.pdf accessed 29 March 2105.

[44] http://www.dnr.state.mn.us/lakefind/showreport_printable.html?downum=51008200&printable=true accessed 29 March 2105.

[45] See http://www.ducks.org/minnesota/minnesota-projects/lake-maria-is-minnesota-duck-rally-success-story, accessed 29 March 2015.

[46] Milton W. Weller, *Freshwater Marshes: Ecology and Wildlife Management* (Minneapolis, University of Minnesota Press, 1994), 71.

[47] Weller, 106.

[48] Weller, 36, 49-51.

[49] For a case, see "Questions raised about wetland development" in *The Independent* (Marshall, Minn.) 2 February 2015 1A, 9A.

[50] "The State We're In." *Star Tribune* (Minneapolis), 16 December 2001, A37-A39.

[51] Marc Reisner, *Cadillac Desert* (New York: Viking, 1983), 12.

[52] http://denr.sd.gov/des/wr/history.aspx accessed 15 April 2015.

[53] "Breaking Down Lewis & Clark Funding" posted at http://listen.sdpb.org/post/breaking-down-lewis-clark-funding accessed 19 April 2015; "Is the Lewis and Clark project a pipeline to nowhere?" posted at http://www.mprnews.org/story/2013/12/02/regional/lewis-clark-water-pipeline accessed 19 April 2015; and http://files.dnr.state.mn.us/aboutdnr/laws_treaties/leg_summaries/legis2001.pdf accessed 29 March 2105.

[54] On one conflict, see "Corps reached one-year compromise on Missouri River," *Argus Leader* (Sioux Falls), 10 April 2003, 1A.

[55] See "Beneath the Surface" at http://minnesota.publicradio.org/projects/2014/01/ground-level-beneath-the-surface/ accessed 19 April 2015.

Chapter 10

Why Would Hunters Quit?

An Examination of Potential Hunting Desertion in Big Sky Country

Stephen L. Eliason

In the United States, wildlife is a collective resource that is held in a public trust, and the state has the responsibility of managing it for the benefit of all citizens.

Hunting has been a popular recreational activity in the United States for much of the nation's history, especially in rural areas.[1] In recent decades, however, hunter numbers have declined to the point that scholars have focused their attention on hunting recruitment and retention,[2] hunting desertion,[3] and the impact a loss of hunters could have on state agencies that manage wildlife.[4] In response to the decline of hunters, special mentoring programs have been implemented in many states in hopes of recruiting and retaining hunters.[5]

It is believed that hunter numbers are declining for a variety of reasons, including social change associated with an increasingly urban society as well as new forms of recreational and leisure pursuits and electronic entertainment.[6] In addition, lack of access to hunting land has been identified as a factor that contributes to declining hunting participation.[7] Research also suggests that individuals could potentially quit hunting due to the spread of chronic wasting disease in wildlife.[8]

Along with the loss of a long-standing cultural tradition, a reduction of hunters will lead to reduced support for wildlife programs and conservation.[9] In their chapter on trends in access and wildlife privatization in *Wildlife and Society: The Science of Human Dimensions*, Brown and Messmer state the following: "Declining hunting participation affects the budgets of many state fish and wildlife agencies because most of their income comes from the sale of hunting and fishing licenses and because federal-aid dollars are tied to participant numbers and related equipment expenditures."[10] Because of the impact declining hunter numbers can have for wildlife funding, it is important for wildlife managers to be aware of factors that could affect an individual's decision to terminate participation in hunting.[11] Everett and Gore state in their study of Michigan youth firearm deer hunters that "As current hunters cease hunting over time owing to various factors (e.g., interest, lack of time, age), the potential for young hunters to be recruited declines."[12] In their article about pro-environmental behavior, published in the *Journal of Wildlife Management,* Cooper et al. make the following observation:

> Our data confirm that, relative to non-recreationists and birdwatchers in rural areas, hunters tend to advocate more often for their preferred activity and articulate the beneficial outcomes it provides to local ecosystems and communities. . . . Our data highlight the conservation contributions of hunters and birdwatchers, showing that both groups are more likely to engage in conservation behaviors than individuals who do not participate in wildlife recreation.[13]

The potential loss of hunters represents an important issue in Montana, a western state that is part of the Northern Plains where hunting is a popular recreational activity.[14] Describing the potential widespread ramifications that might result from a loss of hunters in the state, Gude et al. state, "Declining hunter participation in Montana could have cultural, political, economic, and wildlife management and conservation implications."[15] The purpose of this chapter is to identify factors that would influence active hunters to terminate participation in the sport.

Methods

In 2005 a survey that contained mostly open-ended questions was sent to a random sample of 1,000 resident hunters who purchased a 2004 elk license in Montana. The sample was obtained from Montana Fish, Wildlife and Parks, which is the state agency responsible for managing wildlife and licensing hunters. A total of 255 surveys were returned for a response rate of twenty-six percent.

As noted in Chapter 8, Neuman in his *Social Research Methods* argues for the utility of open-ended questions: "To learn how a respondent thinks and discover what is important to him or her . . . open questions are best. . . . Open-ended questions are especially valuable in early or exploratory stages of research."[16] Individuals in the study were asked the following question: "If you were to quit hunting, what would be the reason(s)?" Hunters were allowed to respond in their own words.

For data analysis, all of the responses provided by hunters were examined and categories were established based on themes that emerged from the analysis. The frequency of responses for each category was noted. Some respondents listed more than one reason, and all of these were included in the analysis. Summarization and interpretation of their responses are provided by the author. Sample responses that illustrate the reasons hunters would quit are provided.

Results

Table 1 reveals the most frequent reasons given by hunters as to why they would cease participation in the activity. The results suggest that Montana hunters are committed to hunting and take it seriously, as three of the top four reasons given for potentially quitting hunting were related to physical impairment and decline of the body. These included health reasons (first, n=87), old age (third, n=31), and death (fourth, n=21). For many individuals in the study, only life-changing events related to health and aging that restricted their mobility would cause them to quit hunting:

> *The only reason I could think of would be health reasons and I was unable to continue.

> *Illness or injury (it would have to immobilize me).

The second most frequent reason given by hunters for potentially quitting was a lack of access to private hunting land (n=43). Much of the good hunting land in Montana where wildlife is found is privately owned, and hunters reported that access to this land has dwindled in recent years:

> *Too hard to find a place to hunt. . . . The ranchers that want the animals harvested off their land because the animals are eating

> their hay should be more helpful to the hunters.
>
> *No places to go because outfitters buy up all private property.
>
> *. . . our ability to hunt is continually limited by the rich [individuals] buying up and locking up Montana.

The fifth and sixth most common reasons listed were that hunting was too expensive (n=20) and there were too many people/crowding (n=12), respectively. Seventh was lack of time (n=10) and eighth was lack of game (n=9). In ninth place, some hunters indicated they would only quit hunting if the practice was made illegal (n=7), while in tenth place other hunters would quit if there was a lack of access to public lands (n=6). Two factors tied for eleventh place on the list of why hunters would quit were: too many hunting restrictions (n=4) and don't need the meat (n=4). In addition to the reasons listed in Table 1, thirty-seven other reasons were provided by hunters less frequently (by three or fewer hunters; many were listed only once). These included things such as complicated regulations, unethical hunters, and a change in interests.

Conclusion

Declining health and aging are a normal and unavoidable part of the human life cycle. A reduction in capacity to endure exertion and strenuous activity coupled with less energy and stamina make it difficult for individuals to engage in rigorous hunting activities such as hiking in steep terrain and packing-out harvested wildlife.

While there are abundant wildlife resources in Montana, there is a lack of public access to private property where much of the wildlife is found. To help remedy this situation, Montana Fish, Wildlife and Parks operates the Block Management program whereby the state pays private landowners who allow free public hunting on their land.[17] However, only a small portion of the state's landowners participate in the program. The commercialization of wildlife also contributes to hunter access problems in the state, as some landowners lease their property to outfitters for the exclusive use of their paying clients.[18]

In the United States, wildlife is a collective resource that is held in a public trust, and the state has the responsibility of managing it for the benefit of all citizens.[19] In *Nature's Trust: Environmental Law for a New Ecological Age*, Wood offers the following description of the public trust doctrine:

> the doctrine rests on a civic and judicial understanding that some natural resources remain so vital to public welfare and human survival that they should not fall exclusively to private property ownership and control. Under the public trust doctrine, natural resources such as waters, wildlife, and presumably air, remain common property belonging to the people as a whole. Such assets take the form of a perpetual trust for future generations. The public's lasting ownership interest in this trust vests in both present and future generations as legal beneficiaries.[20]

The seven principles that guide wildlife management in the United States comprise what is referred to as the North American Model of Wildlife Management.[21] Much of the interest in hunting has been attributed to the democratic manner in which wildlife is allocated and managed in the U.S.[22] According to Condy, "in the capitalist United States, wildlife conservation is socialist (owned and managed by government for the people)."[23]

J. Posewitz notes in *Rifle in Hand: How Wild America Was Saved* that many current trends pose challenges to this North American Model of Wildlife Management:

> We have been drifting into a system of wildlife management that advantages commerce, tolerates exclusion, and creates a class system within the North American hunting community. . . . The threat to our future as hunters is compounded when public trustees yield to the concentrated influence of the minorities seeking privileged access to public resources.[24]

As fewer opportunities are available on private land, hunters are more likely to encounter crowded hunting conditions on public land, especially that which is easily accessible. It is possible that hunters who are unable to get access to private land might experience frustration and discouragement due to hunter crowding and lack of game on public land, thus resulting in their decision to quit. Findings from the research presented in this chapter also suggest that other factors such as increased hunting expenses and crowded hunting conditions in the field could lead individuals to quit hunting, as could lack of time and lack of game.

The results of the research presented in this chapter stress the importance of enhancing hunting opportunities for hunters on private land. In the Block Management tradition, this could involve providing incentives to landowners who allow public hunting on their property. In their contribution to *The Problem of Pleasure: Leisure, Tourism and Crime,* Barclay and Donnermeyer state:

> outdoor leisure opportunities are very much dependent on the amount of available space. . . . As countries increasingly urbanize and greater pressure is placed upon access to natural environments there will be a need to seek ways to nurture relationships between rural landholders and recreationists.[25]

Increased hunting opportunities could also be accomplished by modifying trespass laws on private land in an effort to make access to these lands more "hunter friendly." According to Sigmon in his analysis of hunting and posting on private land, published in the *Duke Law Journal,* Montana is one of "twenty-one states . . . [with] statutes requiring hunters to obtain landowner permission before hunting on private land."[26] Laws could be changed so that hunters could legally enter any private land that is not posted.

The findings presented in this chapter enhance our understanding of conservation and the place of hunting in contemporary society. The most common reasons why hunters would quit hunting include health and physical limitations, lack of access to private land, old age, death, high expenses associated with hunting, too many people/crowding, lack of time, and lack of game. Reversing some of the trends behind the activity's desertion requires access and space.

Frequency of Top Reasons Given by Hunters for Potentially Quitting Hunting

Reason	Frequency
Health	87
Lack of Access to Private Land	43
Old Age	31
Death	21
Too Expensive	20
Too Many People/Crowding	12
Lack of Time	10
Lack of Game	9
Hunting Made Illegal	7
Lack of Access to Public Land	6
Too Many Hunting Restrictions	4
Don't Need the Meat	4

Notes

[1] Arnett and Southwick (2015); Boglioli (2009); Dizard (2003); Eliason (2008); Stedman and Heberlein (2001).

[2] Larson, Stedman, Decker, Siemer, and Baumer (2014); Ryan and Shaw (2011).

[3] Andersen, Vittersø, Kaltenborn, and Bjerke, T. (2010); Applegate (1989); Dietz, Higgins, and Mendelsohn (1996).

[4] Miller and Vaske (2003).

[5] Ryan and Shaw (2011).

[6] Applegate (1989); Heberlein (1991); Robison and Ridenour (2012); Ryan and Shaw (2011).

[7] Miller and Vaske (2003).

[8] Needham, Vaske, Donnelly, and Manfredo (2007).

[9] Ryan and Shaw (2011); Brown and Messmer (2009); Cooper, Larson, Dayer, Stedman, and Decker (2015); Everett and Gore (2015); Miller and Vaske (2003); Montgomery and Blalock (2010); Robison and Ridenour (2012); Winkler and Warnke (2013).

[10] Brown and Messmer (2009), 277.

[11] Applegate (1989).

[12] Everett and Gore (2015), 101.

[13] Cooper et al. (2015), 455.

[14] Eliason (2008); Eliason (2014); Gude, Cunningham, Herbert, and Baumeister (2012); Schorr, Lukacs, and Gude (2014).

[15] Gude et al. (2012), 472.

[16] Neuman (2011), 324-25.

[17] Robbins and Luginbuhl (2005).

[18] Ibid.

[19] Blumm and Paulsen (2013); Blumm and Wood (2013); Decker et al. (2014); Decker et al. (2015); Freyfogle and Goble (2009); Jacobson, Organ, Decker, Batcheller, and Carpenter (2010); Posewitz (1999); Posewitz (2004); Smith (2011); Wood (2014).

[20] Wood (2014), 14.

[21] Heffelfinger, Geist, and Wishart (2013); Mahoney and Jackson (2013); Mahoney, Vahldiek, and Soulliere (2015); Organ, Mahoney, and Geist (2010).

[22] Posewitz (1999); Posewitz (2004).

[23] Condy (2008), 53.

[24] J. Posewitz (1999), 108.

[25] Barclay and Donnermeyer (2012), 90.

[26] Sigmon (2004), 560.

References

Andersen, O., Vittersø, J., Kaltenborn, B. P., and Bjerke, T. (2010). "Hunting Desertion in Norway: Barriers and Attitudes toward Retention Measures." *Human Dimensions of Wildlife* 15(6): 450-66.

Applegate, J. E. (1989). "Patterns of Early Desertion among New Jersey Hunters." *Wildlife Society Bulletin* 17(4): 476-81.

Arnett, E. B., and Southwick, R. (2015). "Economic and Social Benefits of Hunting in North America." *International Journal of Environmental Studies* 72(5): 734-45.

Barclay, E., and Donnermeyer, J. F. (2012). "The Problem of Access: Outdoor Leisure Activities and Access to Private Rural Land." In C. Jones, E. Barclay, and R. Mawby (eds.), *The Problem of Pleasure: Leisure, Tourism and Crime* (77-90). Abingdon and New York: Routledge.

Blumm, M. C., and Paulsen, A. (2013). "The Public Trust in Wildlife." *Utah Law Review* 2013(6): 1437-1504.

Blumm, M. C., and Wood, M. C. (2013). *The Public Trust Doctrine in Environmental and Natural Resources Law*. Durham, NC: Carolina Academic Press.

Boglioli, M. (2009). *A Matter of Life and Death: Hunting in Contemporary Vermont*. Amherst: University of Massachusetts Press.

Brown, T. L., and Messmer, T. A. (2009). "Trends in Access and Wildlife Privatization." M. J. Manfredo, J. J. Vaske, P. J. Brown, D. J. Decker, and E. A. Duke (eds.), *Wildlife and Society: The Science of Human Dimensions* (275-88). Washington, DC: Island Press.

Condy, P. R. (2008). "Conservation—Public or Private, Socialism or Capitalism?" *The Wildlife Professional* 2(2): 52-53.

Cooper, C., Larson, L., Dayer, A., Stedman, R., and Decker, D. (2015). "Are Wildlife Recreationists Conservationists? Linking Hunting, Birdwatching, and Pro-environmental Behavior." *Journal of Wildlife Management* 79(3): 446-57.

Decker, D. J., Forstchen, A. B., Organ, J. F., Smith, C. A., Riley, S. J., Jacobson, C. A., Batcheller, G. R., and Siemer, W. F. (2014). "Impacts Management: An Approach to Fulfilling Public Trust Responsibilities of Wildlife Agencies." *Wildlife Society Bulletin* 38 (1): 2-8.

Decker, D. J., Forstchen, A. B., Pomeranz, E. F., Smith, C. A., Riley, S. J., Jacobson, C. A., Organ, J. F., and Batcheller, G. R. (2015). "Stakeholder Engagement in Wildlife Management: Does the Public Trust Doctrine Imply Limits?" *Journal of Wildlife Management* 79(2): 174-79.

Dietz, N. J., Higgins, K. F., and Mendelsohn, R. D. (1996). "Factors Associated with Declining Proportion of Citizens Hunting in South Dakota." *The Prairie Naturalist* 27(4): 223-36.

Dizard, J. E. (2003). *Mortal Stakes: Hunters and Hunting in Contemporary America*. Amherst, MA: University of Massachusetts Press.

Eliason, S. L. (2008). "A Statewide Examination of Hunting and Trophy Nonhuman Animals: Perspectives of Montana Hunters." *Society and Animals* 16(3): 256-78.

Eliason, S. L. (2014). "Hunting Issues in Contemporary Society: Perspectives of Resident Hunters in Montana (USA)." *Wildlife Biology in Practice* 10(2): 132-48.

Everett, M. W., and Gore, M. L. (2015). "Measuring Flow in Michigan Youth Firearm Deer Hunters: Implications for Measurement and Practice." *Loisir et Société / Society and Leisure* 38(1): 100-09.

Freyfogle, E. T., and Goble, D. D. (2009). *Wildlife Law: A Primer*. Washington, DC: Island Press.

Gude, J. A., Cunningham, J. A., Herbert, J. T., and Baumeister, T. (2012). "Deer and Elk Hunter Recruitment, Retention, and Participation Trends in Montana." *Journal of Wildlife Management* 76(3): 471-79.

Heberlein, T. A. (1991). "Changing Attitudes and Funding for Wildlife—Preserving the Sport Hunter." *Wildlife Society Bulletin* 19(4): 528-34.

Heffelfinger, J. R., Geist, V., and Wishart, W. (2013). "The Role of Hunting in North American Wildlife Conservation." *International Journal of Environmental Studies*, 70 (3), 399-413.

Jacobson, C. A., Organ, J. F., Decker, D. J., Batcheller, G. R., and Carpenter, L. (2010). "A Conservation Institution for the 21st Century: Implications for State Wildlife Agencies." *Journal of Wildlife Management*, 74(2): 203-09.

Larson, L. R., Stedman, R. C., Decker, D. J., Siemer, W. F., and Baumer, M. S. (2014). "Exploring the Social Habitat for Hunting: Toward a Comprehensive Framework for Understanding Hunter Recruitment and Retention." *Human Dimensions of Wildlife* 19 (2): 105-22.

Mahoney, S. P., and Jackson, J. J., III. (2013). "Enshrining Hunting as a Foundation for Conservation–the North American Model." *International Journal of Environmental Studies* 70(3): 448-59.

Mahoney, S. P., Vahldiek, P., and Soulliere, C. A. (2015). "Private Land: Conservation's New Frontier in America." *International Journal of Environmental Studies* 72(5): 869-78.

Miller, C. A., and Vaske, J. J. (2003). "Individual and Situational Influences on Declining Hunter Effort in Illinois." *Human Dimensions of Wildlife* 8(4): 263-76.

Montgomery, R., and Blalock, M. G. (2010). "The Impact of Access, Cost, Demographics, and Individual Constraints, on Hunting Frequency and Future Participation." *Academy of Marketing Studies Journal* 14(2): 115-31.

Needham, M. D., Vaske, J. J., Donnelly, M. P., and Manfredo, M. J. (2007). "Hunting Specialization and Its Relationship to Participation in Response to Chronic Wasting Disease." *Journal of Leisure Research* 39(3): 413-37.

Neuman, W. L. (2011). *Social Research Methods: Qualitative and Quantitative Approaches*. Boston: Allyn and Bacon.

Organ, J. F., Mahoney, S. P., and Geist, V. (2010). "Born in the Hands of Hunters: The North American Model of Wildlife Conservation." *The Wildlife Professional* 4(3): 22-27.

Posewitz, J. (1999). *Inherit the Hunt: A Journey into the Heart of American Hunting*. Helena MT: Falcon.

Posewitz, J. (2004). *Rifle in Hand: How Wild America was Saved*. Helena, MT: Riverbend.

Robbins, P., and Luginbuhl, A. (2005). "The Last Enclosure: Resisting Privatization of Wildlife in the Western United States." *Capitalism, Nature, Socialism* 16(1): 45-61.

Robison, K. K., and Ridenour, D. (2012). "Wither the Love of Hunting? Explaining the Decline of a Major Form of Rural Recreation as a Consequence of the Rise of Virtual Entertainment and Urbanism." *Human Dimensions of Wildlife* 17(6): 418-36.

Ryan, E. L., and Shaw, B. (2011). "Improving Hunter Recruitment and Retention." *Human Dimensions of Wildlife* 16(5): 311-17.

Schorr, R. A., Lukacs, P. M., and Gude, J. A. (2014). "The Montana Deer and Elk Hunting Population: The Importance of Cohort Group, License Price, and Population Demographics on Hunter Retention, Recruitment, and Population Change." *Journal of Wildlife Management* 78(5): 944-52.

Sigmon, M. R. (2004). "Hunting and Posting on Private Land in America." *Duke Law Journal* 54(2): 549-85.

Smith, C. A. (2011). "The Role of State Wildlife Professionals under the Public Trust Doctrine." *Journal of Wildlife Management* 75(7): 1539-43.

Stedman, R. C., and Heberlein, T. A. (2001). "Hunting and Rural Socialization: Contingent Effects of the Rural Setting on Hunting Participation." *Rural Sociology* 66(4): 599-617.

Winkler, R., and Warnke, K. (2013). "The Future of Hunting: An Age-Period-Cohort Analysis of Deer Hunter Decline." *Population and Environment* 34(4): 460-80.

Wood, M. C. (2014). *Nature's Trust: Environmental Law for a New Ecological Age*. New York: Cambridge University Press.

Chapter 11

Conservation on the Northern Plains: *From Farm Field to Biosphere*

Joseph A. Amato

"Man is everywhere a disturbing agent. The harmonies of nature are turned to discord." —George Perkins Marsh, Man and Nature (1864)

Conservation on the Northern Plains, from Wisconsin and the Mississippi into Wyoming and the foothills of the Rockies, takes as many forms as the land is vast and multifold.[1] With its different grasses, soil types and recent geology, variable climate, and immensely diverse surface and ground water resources, the Plains define the language and practice of their conservation. Sharing some common weather and constant wind, and a roughly similar vegetation and topography, this region of varied grasslands and wetlands crosses national borders into Canada and extends from the prairies of western Ontario to the prairie provinces of Manitoba, Saskatchewan, and Alberta.[2] As Kansas historian of the grasslands James Malin emphasized, the Northern Plains and the larger Great Plains have been shaped by diverse patterns of settlement and changing use, too. The face of the Plains belongs not just to the differences of geology and biology but to human activities and material culture, which started with Native burnings of the prairie, involved the coming of European and American civilization, and continued with settlers' efforts to transpose Midwestern agriculture onto the grasslands. As much as it belongs to nature, Plains conservation belongs to different histories, cultures, and politics.[3]

The Northern Plains distinguish themselves as one travels the thousand miles from the Upper Mississippi River Valley to the Rockies. The eastern side of the Plains has older and bigger settlements, with more towns and cities, and developed industry and transportation networks, and is continuous with the tallgrass prairie of the Upper Midwest. The western Northern Plains, conversely, have greater empty spaces, fewer rivers and less surface water, smaller and sparse settlements, and divergent use of drainage and irrigation. With an increasingly dry climate in the west and different soils and shorter and sparser grasses, settlers, correspondingly, allocated a far great percentage of the land to grazing rather than farming and relied sooner and more heavily on irrigation.

Conservation itself has had a different history and mixed meanings on the Northern Plains. Plains conservation's first definition arose out of a mix of national ideas and sensibilities and a varied discourse over separate issues and places. The region was never understood as pristine land like the forests of the West. It was not thought at the time of the first national formulations of conservations (at the end of the nineteenth and early twentieth century) to have much to conserve or preserve aside from the buffalo and few other select species. Accordingly, it fell outside of the pale of the vast federal programs of Theodore Roosevelt's Presidency (1901-1909), whose principal goals were to conserve the great forests of the West for long-term use and to preserve dramatic wilderness and select natural sites as iconic parts of the nation's natural patrimony.

The great sea of grass beyond the Mississippi was conceded unreservedly to the settlers, states, and corporate recipients of a hundred years of federal land grants. Conservation, insofar as it was to come into existence at all, fell to the discretion of farmers, railroads, timbering and mining companies, and to the initiatives of states and municipalities. Early efforts by the latter arose piece-meal and non-systematically, as local governments pursued preserving places, ensuring recreation, and materializing popular sentiment.

In Minnesota, for instance, conservation efforts were associated with preserving select, attractive natural sites, appropriate grounds for memorializing the Civil War and the Dakota War of 1862, and places affording public recreation for new urban centers. With Midwesterners in general following New Englanders, who copied the idealized English model, the municipality of St. Paul established Hidden Falls Park along the banks of the Mississippi in 1887. It was one of the four original parks selected and designed by influential landscape architect Horace Cleveland, whose philosophy was to preserve landscape features while making the site accessible to the public. Notably, Minnesota's first attempt to create a state park in 1885 to preserve Minnehaha Falls was a flop. Entangled in legal appeals and facing a shortage of cash upon resolution, it relied in 1889 on Minneapolis money for purchase of the 173-acre Minnehaha State Park, which was absorbed as a city park. In 1891, the state, however, did succeed in establishing a state park around Lake Itasca to protect the source of the Mississippi and provide recreation, beating out Michigan's 1895 Mackinaw Island State Park on the list of first state parks, headed by the 1885 Niagara Falls Reservation.[4]

Only the drought and Dust Bowl of the 1930s elicited the federal government's interest in conservation on the stricken prairie. Its aim was essentially limited to preservation of the soils and waters through improved agricultural practices on the prairie. The New Deal's land and farm policies did not aim to create vast scenic parks to conserve national inheritance and afford recreation, nor did they seek to preserve unique ecological zones, a concept which arose in post-World War II America with the emergence of environmental science and an awareness of human impact on ecological zones.

This ecological view underlined the importance of the biomes of grasslands and wetlands for the sake of life itself. It was not based on calculating food production for humanity but on a microscopic understanding of what flourishing life required. This view of conservation was antithetical to conservation on the Northern Plains as originally defined by local and state agencies, wildlife groups, conservancies, recreationalists, and agriculturalists.

Definitions

The usage of the word conservation is great and varied. As one would expect from a term implying "saving nature," its meanings are multiple, overlapping, and entwined. Conservation's practices, goals, and ideals are never truly one, or synthetic, cumulative, or complete. They belong to its changing history and to all who for divergent interests and reasons practice, or claim to practice, conservation. The word's definitions can be banal or sublime, nostalgic, or scientific. They can be as confused and contradictory as the parties and institutions that preach and implement conservation. In addition to husbanding resources, designing parks, and caring for historic and natural sites, conservation aims to prevent extinctions and save nature itself. Nature for these purposes can be as vast as a vista in a national park or as microscopic as laboratory research.

Free of reference to walked, hunted, and tilled land, and to the plant and animal life of known waters and fields, conservation puzzles us with abstract concepts. Once elevated to a matter of the fate of regions and entire nations, conservation's meanings lead to higher orders of thought. The very word "nature," which is material yet spiritual, elevates us onto a territory charged with myth and values, yet bristling with scientific theories and claims about life and man's relation to it—what some have called the relation of "the biosphere and the noosphere."[5]

Conservation, in a word, is many things. Its definition still belongs to the stay-at-home Martha of earthly care. It is about the advocacy of wildlife groups, the state and local groups that maintain sites for civic history and public recreation, and the growing private trusts and conservancy groups that set aside tracts of land in perpetuity for a variety of reasons. At the same time, conservation forever toggles between agencies' ideals, the practices of agencies, and new microbiological conceptions of the interdependence of life. Conservation, in effect, belongs to past and present. It continues to express President Roosevelt's earliest notions of preserving forests and iconic landscapes, while being continually thought anew by research.

Conservation on the Northern Plains has taken on the concepts of environmentalism, ecology, and sustainability. Under the influence of the developing natural and applied sciences, conservation has schooled itself in earth and life sciences, and chemistry. With microscopic and macroscopic optics, it examines global matters of life and individual sites. With an expanding "biological imagination," to borrow the title of William Hoffman's recent work, conservation simultaneously takes evidence and hears testimony from hands-on-practice and the most recent scientific, ethical, and political considerations about man's place in the biosphere and his tenuous hold on the earth.[6]

First Federal Definition of Conservation and Wilderness

Because conservation is a diverse mixture of ideas and practices, independent thinkers and governmental agencies, ideologies, and events, its contradictions and ambiguities are best understood as a matter of historical development. Conservation's definition in the United States and on the Northern Plains requires a historical narrative of two centuries.

While romantic artists depicted the lands glimpsed just beyond the Appalachians as immense and majestic, the young Republic moved west for land and opportunity into the rich Ohio Valley and then west and north along the Great Lakes. Democratic hopes and toiling people turned great grasslands into dreams of bountiful gardens.[7]

With the end of the Civil War the nation exploded onto the remaining tallgrass and shortgrass prairie. Within four decades the prairie had been given away to the railroads and settlers.[8] With all of the states of the Northern Plains (Wisconsin in 1848 and Montana in 1889) incorporated into the Union, grasslands conservation was a matter of private agriculture, distant markets, and the laws offered by the Department of Agriculture, established in 1862 and elevated to cabinet status in 1889.[9]

A swelling chorus of national conservationists sang out—and their message was heard across the young literate land. They sang of how quickly the Plains were taken and subordinated to plough and axe, and of how fragile nature was and how great want and greed were. Henry David Thoreau (1817-1862) was an early member of the chorus. His long-cultivated love of a place, Concord, a mere thirty-five miles from Boston, was the point from which he saw the young democracy expand and stand perched to consume the grasslands beyond the Mississippi. Ever pondering where growing populations and reaching railroads would lead, Thoreau suffered the young nation's abrupt assault on nature and the backcountry. He saw the entire American landscape humbled by the power of swelling cities and rampant trains—what historian Leo Marx described as "the machine in the garden."[10]

American scholar, diplomat, and Vermont writer George Perkins Marsh (1801-1882) echoed the plight of the fallen forests of New England. Referencing the destroyed soils and forests of the Mediterranean since Greek and Roman times in his classic *Man and Nature* (1864), Marsh projected a similar fate would soon befall the forests of Michigan and the Great Lakes region. Thinking of the lush lands of Biblical times, Marsh issued his prophetic warning to a nation dazzled and mesmerized by its own expansion—"Deforestation equals desertification."

By the end of nineteenth century the narrative of national advance and settlement was split. Those on behalf of progress advocated a providential narrative. America's manifest destiny of going from ocean to ocean was inevitable and good. An antithetical declensionist narrative, whose warning shot was fired by the threatened extinction of the buffalo, tracked progress's destruction with the spread of the railroad in the aftermath of the Civil War and cited as the evidence the clear-cutting of the forests of Maine, and then Michigan, Wisconsin, and Minnesota. This narrative foresaw the destruction of both nature and human communities in the boundless commercial and technological expansion.[11]

In this debate over progress, two voices offered opposing views of conservation as an act of either preserving or conserving. On one side, Scottish-born and University of Wisconsin-educated naturalist and romantic prophet, John Muir (1838-1914) turned his love of nature into the preservation of the Yosemite Valley and Sequoia National Park, and the founding of the Sierra Club. On the other podium stood Gifford Pinchot (1865-1946). Pinchot insisted that the fate of America turned on the plight of its western forests. They must be conserved and beneficially and productively utilized.[12] An American forester and the first chief of the renamed United States Forest Service (under the Bureau of Forestry within the Department of Agriculture), he sought to conserve federal lands by combating fire, limiting grazing, protecting fish and game, and providing public recreation.[13]

President Theodore Roosevelt (1901-1909) was the godfather of conservation born of national sensibility and legislation. Self-styled big game hunter, adventurist, and soldier, he was of militant faith and took on the world in a struggle that joined national pride and aggrandizement. North Dakota speculative rancher, municipal inspector of public corruption, and critic of greed and monopolies, he joined ranks with moral and aesthetic conservationists. Hunting and ranching the landscape on North Dakota's Little Missouri in the years 1883-1887, Roosevelt knew both the killing power and the frailty of nature—he saw it in frozen and starved cows on his range and the buffalo and other wildlife he shot there and in Africa.

He responded with a program of conservation. It was first based on a preservation of all national resources, first and foremost among them the nation's forests. Conceding an agriculture based on individual rights and also the public's right to enjoy (to hunt, camp, and sightsee), he legislated on behalf of parks, scenic sites, and monuments, and preserved vast tracts of government land from settlement and exploitation. He proposed the Newlands Reclamation Act of 1902, which set the federal government to building dams to help small farmers with irrigation, and put 230 million acres under federal protection.[14]

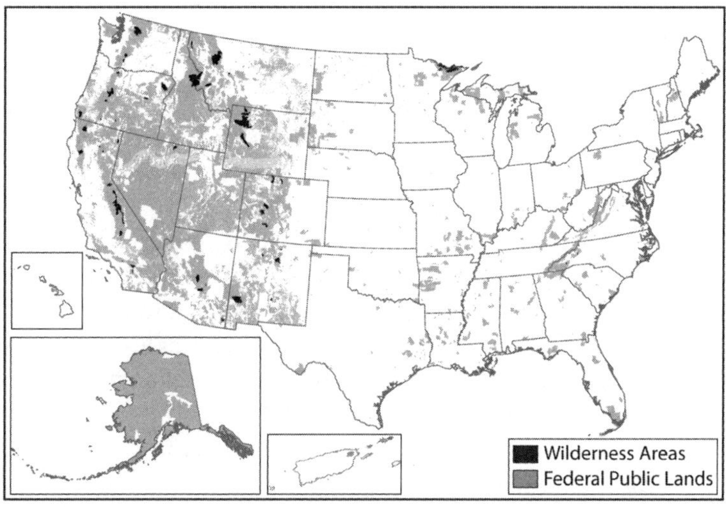

Map I.1 National Wilderness Preservation System, 1964. When Congress established the wilderness system in 1964, it protected 54 wilderness areas encompassing 9.1 million acres, all in the national forests. *Note: maps of Alaska, Hawaii, and Puerto Rico not to same scale.*

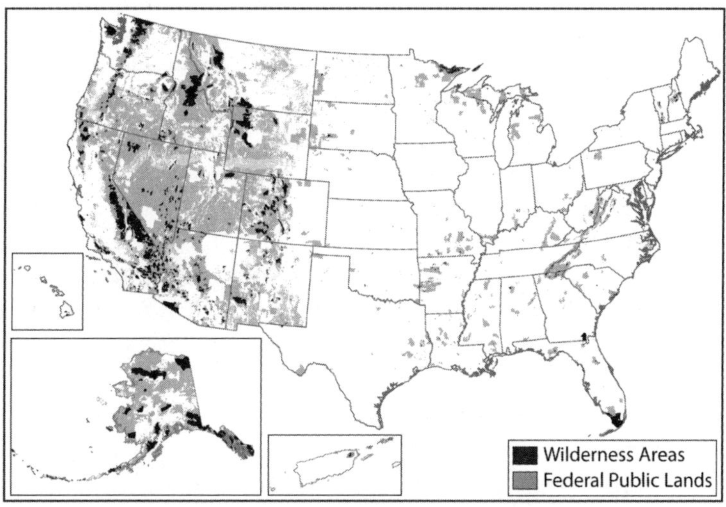

Map I.2 National Wilderness Preservation System, 2009. By 2009, Congress had expanded the wilderness system to 757 areas encompassing 109.5 million acres (57.4 million acres of which are in Alaska). *Note: maps of Alaska, Hawaii, and Puerto Rico not to same scale.*

U.S. Federal Lands shown in gray, and wilderness areas within those lands are shown in black. This map is from James Morton Turner, *The Promise of Wilderness: American Environmental Politics since 1964* (Seattle: University of Washington Press, 2012). *Map provided courtesy University of Washington Press.*

Supplemental legislation under President Roosevelt established the Forest Service, the administrative spine of his conservation programs. He "established five national parks," eighteen national monuments, fifty-one bird reserves, four game preserves, and, in accordance with the prescripts of John Wesley Powell, designated 150 national forests.[15] He focused conservation's optics westward, toward the greater West, including the territory of Alaska, where he found great reserves of land, towering mountains, abundant forests, and expansive deserts and ocean shores that typified the American idea of nature as sublime and majestic. Roosevelt, in effect, initiated and anchored conservation in Western lands and their federal preservation.[16] It was this Western patrimony that, more than a half century later, in 1964, President Lyndon Johnson expanded with the National Wilderness Preservation System bill.[17]

The western concept of conservation did not frame the Midwest and prairie grasslands, which were without significant forests. Their rivers and valleys, lakes, wetlands, and prairie potholes had already been irrevocably conceded to settlers, veterans, states, and companies, and the nation still remained intent on giving away those lands that would extend settlement and expand the potential of the young democracy.[18] By the time New Mexico and Arizona were granted statehood in 1912, little Midwestern and Northern Prairie land belonged to the government's vast reserve.[19]

As much as Roosevelt directed his conservation toward the protection of the virgin landscape of the West, he nevertheless advocated that states should reserve forests, soils, lands, waters, and waterways for their own sake and the strength of the nation. He realized that, on the Plains and Prairies, the state and private claims superseded federal powers. He was left exhorting from the bully pulpit.[20]

With federal conservation legislation oriented to the Far West, conservation on the Northern Plains was in the hands of farmers, health officials, city, county, and state reformers, and agents of early departments of natural resources. Local and state legislators, taking their cue from the federal government and neighboring states, extended and exercised their local and state sovereignty to protecting and developing state-owned forests, waterways, parks, monumental sites, and public health. Conservation on the Northern Plains in the first decades of the twentieth century was inaugurated by state departments of forestry, wildlife, and waters in departments of natural resources in Wisconsin, Minnesota, Iowa, North and South Dakota, and Montana.[21] Each state dedicated itself to conserve forests and regulate mining, while establishing parks, protecting fishing and hunting, and offering public recreation.[22]

Second Federal Definition of Conservation

The federal government entered conservation a second time. This time it came with a direct focus on the grasslands and plains. Under President Franklin D. Roosevelt (1933–1945), conservation policies came as part of the New Deal's reaction to a society caught in the throes of the Great Depression. It came from a government seeking to revive and revitalize the entire nation—to awake the full productivity of industry, resources, and people. On the Prairie and Plains, government affirmed its prowess in the face of the worst drought ever recorded. The "New Dealers" narrated the story of agricultural disaster on the Prairie, not as one born of nature and weather but as one born of poor farming—plowing and planting fence-row to fence-row and overgrazing the grasslands. Federal conservationists traced the source of erosion to bad farming and grazing practices.[23]

There were dissenting conservationists. Professor James Malin, Kansas local and grasslands historian, spent a good portion of his career arguing against the views of the "climax conservationists," those who argued for that "mythical, idealized condition, in which natural forces, biological and physical, were supposed to exist in a state of virtual equilibrium, undisturbed by man." He believed they had exaggerated the tragedy of the 1930s and had wrongly concluded that farming had no place on the High Plains. In particular he lambasted the highly popular documentary film *The Plow that Broke the Plains,* made in 1937 by Pare Lorentz for the Farm Security Administration, as "sensationalized propaganda that had left an indelible slur on the farmer's good name." Malin argued to the contrary that agricultural enterprise—especially large-scale mechanization—was "a constructive step forward." "Nature," in Malin's assessment, according to historian Donald Worster, "needed plowing up, and even a little blowing dirt now and then to remain vigorous and fertile."[24]

The Plains and Prairies, no doubt, belonged to the raisers of wheat, corn, hogs, and beef for distant markets. Already before the First World War, farmers as far west as western Iowa and Minnesota opened and began to ditch and drain their fields and wetlands for greater production of corn, which had displaced wheat.[25] The narrative of full production, accepted by the majority of farmers, did not include blame for their own greed or overproduction. Growers accounted for bad times on the Northern Plains in the 1870s and again in the 1890s, citing bad climate, on the one hand, and price fixing of the railroads and markets on the other hand. They argued that market agriculture meant more food and money, higher land values, roads that limited the spread of fires, and drainage that resulted in less water seeping into the lowlands and fewer malaria-transmitting mosquitoes. Mining and lumbering on the edges and in the basins of the Plains equaled more materials for the advance of civilization. These arguments inoculated most farmers against blame for their farming practices up through the 1930s and beyond.

Despite the consensus of the majority of farmers and ranchers that the source of the land's troubles lay in either uncontrollable weather or the manipulations of outside markets, proponents of reform disagreed. Believing that problems of all sorts yielded to analysis and solution, reformers contended that farmers had recklessly ploughed and grazed their lands into the Dust Bowl. As an initial political response, Congress passed the Soil Conservation and Domestic Allotment Act of 1935 (amended and passed in 1936) for the express purpose of encouraging the use of soil resources in such a manner as to preserve and improve fertility, promote economic use, and diminish the exploitation and unprofitable use of soil resources. The legislation also had provisions to protect sharecroppers and tenant farmers by requiring landlords to share the payments they received from cutting back production, while carrying a directive to save the soil in the High Plains from being blown away by dust storms.[26]

New Dealers strengthened the government's hold on federal lands to save it for the future. Affecting vast federal lands (65 million acres in all) beyond the hundredth meridian, the Taylor Grazing Act of 1934 aimed to stop injury to the public grazing lands by preventing overgrazing and soil deterioration, and by providing for their orderly use, improvement, and development. (This Act was pre-empted by the Federal Land Policy and Management Act of 1976.) They offered incentives for land retirement, forest restoration, and hydropower for farm and industry, while helping expand parks and recreation. All of this encapsulated the New Dealers' dream that one-third of America's people would continue to live with equality and hope on the land.

The Resettlement Administration (RA), the vanguard of the New Deal's reformist plans for the Plains, was the brainchild of the technocrat, close presidential advisor, and Commissioner of Agriculture Professor Rexford Tugwell. The RA had four divisions: Rural Rehabilitation, Rural Resettlement, Land Utilization, and Suburban Resettlement. Never fully funded by a Congress unwilling to go down the path to what would be considered "a socialism of the countryside," Tugwell's goal of moving 650,000 people from 100 million acres of agriculturally exhausted land went largely unrealized. Ultimately, the Resettlement Administration moved only a few thousand people from nine million acres of Great Plains land and built several greenbelt cities.[27]

The New Deal reformist philosophy harnessed conservation to the task of delivering social justice. It did this under the century-long banner of rural development. Its program of conservation as transformation came steeped in older beliefs that vegetation changes the climate.[28] These beliefs were allied to an activist hydrology, which reiterated the charge of the Army Corps of Engineers and argued that harnessing rivers and building canals could produce fertile valleys and facilitate commercial transportation and hydroelectric energy.

In *This Land, This Nation: Conservation, Rural America, and the New Deal* (2007), Sarah T. Phillips contends that at first blush the New Deal's conservation programs were simply a set of rural anecdotes about bad times on the land and an array of particular and local accomplishments achieved by the New Deal's Conservation Corps and their diverse programs.[29] But for Phillips conservation belonged to the New Dealers' progressive and moralizing narrative. And this narrative was more than another compromise with commanding capitalism or a simple exercise in efficient government, as prescribed by Pinchot and praised by historian Samuel P. Hays in his *Conservation and the Gospel of Efficiency.*[30] Instead, by the progressive lights of the New Deal, government "had an obligation and a mandate to expand the economic and political opportunities of rural people by means of conservation policy."[31]

Environmentalism and Ecology

Conservation, ignored during the Second World War, emerged in the post-war era as a divided and fractured discourse. Diverse federal and state agencies still clung to traditional missions. Farmers and ranchers, hunters, fishermen, and naturalists followed their independent ways. Land and parks, even those dedicated to preservation, were increasingly occupied with growing numbers of visitors and vacationers in the post-war prosperity. On the eastern end of the Northern Plains, flood control still absorbed the attention of conservationists, while drought on the western end called for expanded irrigation projects.

Far beyond the orbits of conservation's daily practices and concerns, another more dramatic discussion arose. Its axis was an ever more powerful humanity versus an increasingly vulnerable nature. This sensibility, awakened by a sense of pending apocalypse, warned of danger in every corner of the globe as humanity seemed to threaten nature itself with its weapons, growing Third World populations, and an escalating exploitation of the earth's lands, waters, and animals.

By the 1950s and 1960s conservationists of all quarters—Prairie and Plains conservationists included—could not deafen themselves to this sensibility or divorce their understandings from a full-blown global environmentalism, which was supported by a whole complex of specialized biological and natural sciences. Prophecy and science suggested that life across the globe was under attack, and this attack now included the soils and grasses and wetlands and waters of the Northern Plains.

The scientific and ethical eyes of this global environmentalism were the concepts of ecology. While ecology received its first sight in the nineteenth century, only in the twentieth century did ecology turn its gaze toward the microcosmic and literally the invisible. This was thanks to the new light cast by the developing sciences of chemistry, microbiology, and genetics. Ecology's optics were rooted in the spiritual vision that all life belongs to a community. Surely tempering, if not contradicting, Darwin's harsh principle of the survival of the fittest, ecology depicted all life as belonging to mutual supporting biotic communities. Worthy of an ethic higher than self-interest and utilitarian ends, ecology located its foundational metaphor in its very name. Derived from the Greek word *oikos* (home) and *logoi* (study), ecology advocated that species exist in and must be studied in their habitat, their home. A term first coined by the German thinker Ernst Haeckel in the second half of the nineteenth century, ecology, a type of environmental geography, declared in simplest tautological terms that all life had its life in relation to other life.[32]

In the spirit of the great geographer, explorer, and naturalist Alexander von Humboldt (1769-1859), naturalists, inspired by ecology, defined homes and taxonomies of plants in terms of altitude, climate, and terrain. In the structure first articulated by Carl Linnaeus and then filled in by ardent naturalists such as Darwin and amateur botanists such as Thoreau, a host of European, British, and American scientists began to construct a compendium of plants and animals based on zones of life.[33]

Aldo Leopold (1887-1948), by contrast, made nature and its processes, not man's goals and works, the measure of value. A life-long forester, ecologist, professor, and conservationist, having worked for the revived Audubon Society in the early 1930s, Leopold gained significant attention in the conservation community with his call for a national inventory of threatened species.[34] Leopold's national notoriety arose above all from a single book—his 1949 *A Sand County Almanac*. Based on seasonal portraits of life on his farm near Baraboo, Wisconsin, Leopold offered "a land ethic." Setting himself in opposition to the economic and utilitarian conservationists, he thought in terms of flora and fauna and their balance in nature. He imputed intrinsic importance to all species, finding in their reciprocal balance with soil and water, a biotic community, which is worthy of preservation for life's own sake. In the opening lines of an address, he made the following declaration:

> In pioneering times wild plants and animals were tolerated, ignored, or fought, the attitude depends on the utility of the species. Conservation introduced the idea that the more useful wild species could be managed as crops but the less useful ones were ignored and predaceous ones fought, just as in pioneering days. Conservation lowered the threshold of toleration for wildlife, but utility was still the criterion of policy to species rather than any collective total of wild things. . . . The proof of this [economic conservation, Leopold continued] is the bony framework of any campus or capitol: department of economic entomology, divi-

> sion of economic mammalogy, chief of food habits, and research professor of economic ornithology. These agencies were set up to tell us whether the red-tailed hawk, the grey gopher, the lady beetle, and meadowlark are useful, harmless, or injurious to man. [35]

For Leopold such man-centric reductionism had nothing to say if the criterion of ecology was the biotic community as confirmed by science and affirmed by the value of nature's integrity. Or again to draw on Leopold's 1939 address to a joint session of the American Foresters and the Ecological Society of America, "The Biotic View of the Land": "The emergence of ecology has placed the economic biologist in a peculiar dilemma: with one hand he points out the accumulated findings of his search for utility, or lack of utility, in this or that species: with the other he lifts the veil from a biota so complex, so conditioned by interwoven cooperation and competitions, that no man can say where utility begins or ends. No species can be 'rated' without tongue in the cheek."[36] With the endurance of the food chain and cycle of life as his measure of the good, and with human disruptions judged as violent, Aldo claimed no one, conservationists included, knows what is the correct equation regarding nature's biotic circuitry and human actions.

The Culture of Ecology

If ecology challenged conservationists to weigh the worth of microbiotic units on one hand, global environmentalism, on the other hand, challenged the conservationists to value nature in its vastness. The movement asked people to value the whole earth above the needs of a populace ever greedier for land, water, and resources.[37]

In the 1950s and 1960s, this dualistic view of the small and great intensified and focused on the use of the soil and water. Ecology was born in the 1930s from the convergence of the newer academic disciplines of biochemistry, genetics, microbiology, virology, and even physics.[38] Relying on microbiology, which scrutinized the molecular interactions of all facets and phases of life, soil science itself developed in relation to advancing genetics, synthetic fertilizers, and pesticides, transforming farming of all sorts into a matter of chemistry.

At the same time that the soil, water, and their micro-biotic relations were appreciated as conditions for plant and animal life, global food demands called for profoundly increased human intervention through artificial manipulations and synthetic enhancement. Starting in the 1940s and blooming in the 1960s, the Green Revolution sought increased agriculture production for the Third World.[39] Green Revolution adaptations in genetics and synthetic fertilizers, in addition to a mechanical revolution on the farm and increased drainage systems, also brought increased use of lands on the Northern Plains. Intense farming meant, if not exhaustion, the re-composition of soils and increased use and contamination of water (especially from nitrates and pesticides). Increased monocultural agriculture turned fields into factories and resulted in the dramatic diminishment of habitats, wetlands, scrublands, and all plants and animals commercially deemed "extraneous."

Conservationists on the Northern Plains could not overlook these changes, and they responded with a range of answers. Aside from banning certain chemicals, they developed set-aside programs for vulnerable lands and proposed green zones to protect the land against erosion. State game and fish agencies protected species threatened with extinction, while leasing and regulating others for hunting, fishing, and trapping. At the same time, other agencies protected state wetlands and rivers, while research centers experimented with the restoration of prairie grasslands through controlled burnings.

The Truth and Rhetoric of the Prophet

In the 1960s, conservation expanded beyond select places and resources, and crossed into new territory. Conservation, if not mutated earlier, was put into a different context and transformed. Naturalists, environmentalists, ecologists, and concerned citizens put life itself at the head of the agenda. Faced with the rhetoric of this agenda, politicians could no longer be indifferent to the fate of places and life. Even historians joined natural scientists, anthropologists, and geologists in finding themes for their work in ecology and environmentalism.[40] Starting with human dependency on soils, plants, and animals, historians began to write on the movement of plants or on single crops.[41] A concern for forms of life and effects on larger wholes became the basis for a yet unnamed movement forming from a confluence of ecology and sentiment.

Initially, the rhetoric did not find an audience close to field and pond. Farmers, ranchers, gardeners, birdwatchers, and hunters on the Northern Plains, however dedicated and singular their conservation frame, remained entirely indifferent to the new ecological vigil. Moreover, the new sensibility grounded in abstract concerns did not penetrate the busy minds of the masses. The dire warnings did not threaten the abundance, comfort, and leisure they enjoyed.

Over the course of the 1950s, 1960s, and 1970s, the sense of urgency and the universality of the message intensified. The extended reach of multiplying intercontinental missiles increased the fear of radiation, with its threat of poisoning all land, water, and air, and inciting the monstrous mutations of life. The environmental turned chemical and personal when 7,000 thalidomide-deformed infants were discovered in West Germany in 1957 and Strontium 90 was found at toxic levels in milk in 1961. Sounding a different note, Paul Ehrlich predicted the explosive threat of "the population bomb," to cite the influential title of his 1968 book. Fear of impending cataclysm and doom permeated the country, and the fear of both the known and yet unknown created an audience for environmentalism among common men and women.

If a single thinker from the post-war expressed this growing and invisible threat to nature and life, she was scientist, amateur bird watcher, and government employee Rachel Carson.[42] A marvelous writer and rhetorician, she delivered a stark warning: society was poisoning its land and waters and destroying habitats and eliminating life. Carson initiated her work in *The Sea Around Us* (1951) with the thesis that we spoil the sea we don't understand.[43] Drawing on the work of her teachers and other maritime scholars, Carson showed that the waters of the sea, no matter their sunless depths, are not safe burial grounds. Their currents and surface winds circulate the poisons they receive. The sea, the origin of life since their basins were ripped from the earth and cast into the skies, is not a sealed vault but a medium that moves molecularly in and out of all life.

Eleven years later, Carson's *Silent Spring* (1962) announced the dawn of ecological conscience. In that singular work, selecting varied evidence about industry, chemistry, and their effect on microbiotic systems, she argued that our chemicals are killing off life. She made her case particularly regarding the immense use of the highly touted post-war insecticide, the synthetic chemical DDT (dichlorodiphenyltrichloroethane), which had won its spurs combating malaria and typhus among soldiers and civilians during the war and found beneficial use across the world. Carson's most compelling evidence was broken eggshells. It showed that DDT entered waters, took hold in the tissue of fish, and was passed through the food chain to the raptors, which were at the top of the feeding chain. Concentrated DDT in their systems denigrated the production of calcium required for the production of strong eggshells and incubation of young chicks. Her accusation against DDT questioned the use of all chemicals in plant and insect control. It implied that the chemical that killed "weeds" (non-economic plants) and "pests" (unwanted arthropods, insects, spiders, and the dreaded mosquito) poisoned the entire food chain. Her argument did not entertain consideration of the benefits of DDT and led her harshest critics to refer to "the toxic legacy of Rachel Carson."[44]

Beyond the complex scientific debates that surrounded the subject of DDT as a form of human self-poisoning, Carson had written a terrifyingly dark story.[45] It is a kind of detective story, an environmental *Arsenic and Old Lace*. In the guise of being a nurturing society, America poisons Mother Earth. The very question of who is poisoning what became a part of America's continuing self-examination. The title of Lewis Regenstein's 1982 book succinctly expressed our sins: *America, the Poisoned: How Deadly Chemicals Are Destroying Our Environment, Our Wildlife, Ourselves, and How We Can Survive.*[46]

Carson and other environmentalists fertilized imaginations and invigorated passions. Invisible human work now struck terror into hearts, and the reactions based on this fear spread across the nation.[47] Fueled by the counter-culture of the 1960s and early 1970s, various movements allied themselves with nature against nation and technology. The threat of nuclear war and the spectacular growth of synthetic bio-chemistry generalized the declensionist environmental narrative: mankind was not progressing but was en route to destroying itself.

Radicalized and cause-driven campuses discovered activist ecology on Earth Day, first proposed in 1970. Protestors and advocates of all stripes rallied around the cause, calling for an end to pollution, a return to the land, natural living, organic farming, the founding of food co-ops, and environmentally friendly products. Rich with such metaphors as "natural" and "organic," the movement spawned a love of the small, the beautiful, and communal.

Common environment parlance complained of the wasteful, synthetic, corporate, and artificial. The hideous and devastating oil spill in Santa Barbara Channel in 1969, the largest oil spill to date to have occurred in the waters off California, offered further evidence of antithesis of capitalism and nature. As documented in the 1991 book *Save the Earth,* the movements emblematized by Earth Day marked an irrevocable change in sensibilities.[48]

Conservation Redefines Itself

Conservation, defined by place, agency, scientific theory, and changing sensibilities, absorbed new meanings as it came into contact with emerging forms of ecology and environmentalism. Already altered in practice on farms and parks, in national forests, grasslands, and wilderness areas, conservation now was seen through advancing scientific interpretations, expanded ethical concerns, and the agendas of environmentalists. Conservation's meaning was popularized as it spread from the intelligentsia to mass culture and politics.

The agendas of conservationists of the Northern Plains were many from the outset. They were not unified in use or practice. There was a gap between farmers and government agencies. Conservation had different connotations depending on geographic, social, and scientific axes. Excluded initially from the federal government's concern for forest, mountain, scenic, and historic lands and sites, conservation entered the Plains through the actions of diverse farmers, legislators, hunters, fishermen, and recreationists. Nevertheless, there was from the beginning a consensus that the Plains, unlike the West, had been tamed and settled.

In the post-World War II era, this view was reversed. In the spirit of Leopold and Carson, the Prairies in particular were grasped as rich and distinct biomes, made up of grasslands and wetlands. These intersecting biomes joined with the Great Plains and crossed the border into Canada. Conservation acknowledged the wetlands for their gift of pure and life-giving water, the grasslands for their creation of deep and rich soils and their indispensable role in transforming light and minerals into food, and a life-supporting atmosphere and climate for their release of oxygen and retention of carbon.

Certain environmental appraisals of the conditions of the grasslands reinforced a declensionist view of American history, and they rooted many conservationists in a nostalgic belief in lost natural patrimony. The sensibility, which feasted on "endless realms of bountiful grass" and celebrated marshes and swamps, harshly judged imposing industries and mono-cultural, chemical, and mechanized farming. As noted earlier, this form of conservation regretted the plough and the coming of the Euroamerican, and it did so against the myth of an original and enduring harmony between Native Americans and nature.

Conservation on the Northern Plains, which up until recently focused principally on agricultural erosion and run-off, has entered an ever more complicated world. It must now monitor commercial agriculture, which genetically manipulates plant biology and uses synthetic chemistry for its fertilizers and pesticides. Conservation no longer separates local and global when the issue is the exhaustion of soils, the pollution and depletion of water, and the extermination of native flora and fauna. Conservation today joins transcendent worldviews and ever-querying empirical sciences.

Ecology and environmental sciences broadened the spirit of conservation on the Northern Plains. Both have brought changes to conservation's traditional identity, which lay in governmental agencies that established natural reserves, regulated rivers and lakes, created parks, and protected fish and game as well as wildlife threatened with extinction. Contemporary practitioners have directed conservation towards the reintroduction of native species and the restoration of ecological zones such as prairie grassland, wetlands, and river basins. Relying on microbiology for soil science, hydrology, and toxicology, they monitor discharges and wastes for pollution and contamination. In recent decades conservationists have been on alert about the intrusion of "pests," "weeds," and "exotic invaders." With the help of multiple agencies, they launch campaigns against such unwanted exotic invaders as Zebra mussels, Eurasian milfoil, Asian carp, and hosts of intrusive mollusks, ticks, worms, and blights. In the direct service of the environment, conservationists have lobbied for legislation against a widening spectrum of chemical pollutants and toxins and hold their university laboratories to account for a decline in frogs, snakes, and turtles, and the dwindling numbers of pollen-spreading bees. While continuing to toil to preserve and restore, conservationists have had to resign themselves to the reality of human disturbances and transformations of nature.

The vast, developing, and shifting agendas of environmentalism have exceeded the patchwork of agencies and sciences dedicated to conservation. Competing scientific approaches, differing commercial and political interests, and contested borders between governmental agencies, and non-profit environmental advocacy groups have compounded the issues pertaining to conservation. Field observation, scientific sensibilities, and state and federal legislation introduce fresh issues. Hunters, fishermen, recreationalists, and industries have divergent interests and frequent quarrels over the use and conservation of resources. Constantly in play are debates over recreational and commercial use of public lands and parks. Rivers and surface and ground waters require conservationists to mediate between municipal protection and the integrity of farmers' property. Flood control, drainage, and irrigation involve a tangle of agencies and excite local and regional wars between public and private holders, upstream and downstream residents, and city water use and discharge versus farmers' need to obtain and discharge water.

Conservationists must recognize that the grasslands and wetlands of the Northern Plains still exist largely in private hands. They must accept malleable and negotiable farm policy. They must concede that sometimes they are spectators of county, state, and federal legislators, and stand aside and watch the protracted negotiations and see-saw course of farming set-aside programs. Independent conservationist farmers who wish to secure their land for posterity must look to the actions of non-profit groups like the Nature Conservancy or other emergent private or state land trusts that purchase or hold lands in perpetuity. (The lands are held by local and regional land trusts, national conservation groups and state, general, and federal agencies, and, as of June of 2014, there are forty million acres of private land protected through conservation easements in the United States.)[49]

In the last few years conservationists have witnessed a truly dramatic struggle between those looking to conserve the land and those wanting, with government support, to put it in full production. The government, disposed to keep agriculture competitive in the world market, has also espoused a policy of green energy. Not without ironic consequences, it has affirmed its "greenness" in a variety of ways: funding the ethanol industry, the sale of ethanol at the pump, and corn raised for ethanol. The first deleterious effect of government support of ethanol came with soaring corn prices, which reached an extraordinary $7.63 a bushel in August 2012. Prices created a true "corn rush," which induced farmers to throw all the land they could get their hands on into corn production. They took land out of grazing and put it into crops, and they did the same with their government-supported, sure-money-in-the-bank, set-aside lands, removing them from dedication to battling erosion, serving flood control, and increasing natural habitat, and gambling them away on presumed ever-higher crop prices. Corn production was also fed by advancing genetics, which dramatically increased yields and created plants immune to Monsanto's most effective systemic herbicide, Roundup. The farmers of the Northern Plains planted row-to-row, and corn as a crop reached to the Missouri River. South Dakota grass, grazing, and hunting land was entered into production. The prime pheasant-hunting grounds of the Prairie largely vanished in the fall of 2013. The plight of the pheasant in South Dakota followed that of Iowa and Minnesota.

Hunters and conservationists lamented the loss of habitat. Mono-cultural fields no longer served plants and insects, according to many observers who assessed the steady disappearance of frogs, snakes, butterflies, and, above all, the "golden" honeybee. Select scientists contended that the government's support of ethanol added to global warming. They argued that expanded chemical and mechanical farming releases far more carbon than is saved by the use of ethanol. Additionally, government-sponsored ethanol plants have made heavy use of water for processing. From one perspective, the search for "green energy" echoes a century-long Plains dream: energy self-subsistence by what we plant rather than the carbon-laden oil we import.[50] As violent as its ascent, ethanol followed a precipitous descent, with corn prices dropping to $3.38 in September 2014, lower than the $3.50 level of 2010.

Other issues on the Plains cry out for the conservationist's attention. There is the accelerating exhaustion of ground water and central aquifers by farms, cities, towns, and industries. Chemicals contaminate soil and pollute waters. A new form of mining for oil and natural gas, hydraulic shale fracking in North Dakota, threatens ground waters as the once-proposed burial sites for nuclear materials did. From western Minnesota to the High Plains, the issue of available water has become urgent. The dry regions of the Northern

Plains and the entire Upper Midwest continue to produce concerns about the conservation of surface and ground water for future life.

Beyond the question of flora and fauna, soils and waters, conservationists increasingly face the challenge of tempering climate change. Conservation of all sorts is dwarfed by changing weather patterns, melting polar ice caps, rising seas, and threatened coastlines. Global problems, real and projected, swallow local and regional issues. There are droughts in sub-Saharan Africa, the clearing of the Amazon Rainforest, and the tsunami and nuclear meltdown in Japan, the destructive search, pumping, and transmission of oil, and industrializing and coal-fired Third World states like India and China. Simultaneously, the world's clock ticks with exterminations of species, loss of entire habitats, and the demise of traditional peoples.

On the Northern Plains, we can no longer deny that we are at the end of the Holocene and have entered fully into the era of the Anthropocene. Conservation, despite its divisions and frailties, now stands for the survival of humanity.[51]

Notes

[1] For an agricultural description of the different zones of the Northern Plains as formed east to west out of the Central Feed Grains and Live Stock Area, Central Great Plains Winter Wheat and Range Region, and Western Great Plains Range and Irrigated System, see *Land Resource Regions and Major Land Resource Areas of the United States, the Caribbean, and the Pacific Basin,* United States Department of Agriculture Handbook 296, issued 2006. For the "Great Plains and Prairies," see Chapter 11, Stephen S. Birdsall and John Florin, *An Outline of American Geography: Regional Landscapes of the United States* (Washington, DC: Information Agency, 1998).

[2] Ed. Arnold Van Der Valk collection *Northern Prairie Wetlands* (Ames, IA: University of Iowa State Press, 1989) serves as a useful introduction to the geography and ecology of the wetlands, which cut a large swathe from central Iowa, across western Minnesota and the eastern Dakotas, entering into the southern and central Canadian provinces, Manitoba, Saskatchewan, and Alberta.

[3] For an introduction to James C. Malin's probing work on the Plains and Prairies as places created by the human act of settlement and agriculture, see his *History and Ecology: Studies of the Grasslands,* ed. Robert P. Swierenga (Lincoln: University of Nebraska Press. 1984), esp. Swierenga's Preface, xiii-xxiv, and Introductory Essay, 2-20. Also, for the introduction of agriculture from the east to the Midwest and Grasslands, see John Frazer Hart, *The Land*

That Feeds Us (New York: Norton, 1991), 104-62, and John C. Hudson, *Making the Corn Belt* (Bloomington: Indiana University Press, 1994).

[4] By the late 1860s, a small band of early environmentalists, concerned over the river's waning flow, founded the Free Niagara movement. The movement held that the natural beauty of the land surrounding the falls should be protected from commercial interests and exploitation and remain free to the public. After more than fifteen years of pressure, the Free Niagara crusaders achieved victory with the Niagara Appropriations Bill of 1885. For Muir as a spiritual founder and prophet of the conservation movement, see Stephen Fox, *The American Conservation Movement: John Muir and his Legacy* (Madison, WI: University of Wisconsin Press, 1985).

[5] For an introduction to the relation of work on the biosphere and noosphere—life and society—and the work of such thinkers as Henri Bergson, Teilhard Chardin, Edouard LeRoy, and Vladimir Vernadsky, see eds. Paul R. Samson and David Pitt, *The Biosphere and Noosphere Reader: Global Environment, Society, and Change* (London: Routledge, 1999).

[6] William Hoffman and Leo Furcht, *The Biologist's Imagination* (New York: Oxford University Press, 2014).

[7] For the landscape as vision of a dynamic new nation, see Roderick Nash, *Wilderness and the American Mind*, 3rd edition (New Haven, CT: Yale University Press, 1983).

[8] The Homestead Act of 1862 gave away 160 acres of western land for the price of filing a fee and living on the land for five years. In the last half of the nineteenth century, 200 million acres were available from the railroad reserve of gifted lands. In 1850 there were 1.5 million farms, and by 1900 there were 5.75 million farms in the nation.

[9] Harold Steen, *The U. S. Forest Service: A History* (Seattle: University of Washington Press, 1976), 5.

[10] For a short description of Thoreau's walking, botanizing, and description of American landscapes, see Joseph A. Amato, *On Foot: A History of Walking* (New York: New York University Press, 2006), esp. 141-47. A single influential work on disjuncture between society and nature was Leo Marx, *The Machine in the Garden* (New York: Oxford University Press, 1964).

[11] For the alarm and growing concern about the extinction of animal life, see Chapter 3, "Sounding the Alarm About Continental-Wild Life Concern," of Mark V. Barrow's *Nature's Ghosts from the Age of Jefferson to the Ages of Ecology* (Chicago: University of Chicago Press, 2009), 78-107; for the story of the role of the bison in sounding the warning of man-made extinction, see 92-94.

[12] For discussions surrounding forestry and the origin of the U.S. Forest Service, see Steen, *U. S. Forest Service*, 9-10.

[13] For a discussion of the difference between Muir's commitment to preservation and Pinchot conservation of regulated use, see Roderick Nash, *Wilderness and the American Mind*, esp. Chapter 8, "John Muir: Publicizer,"122-140 and Chapter 10, "Hetch Hetchy," 161-181. For a discussion of Pinchot and his relation to national forestry, see Harold T.

Pinkett, *Gifford Pinchot: Private and Public Forester* (Urbana: University of Illinois Press, 1970), esp. the introduction, 1-20, and conclusion.

[14] In the United States there are 155 National Forests containing almost 190 million acres (297,000 mi^2/769 000 km^2) of land. These lands comprise 8.5 percent of the total land area of the United States, an area about the size of Texas. Some eighty-seven percent of National Forest land lies west of the Mississippi River; Alaska alone accounts for twelve percent of all National Forest land. This note is a composite of two well-documented *Wikipedia* articles, "The Conservation Movement" and "United States National Forests."

[15] For a short history of national parks, which presently number 59 and were only 3—Yellowstone, Sequoia and Yosemite—at the time Roosevelt took office and before he signed in 1906 the empowering act that allowed him to proclaim at one stroke eighteen national monuments, many of which Congress turned into national parks, see Stewart Udall's "Introduction," *National Parks of America* (Waukesha, WI: Country Beautiful Corporation, 1972), 9-15. See also https://www.nps.gov/thrb/learn/historyculture/trandthenpsystem.htm accessed 30 July 2016.

[16] To grasp how the loss and hope of the restoration of forests focused and rallied early federal and state conservations, see Joel Orth, "Directing Nature's Creative Forces: Climate Change, Afforestation, and the Nebraska National Forest," *Western Historical Quarterly* 42 (Summer 2011), 197-217.

[17] Placed under the supervision of the National Park Service, U.S. Forest Service, U.S. Fish and Wild Life Services, and the Bureau of Land Management, the bill produced a culling of federal lands that could be deemed wilderness, which in the words of the 1964 bill would be places where the earth and community of life are "untrammeled by man, where man himself is a visitor who does not remain" and "an area of undeveloped Federal land retaining its primeval character and influence, without permanent improvements or human habitation, which is protected and managed so as to preserve its natural conditions." In the subsequent fifty years, 758 wilderness areas have been designated. They presently total 109,511,038 acres or about 4.5 percent of the area of the United States, "National Wilderness Preservation System," in *Wikipedia*.

[18] Beginning in the early 1800s, bounty land and homestead laws were enacted to dispose of federal land. Several different types of patents existed. These included cash entry, credit, homestead, Indian, military warrants, mineral certificates, private land claims, railroads, state selections, swamp, town site, and town lots. A system of local land offices spread throughout the territories, patenting land that was surveyed via the corresponding Surveyor General's office of a particular territory. This system gradually spread across the entire United States. With the exception of the Mining Law of 1872 and the Desert Land Act of 1877 (which was amended), all have since been repealed or superseded by other statues, "Bureau of Land Management," *Wikipedia*.

[19] "Federal Lands," *Wikipedia.* In March 2012, federal lands equaled 2.27 billion acres, about twenty-eight percent of the total of the country. Most public lands are located in western states, and especially Alaska. The Bureau of Land Management (BLM) is an agency within the United States Department of the Interior that administers American public lands totaling approximately 247.3 million acres, or one-eighth of the landmass of the country. The BLM also manages 700 million acres (2,800,000 km^2) of subsurface mineral. U.S. land is also managed by the Bureau of Indian Affairs, Bureau of Reclamation, Department of Agriculture, United States Fish and Wildlife Service, National Park Service, the United States Forest Service, and the Department of Defense, Army Corps of Engineers, and the Tennessee Valley Authority.

[20] For a major example of Roosevelt exhorting the states to care for their lands and seeking to spread conservation beyond forest and beyond federal jurisdiction to care for their lands, see Theodore Roosevelt's Conference of Governors, http://en.wikipedia.org/wiki/Conference_of_Governors.

[21] For early approaches to wildlife in Minnesota, see Evadene Burris Swanson, *The Use and Conservation of Minnesota Wildlife, 1850-1900,* Foreword by Aldo Leopold (St. Paul: Department of Natural Resources, 2002). For the articulation of Minnesota conservation, see "Minnesota Department of Natural Resources," *Wikipedia.*

[22] Minnesota is one example of a state's articulation of conservation. With sixty-seven state parks, and seven state recreation areas, the park system (originally administered by the Forestry Division and the second oldest in the nation after New York's) began in 1891 with Itasca State Park. An earlier effort in the 1880s to incorporate Minnehaha Falls as a state park ended with beginning a Minneapolis city park. For the history and interest of municipality in the creation of parks, see Galen Cranz, *The Politics of Park Design: A History of Urban Parks in America* (Cambridge MA: The MIT Press, 1989).

[23] For an analytic study of how government sought mistakenly to narrate nature, ignoring the fact that farming failures followed the drought and its conditions, not vice-versa, Geoffrey Cunfer, *On the Great Plains: Agriculture and Environment* (College Station: Texas A & M Press, 2005).

[24] Malin's critique of the climax conservationist is quoted here by Donald Worster, *Nature's Economy: A History of Ecological Ideas,* 2nd ed. (Cambridge: Cambridge University Press, 1994), 215, 242–49.

[25] See John Frazer Hart, *The Land That Feeds Us,* and John C. Hudson, *Making the Corn Belt.*

[26] From "The Soil Conservation and Domestic Allotment Act," *Wikipedia.*

[27] "Resettlement Administration," *Wikipedia.* Professor Geoffrey Cunfer's e-mail to the Author of September 15, 2014: "Tugwell's Land Utilization Program (LUP) was the earliest effort I know of government bringing conservation to the Great Plains and the far western edge of the Northern Plains." Unable, as he explained, to control private lands, "the government's solution was to buy land." The federal government bought millions of acres

of farmland and created, under the 1937 authorization of the Bankhead-Jones Tenant Act, the first National Grasslands, which parallel much vaster tracts of land designated by U.S. National Forests and were to be managed on a conservation basis. Cunfer critically examines the limited application of one of three North Dakota grasslands: North Dakota's Little Missouri National Grassland, in his article "The New Deal's Land Utilization Program in the Great Plains," *Great Plains Quarterly* 21 (Summer 2001): 193-210. After the Land Utilization Program the next government effort at conservation on the plains came with the Soil Bank in the early 1950s, and then, most comprehensive of all, the Conservation Reserve Program, 1985 to the present. This program and other conservation programs experienced notable reductions in the 2014 Farm Bill.

[28] For an examination of an earlier government experiment in 1901 predicated on the assumption of the beneficence of forests in changing climate, see Joel J. Orth, "Directing Nature's Creative Forces: Climate Change, Afforestation, and the Nebraska National Forest," *Western Historical Quarterly*, 42 (Summer 2011), 197-217.

[29] For a study of the Civilian Conservation Corps and its ties to the American Environmental Movement, see Neil M. Maher, *Nature's New Deal* (Oxford: Oxford University Press, 2008).

[30] Samuel P. Hays's *Conservation and the Gospel of Efficiency: The Progressive Conservation Movement, 1890-1920* (Cambridge, MA: Harvard University Press, 1959).

[31] Ibid., 9.

[32] For a brief note on the origins of ecology, see Worster, *Nature's Economy,* 192-93.

[33] For the development of animal ecology as a geographic determination, see the second English edition of Richard Hesse, *Ecological Animal Geography* (Chicago: University of Chicago Press, 1951). It is a revision of the 1937 and 1924 German editions of *Tiergeographie auf oekologisher Grundlage,* which was preceded by his 1913 article, "The Ecological Foundations of Animal Distribution." In Part One of *Ecological Animal Geography* Hesse takes up "the Ecological Foundations of Zoögeography. He considers classification by characteristics as tied to geography and biotic community (or *biocenosis*), along with its physical environment (or *biotope*). In Part Two he takes up marine animals and the chemistry of the sea and the biotic divisions of the oceans by depths. In Part Three the subject is running, standing, and other inland waters, and Part Four focuses on the distribution of animals across regions, with a section on "Grassland and Desert Communities."

[34] For a discussion of Leopold's role at the revivified Audubon Society, see Barrow, *Nature's Ghosts*, 276-79.

[35] Aldo Leopold, "A Biotic View of Land," *Journal of Forestry*, 31, No. 9 (1939), 727.

[36] Ibid., 727.

[37] The dimensions in question were offered in 1956 by the two-volume work *Man's Role in the Changing Face of the Earth.* Introduced by historical

perspectives suggested by "Man's Tenure of the Earth," which covers human agency and antiquity and the expansion of human culture, it proceeds under the rubric "Through the Corridors of Time," treating fire as a first human agency, early food production, hydraulic civilizations, antiquity's effect on the land, clearing of the European woodlands, the changing face of the "dry belt" of Asia, changes in climate, vegetation, and human adjustment in Saharo-Arabian belt, land use in the tropics, and a piece on the grasslands of North America by James Malin, and finally pieces on the age of using fossil fuels and spreading urbanization. The second volume takes up the effects of man on the seas, coastlines, and ground and surface waters. It also considers human wastes and their treatment, urban-industrial demands on the land, possible alterations of the climate, and of particular interest to conservationists, and varied human modifications of biotic communities by agriculture, grazing, clearing of forests, new exotic plants, and man as an agent in the spread of organism. The conclusion, on prospects for nature and man, considers growth of population, limits of raw materials and fuels, and "technological denudation."

[38] For the confluence of diverse microscopic sciences, see "Microbiology." *Wikipedia.*

[39] The Green Revolution in particular is identified with Professor Norman Ernst Borlaug (1914-2009) who, having studied biology, plant pathology, and genetics at the University of Minnesota, directed his agricultural research position in Mexico to the development of semi-dwarf, high-yield, disease-resistant varieties of wheat. "Norman Borlaug," *Wikipedia.*

[40] For perspectives on modern environmental impact, with an excellent bibliography, see Donald Worster, ed., *The Ends of the Earth* (Cambridge: Cambridge University Press, 1988). For history as a story of landscape, crops, and society and its animals, see the production of the French *Annales* School, origin in 1929, beginning with the works of Marc Bloch, *French Rural History* (Berkeley, Calif: University of California Press, 1966; orig. French, 1931) and *Feudal Society*, 2 vols. (Chicago: University of Chicago Press, 1961; orig., 1939). On contemporary history, see Carole Crumley, ed., *Historical Ecology: Cultural Knowledge and Changing Landscapes* (Santa Fe, NM: School of American Research Press, 1997); for environmental and ecology's cumulative effect, see J. R. McNeill and William McNeill, *The Human Web* (New York: Norton, 2003); for anthropology's commitment to a history of agriculture, foods, and materials, see a recent collection, Andrew Shryock and Daniel Lord Small, eds., *Deep History* (Berkeley: University of California Press, 2011).

[41] For one classic introduction to plants and their migration, see Alfred Crosby's *The Columbian Exchange: Biological and Cultural Consequences of 1492* (Westport, CT: Greenwood Press, 1972); for a study of a single crop that mingles history, migration, and cultures, see Sidney Mintz, *Sweetness and Power: The Place of Sugar in Modern History* (New York: Viking, 1985).

[42] For two biographies, see Mark Hamilton Lyttle, *The Gentle Subversive* (Oxford: Oxford University Press, 2007) and William Souder, *On a Farther Shore* (New York: Broadway Books, 2012).

[43] Rachel Carson, *The Sea Around Us* (Oxford: Oxford University Press, 1950).

[44] Gathering some of the literature critical of Rachel Carson is a recent article called "The Toxic Legacy of Rachel Carson," *First Things*, April 27, 2015: http://www.firstthings.com/blogs/mullarkey/2015/o4/the toxic-legacy-of-Rachel-carson.

[45] For a study of the debate that developed around DDT, see Thomas R. Dunlap, *Scientists, Citizens, and Public Policy* (Princeton: Princeton University Press, 1981).

[46] Lewis Regenstein, *America, The Poisoned* (Washington, D.C.: Acropolis Books, 1982). For a regional environmentalist's perspective, see Herbert Krause, *Birding in the Northern Plains: The Ornithological Writings of Herbert Krause*, edited by Ronald R. Nelson (Sioux Falls: Center for Western Studies, 2008).

[47] For humanity's descent into the world of the small and invisible, see Joseph A. Amato, *Dust: A History of the Small and the Invisible* (Berkeley: University of California Press, 2000) and William Hoffman's *The Biological Imagination* (Oxford: University of Oxford Press, 2014).

[48] Sporting a foreword by the Prince of Wales and an introduction by actor, director, and environmentalist Robert Redford, *Save the Earth*'s table of contents expresses environmentalism's commitment to places, species, micro-habitats, or regional human/natural environments. Short essays by more than fifty notable figures from the contemporary political and entertainment world dwell on facts and facets of endangered life. The indigestible lists of tragedies and imminent disasters include "the extinction of tribal peoples," "ozone depletion," "expanding world populations," loss of "biodiversity" (with the purported disappearance of "50 to 100 species daily"), "air pollution" (with extending highways and increasing vehicles, and mounting industries and cars), "diminishing croplands and agricultural production, despite use of fertilizers and pesticides," "failing fisheries," and "disappearing rainforests." Its inventory includes the diminishment of grasslands, croplands, rivers, lakes, and wetlands.

[49] The largest American environmental non-profit, The Nature Conservancy, founded in 1951 and now with over a million members, annual revenue of more than $550 million, and projects in thirty-five countries, including all fifty states, has spent nearly a billion dollars to protect three million acres through land easements and spent five times that amount in direct purchases. Aside from extensive maritime projects, it claims to have protected the sum of 6.5 million acres, directly and in cooperation with others, in the shared purchase of easements, while protecting a total of twenty million acres in the United States and 120 million worldwide, *Nature Conservancy* (October/November, 2014), 42–43.

[50] The search for a botanic—"a green-prairie-way"—around oil and Rockefeller is a dream that dates from the 1920s. Henry Ford and his Dearborn Conferences of 1934 and 1935 sponsored this and several other green dreams of plant energy and materials. The early 1980s saw a parade of promising plants and methods for the sake of alternative energy. Joseph A. Amato offers a history of the scam built around the Jerusalem artichoke as the magic road to ethanol, American energy independence, and wealth for American farmers, in his *The Great Jerusalem Artichoke Circus* (Minneapolis: University of Minnesota, Press, 1993), 5-14. For the relation between ethanol and grasslands, see the side bar on page one of R. Brooke, G. Fogel, A. Glaser, E. Griffin, K. Johnson, "Corn Ethanol and Wildlife: How increases in corn plantings are affecting habitat and wildlife in the Prairie Pothole Region" (published by the National Wildlife Federation, Reston, VA 2010). Posted at http://www.nwf.org/pdf/Wildlife/01-13-10-Corn-Ethanol-Wildlife.pdf_accessed 27 March 2016. Davide Gill-Austern, "The Impact of Rising Corn Prices on the Conservation Reserve Program: An Empirical Model," *Undergraduate Economic Review*: Vol. 7: Issue 1, Article 22 (2011): 3-5, 25 posted at: http://digitalcommons.iwu.edu/uer/vol7/iss1/22 accessed 27 March 2016: 3-5; and Xiaoguang Chen and Madhu Khanna, "Indirect Land Use Effects of Corn Ethanol in the U.S: Implications for the Conservation Reserve Program," Selected Paper prepared for presentation at the Agricultural & Applied Economics Association's 2014 AAEA Annual Meeting, Minneapolis, MN, July 27-29, 2014, 16, 18 posted at http://ageconsearch.umn.edu/bitstream/170284/2/2014%20AAEA.pdf_accessed 27 March 2016; and Daniel Hellerstein and Scott Malcolm, "The Influence of Rising Commodity Prices on the Conservation Reserve Program" *Economic Research Report* No. (ERR-110) 44 pp, February 2011 posted at http://www.ers.usda.gov/publications/err-economic-research-report/err110.aspx accessed 29 March 2016.

[51] Climate engineering "is shaking up our traditional understanding of ethical requirements of environmental responsibility in the twenty-first century, particularly the presumption that human intervention in and manipulation of nature is inherently wrong," Ben A. Minter, "Geoengineering and Ecological in the Anthropocene," *BioScience*, 62: 10 (October 2012), 857.

Afterword

Anthony J. Amato

For many, the term conservation has come to preclude action, but the new conservation accepts action and even requires exertion.

Eleven essays have trekked across the Northern Plains, and each has made stops at sites of efficiency, nature, legacy, and perpetuation. The essays have followed a path that extends from the past to the present and into the future, and their venture in the grassland has reopened the territories of use and nature, past and present. Conservation has been their steady heading in a land of uncertain definitions and ambitions.

The essays have discovered conservation on the land and in the mind of this region. In fact, there has been and is a distinct Plains conservation, and its practice has depended on the work of citizens, scientists, and officials. Conservation in its many forms retains value in everyday moments on the Prairie, and, when at the foundation of bioregionalist and re-wilding efforts, it has enhanced value for people and places. Cast as managed, damaged, giving, or thriving, the Plains hold out hope if only for the sake of knowledge. These rural areas in America's remote midsection conserve nature's past and present possibilities, efficient and inefficient. The understandings of use and nature opened by conservation in the Plains promise to benefit science and policy. The efficacy of a new public conservation on the Prairie will depend on approaches that go beyond preservation and address origins and efficiency in scientific contexts.

Conservation's capacity to serve alternately as both a check on use and an imperative to use is perhaps its greatest asset. In the age of excess and consumerism, conservation is a call for frugality, to check consumption on the local and the global scale.[1] In a time of hedging, conservation as a call to make the most can encourage radical action. In an age of skepticism, it forces citizens to reengage and consider the value of projects that are above them or beneath them. For many, the term conservation has come to preclude action, but the new conservation accepts action and even requires exertion. As Ian Rotherham stresses, "Nature conservation as a leisurely activity can help . . . a deleted nature, but, in the long term, something more radical will be required."[2] Conservation should not tread lightly on the beaten paths. Its way is the path of extremes and possibilities.

Notes

[1] George Perkins Marsh noted the connection between conspicuous consumption and demands on the environment, See his *Man and Nature, Or Physical Geography as Modified by Human Action,* 1864 (Cambridge, Mass.: Harvard University Press, 2000), 28-29.

[2] Ian D. Rotherham, *Eco-history: An Introduction to Biodiversity and Conservation* (Winwick, UK: White Horse Press, 2014), 117.

About the Authors

Anthony J. Amato is an associate professor in the Social Science Department at Southwest Minnesota State University. He received a Ph.D. in history from Indiana University. Over the years, his scholarship and publications have addressed other places and cases where economy, environment, and culture converge. He has brought an interdisciplinary outlook to research topics ranging from river management to beekeeping to household budgets. His papers have been delivered at national and international conferences, and his publications have appeared in national and international books and journals. He was co-editor of the acclaimed book *Draining the Great Oasis: An Environmental History of Murray County, Minnesota.*

With a Ph.D. in History from the University of Rochester in 1970, and post-doctoral study at U.C.L.A, **Joseph Anthony Amato** taught history at several colleges, including almost forty years at Southwest Minnesota State University, from which he retired as Professor Emeritus of History and Dean of the Center for Rural and Regional Studies. Aside from writing, editing, co-authoring, and publishing many books on small towns, rural culture and ethnicity, regional demographics, and Midwestern life, he has written more than twenty other books, including memoirs on golf and bypass surgery. His books on local, family, and regional history include *When Father and Son Conspire: A Minnesota Farm Murder; The Great Jerusalem Artichoke Circus: The Buying and Selling of the American Dream;* and *Rethinking Home: A Case for Local and Regional History.* His books in intellectual and cultural history include *Mounier and Maritain: A French Catholic Understanding of the Modern World; Guilt and Gratitude: A Study of the Origins of Contemporary Conscience; Victims and Values: A History and a Theory of Suffering; Dust: A History of the Small and Invisible; On Foot: A History of Walking;* and *Surfaces, A History* and *The Book of Twos: The Power of Contrasts, Powers, and Polarities.* His second book of poetry, *My Three Sicilies,* and *Everyday Life: A Short History of its Long and Extraordinary Making* have recently come out.

Dennis Anderson has been the *Minneapolis Star Tribune* outdoors editor and columnist since 1993, before which he held a similar position at the *St. Paul Pioneer Press,* beginning in 1980. He holds a bachelor's degree in English from the University of Minnesota,

Morris, and a master's degree in journalism from the University of Minnesota, Twin Cities. He has been a finalist for the Pulitzer Prize, has won the Scripps Howard Foundation national journalism award for environmental reporting, and twice has won the Frank Premack Award for public service reporting in Minnesota. He and his wife, Jan, live in the St. Croix River Valley, which divides Minnesota and Wisconsin northeast of the Twin Cities. Their older son, Trevor, is a recent graduate of the University of Montana, where their younger son, Cole, is a student.

Peter Carrels is Communications Coordinator for the University of South Dakota and the USD Sanford School of Medicine. Peter Carrels has worked as an environmental activist and environmental writer/journalist since 1979. Much of his work has emphasized water issues and rivers. Carrels is a native of Aberdeen, South Dakota, and he and his wife moved to Sioux Falls, South Dakota, from Aberdeen in 2015. He is also a graduate of the University of St. Thomas, St. Paul, Minnesota. Carrels traces his interest in prairie ecosystems and agricultural grasslands to his friend Michael Melius, a writer, farmer and naturalist. "Michael introduced me to the ecological bounty and values of grasslands, and he was sounding the alarm through his own poignant, heartfelt writing about disappearing prairie long before it became a popular conservation issue," notes Carrels. "He inspired, encouraged and supported my project to interview and write about grassland farmers in our part of the world. Those interviews are the basis for my essay in this book."

Stephen L. Eliason is a Professor of Sociology in the Department of Social Sciences and Cultural Studies at Montana State University Billings, where he teaches courses in sociology and criminal justice. He earned B.A. and M.A. degrees in sociology at Utah State University and received his Ph.D. in sociology at Oklahoma State University. His research interests include the study of conservation law enforcement, hunting in contemporary society, and those employed in the hunting industry. His work has been published in a variety of journals including *American Journal of Criminal Justice, Deviant Behavior, Human Dimensions of Wildlife, Journal of Rural and Community Development, Society and Animals, Journal of Social Psychology, Wildlife Biology in Practice,* and *Wildlife Society Bulletin.*

Andrea Glessner received her doctorate from North Dakota State University in 2014. Her studies emphasized Great Plains history, the history of the American West, Public History, and Rangeland Management. In her dissertation she analyzed how public perceptions of wild horses have changed since the early twentieth century, particularly since the passage of the Taylor Grazing Act. Government management of wild horses, particularly those living on ranges throughout the American West, has led to controversial discussions about how these animals can be maintained for future generations. It is a subject that incites an array of opinions. Dr. Glessner continues to study wild horses and also teaches part-time for Cowley County Community College and Western Wyoming Community College. In addition, she co-coordinates the Rural and Agricultural Studies section of the Western Social Sciences Association. She resides in Wichita, Kansas, with her husband and their dog, Cleo.

Linda M. Hasselstrom ranches and is resident writer at Windbreak House Writing Retreat. She has advised writers at the University of Minnesota, has been visiting faculty at Iowa State University, Ames, and is an advisor to Texas Tech University Press. A founder of International League of Conservation Writers, she is Special Consultant to the Rural Lit RALLY initiative, SUNY Buffalo, New York. Her ranch hosts the Great Plains Native Plant Society's Plains Garden and a Rocky Mountain Bird Observatory riparian protection area. Awards won by her fifteen published books include *Dirt Songs: A Plains Duet* with Twyla Hansen, Nebraska Book Award (poetry); *Between Grass and Sky*, WILLA Finalist, Women Writing the West; *Bitter Creek Junction*, WILLA Finalist, Women Writing the West, and Wrangler, National Cowboy & Western Heritage Museum. Readers can follow her work at: www.windbreakhouse.com; www.Facebook.com/WindbreakHouse; and windbreakhouse.wordpress.com.

William Hoffman has been a writer and editor at the University of Minnesota for more than thirty years. He has worked closely with faculty in genetics and bioengineering and with the medical technology and bioscience industries. He is co-author with Leo Furcht, M.D. of *The Stem Cell Dilemma*; *The Biologist's Imagination: Innovation in the Biosciences*; and "Divergence, Convergence, and Innovation: East-West Bioscience in an Anxious Age," in *Asian Biotechnology and Development Review*. He is also author of "The Shifting Currents of Bioscience Innovation," in *Global Policy*, part of a special section on geo-technologies.

Miles D. Lewis was born and raised in rural central Montana, where he grew up on a cattle ranch near the town of Two Dot. After serving in the Marine Corps, he enrolled in classes at Montana State University Billings, eventually graduating with a B.A. degree in history in 2000. Two years later he earned a M.Ed. in Interdisciplinary Studies-Teaching History, also at MSU. Miles holds an M.A. in the American West and Ph.D. in Great Plains History, with minor fields in Modern German and World History, from North Dakota State University. His substantive research interests are in regional history as a methodology, agricultural history (particularly apiculture), and historical memory and identity from a grassroots perspective.

Lisa Payne Ossian is Professor of History at Des Moines Area Community College in central Iowa. Ossian earned her master's degree in women's studies at Eastern Michigan University and her doctorate at Iowa State University in agricultural history and rural studies. She currently serves as president to the Women & Gender Historians of the Midwest and has been elected once to the National Education Association's board and twice to the State Historical Society of Iowa board as well as selected for the Hoover Presidential Education Committee, OAH Committee on Community Colleges, NEA's *Thought & Action,* and Humanities Iowa Speakers' Bureau. Her three books—*The Home Fronts of Iowa, 1939-1945; The Forgotten Generation: American Children and World War II;* and *The Depression Dilemmas of Rural Iowa, 1929-1933*—were published by the University of Missouri Press. She is currently researching and writing her next book tentatively titled *'The Grimmest Spectre': The World Famine Emergency, Herbert Hoover's Mission, and the Invisible Year, 1946.* She has presented her current and past research at a number of national and international conferences.

Barry L. Stiefel is Associate Professor in the Historic Preservation & Community Planning program at the College of Charleston. He has also taught occasional classes at Clemson University, Tulane University, and Roger Williams University, and is an External Research Associate at Carleton University in Canada. Stiefel completed his Master of Urban Planning (Environmental Planning specialization) from the University of Michigan and Ph.D. in Historic Preservation from Tulane University, where he became interested in the overlapping issues of cultural and natural heritage conservation. Stiefel has also published several articles, edited volumes, and books related to heritage preservation issues, in addition to consulting on these issues.

Index